Cambridge Lower Secondary

Maths

STAGE 9: TEACHER'S GUIDE

David Bird, Belle Cottingham, Alastair Duncombe, Amanda George, Annabel Lewis, Deborah McCarthy, Claire Powis, Fiona Smith

Series Editors: Alastair Duncombe, Caroline Fawcus, Sarah Sharratt

Collins

William Collins' dream of knowledge for all began with the publication of his first book in 1819.

A self-educated mill worker, he not only enriched millions of lives, but also founded a flourishing publishing house. Today, staying true to this spirit, Collins books are packed with inspiration, innovation and practical expertise. They place you at the centre of a world of possibility and give you exactly what you need to explore it.

Collins. Freedom to teach.

Published by Collins
An imprint of HarperCollinsPublishers
The News Building
1 London Bridge Street
London
SE1 9GF

Browse the complete Collins catalogue at
www.collins.co.uk

British Library Cataloguing in Publication Data.
A catalogue record for this publication is available from the British Library.

Authors: David Bird, Belle Cottingham, Alastair Duncombe, Amanda George, Annabel Lewis, Deborah McCarthy, Claire Powis, Fiona Smith
Series editors: Alastair Duncombe, Caroline Fawcus, Sarah Sharratt
Publisher: Celia Wigley/Elaine Higgleton
Commissioning editor: Karen Jamieson/Lisa Todd
In-house project editor: Letitia Luff
Managing editor: Wendy Alderton
Project manager: Karthikeyan at Jouve
Copyeditor: Alison Walters
Collator and Proofreader: Jan Schubert
Answer checker: Nicholas Mason
Illustrator: Ann Paganuzzi
Cover designer: Gordon MacGilp
Cover illustrator: Maria Herbert-Liew
Typesetter: Jouve India Private Limited
Production controller: Sarah Burke
Printed and bound by: CPI Group UK

Acknowledgements

The publishers gratefully acknowledge the permission granted to reproduce the copyright material in this book. Every effort has been made to trace copyright holders and to obtain their permission for the use of copyright material. The publishers will gladly receive any information enabling them to rectify any error or omission at the first opportunity.

All exam-style questions and sample answers have been written by the authors.

Contents

Introduction

This highly supportive Teacher's Guide provides step-by-step, detailed notes and a wealth of ideas on how to use the *Collins Cambridge Lower Secondary Maths* series effectively with students. Problem-solving tasks are clearly signposted, as well as opportunities for adaptation and extension so that lessons can be adapted to suit the needs of individual students.

For every chapter:
Useful list of learning objectives clearly displayed

Prior knowledge assumptions listed, so students can be encouraged to build on what they already know

Starter ideas given, to help get the lesson going and get students thinking about the topic

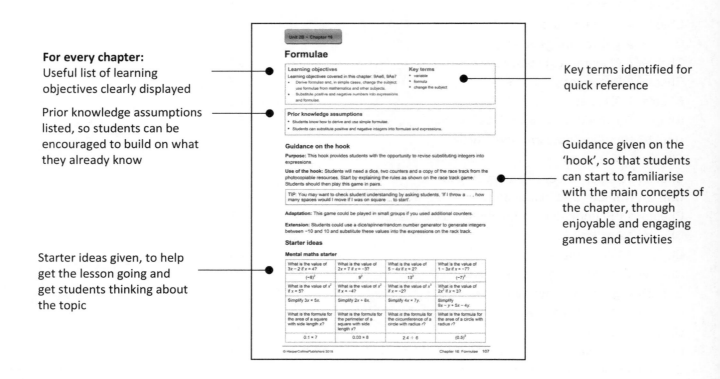

Key terms identified for quick reference

Guidance given on the 'hook', so that students can start to familiarise with the main concepts of the chapter, through enjoyable and engaging games and activities

Common misconceptions identified, to help avoid pitfalls

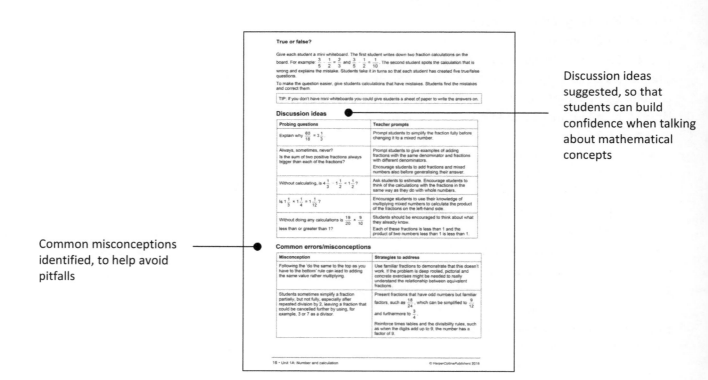

Discussion ideas suggested, so that students can build confidence when talking about mathematical concepts

Suggestions for end-of-chapter quizzes and activities, to enhance mental maths skills

Technology recommendations, to support students with online work

Ideas for investigation and research tasks, to extend learning

Fix and *stretch* ideas given, for developing conceptual understanding

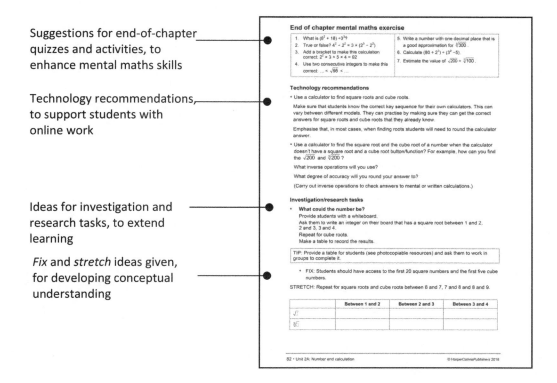

In addition to the many useful features identified in the reduced pages shown, the following supporting materials can be found, free-to-download, at **www.Collins.co.uk/CCLSM**.

For students to access:

- 36 x consolidation exercises (one per chapter), for embedding concepts covered in each chapter*
- 9 x review units (one per unit), so students can check their progress at the end of a block of work*

For teachers to access:

- 36 x end-of-chapter tests, to monitor and assess students' progress*
- 50+ photocopiable resources to accompany Teacher's Guide activities, to support teaching of core mathematical concepts
- Answer keys for all exercises (Student's Book, Workbook and the above listed, free, online exercises and tests)

More information on how and when to use these materials can also be found online at the above address.

* This material has not been through the Cambridge International endorsement process.

Directed numbers

Learning objectives

Learning objectives covered in this chapter: 9Ni1
- Add, subtract, multiply and divide directed numbers.

Key terms
- directed number

Prior knowledge assumptions
- Students can add and subtract integers
- Students can multiply and divide integers.

Guidance on the hook

Number grid   *Problem solving*

Purpose: The hook requires students to notice the relationship between the numbers in the grid whilst revisiting prior knowledge of adding, subtracting, multiplying and dividing positive and negative integers.

Use of the hook: Give pairs of students a copy of the grid and ask them to look at the yellow cross and the numbers in the yellow boxes. Can they see how they are related? Allow students time to explore the different calculations that they can make.

Adaptation: If students are unsure where to start, ask them to look at these calculations $-6 + -20 = ...$, $-12 + -14 = ...$, $2 \times -13 = ...$. Can they spot these numbers in the grid? What do they have in common? How do they differ? You can start with the numbers in the blue grid as the numbers are smaller $-8 + -10 = ...$, $-2 + -16 = ...$, $2 \times -9 = ...$

BEWARE: Some students may not be sure how the negative signs affect the outcomes of addition and multiplication problems. Explain any misconceptions students may have and provide more practice to ensure that students are confident with the addition and multiplication of negative integers before starting to work with directed numbers.

Extension: In addition to creating their own questions related to this context, you can give students grids with bigger numbers for more challenging calculations.

TIP: Ensure that you reinforce the idea of writing down the number facts that they make. This will help them generalise the rule that the numbers of each colour follow.

Starter ideas

Mental maths starter

Calculate $-25 - -20$	The temperature is $-11°C$. It drops by 20°. What is the new temperature?	What is 90 less than 4?	What is 40 less than -6?

Calculate −10 + 25.	What temperature is 3 degrees warmer than −15°C?	What temperature is 10 degrees warmer than −20°C?	What temperature is 5 degrees warmer than −27°C?
Calculate −24 ÷ −8.	What temperature is 7 degrees colder than −13°C?	What temperature is 9 degrees colder than −9°C?	What temperature is 25 degrees colder than −11°C?
Calculate −7 × −4.	What is −18 + −6?	What is 8 − −3?	Calculate −15 × 2.
Calculate 12 ÷ −4.	Calculate −9 × 8.	Calculate 10 × −8.	Calculate −6 × 9.
Calculate 42 ÷ −7.	Calculate 45 ÷ −5.	Calculate −81 ÷ 9.	Calculate −7 × −4.

Start point check: Number lines

Display some vertical number lines.

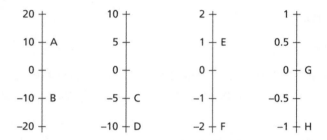

Ask students to point out where different numbers should be, for example: +6, −3, −9.

Ask students for the difference between two points on the scale, for example ask 'How much higher is point A than point B? What is the difference between points C and D?'

Repeat with other numbers, including fractions and decimals, for example: 'Where is −0.6, $-\frac{1}{2}$ and so on.

> TIP: Students have not learned to add and subtract negative decimals and fractions yet, however they should be able to position the different negative decimals and fractions on the number line.

> TIP: You could provide students with a copy of the number lines (photocopiable resources) and ask them to mark the points on each of them.

Making numbers

Write four consecutive numbers. Make two of them positive and two of them negative, for example: −2, −3, 4, 5.

Ask students to create calculations using one of the operations (+, −, ÷, ×).

- How many different calculations can you make?
- How many different answers do you get?

Extension: Would you get any new answers if you could use brackets and use all the operations (+, −, ÷, ×)?

Discussion ideas

Probing questions	Teacher prompts
What do multiplying, dividing, adding and subtracting positive and negative integers have in common with multiplying, dividing, adding and subtracting directed numbers?	Ask students to compare 'calculating with positive integers' to 'calculating with positive decimal numbers' first.
How many different numbers can you make by using −3, −0.8, ×, ÷ , + or −?	Encourage students to use their knowledge of adding, subtracting, multiplying and dividing positive and negative integers (e.g. use −3 × −8 = 24 to work out −3 × −0.8).
How many different ways can you show that −6.9 + 3.1 ≠ −10?	Students can show this directly by calculating both sides. Alternatively, they could use a number line to show the addition of −6.9 and 3.1. Or they could use a thermometer and show what the temperature of −6.9°C will be after an increase of 3.1°C.
Convince me that $\frac{-1}{2} \times 10 = \frac{1}{2} \times -10$.	Students can show this directly by calculating both sides. This could be a good opportunity to recap on their previous knowledge from Year 8 of multiplying and dividing positive and negative numbers. (+ × + = +) (+ × − = −) (+ ÷ + = +) (+ ÷ − = −) (− × + = −) (− × − = +) (− ÷ + = −) (− ÷ − = +)

Common errors/misconceptions

Misconception	Strategies to address
Students often try to memorise rules such as 'two minuses make a plus', and then apply them incorrectly. For example, they may mistakenly think that −3 − 0.5 = 3.5 because two negatives make a positive.	Express negatives as 'negative three', not 'minus three'. Use 'take away' or 'subtract' for the operation. −3 − 0.5 = −3.5 as we are taking away 0.5 from (or adding −0.5 to) −3. Link working with directed numbers to working with integers and explain that all the techniques for working with integers apply to directed numbers also.
Specifically, 'rules' that work for multiplication may be inappropriate for addition. For example, −0.3 × 3 = −0.9, however −0.3 + 3 = −2.7 is not correct.	Encourage students to think carefully about the appropriate method and check that any answer looks sensible. They could use a number line to check each calculation. +1 +1 +1 0 −0.3 0.7 1.7 2.7 −0.3 −0.3 −0.3 −0.9 −0.6 −0.3 0
Students will sometimes forget to write the negative sign when reading from a scale or a number line. For example, believing that −10 + 20 = 30.	Emphasise the importance of checking answers and using estimation to see that the answer makes sense. For example, −10 + 20 cannot be 30. Remind students to think of the temperature. If the temperature is −10°C and it becomes 20 degrees warmer, what will the temperature be?

Developing conceptual understanding

9Ni1 Add, subtract, multiply and divide directed numbers.

- FIX: You could give students calculations with positive decimal numbers, then take it in turns to change one or both of them to negative numbers. For example, you could start with 0.2 + 0.6 = 0.8. Ask students to think how the answer will change if one or both of the numbers being added is changed to a negative number. Write down
−0.2 + 0.6 = … 0.2 + −0.6 = … and −0.2 + −0.6 = …

- Encourage students to use a number line to justify their answers (it could be a horizontal or vertical number line).

STRETCH: To make this more challenging, students could use laws of arithmetic to simplify calculations with directed numbers, for example: $\dfrac{3}{10} - \dfrac{1}{15} + -\dfrac{3}{5}$.

- FIX: When subtracting directed numbers, encourage students to look at the difference between the positions of the two numbers on a number line.

- FIX: For multiplication and division, you will initially need to restate questions using simple language. For example, for −0.3 × 4, ask 'Four groups of negative 0.3 make how many altogether?'

- FIX: Use multiplying and dividing of integers to derive number facts about decimals and fractions. For example, if −3 × 4 = −12, then −0.3 × 0. 4 will be 100 times smaller.

STRETCH: To make this more challenging you could use 'missing number questions' where students need to work backwards to find the missing numbers. For example −0.2 × … = 0.08

End of chapter mental maths exercise

1. True or false? $-25 \times \dfrac{3}{5} = 15$ 2. Calculate −10 ÷ −0.01 3. Work out (0.5 − −2)²	4. Work out $\dfrac{8 - -2}{-10 \times -2}$ 5. $\dfrac{11}{15} + -\dfrac{3}{5}$ 6. Use >, < or = to complete this calculation: $-\dfrac{3}{8} - \dfrac{1}{8}$ …….. $-\dfrac{1}{4}$

Technology recommendations

- Ask students to use their calculator to work with directed numbers. Students need to pay attention when inserting '− − ', as sometimes they forget to insert the second 'minus sign'.

- Ask students to use the internet to research the average temperatures at the North and South Pole during last year. Ask students to make a table showing the average temperature for each month.

  They should use their table to calculate the average temperature in the North Pole and the average temperature in the South Pole.

  Ask students to make three comparisons questions based on their table.

TIP: Students can use a number line to show their results.

STRETCH: Make three true/false questions based on the table.

Investigation/research tasks

- **Magic Square**   *Problem solving*

  Draw the magic squares on the board. Separate the class into three groups and provide them with a printout. Ask students to complete them.

-0.3		
	-0.2	0
0.1		-0.1

-0.4		
	-0.1	
	-0.3	0.2

0	$-\frac{7}{8}$	
$-\frac{5}{8}$		
$-\frac{1}{2}$		

- FIX: Encourage students to figure out which number everything has to add to.

  STRETCH: Give students an empty magic square and ask them to make their own 'directed number magic square'. Share the magic squares that the students make with the whole class and solve them.

  > TIP: This can be run as a game with students playing in teams with 5 points being awarded for completing the magic square correctly.

  > TIP: You can give each student a copy of the magic squares (available as a photocopiable resources). They can work individually or in groups of three to solve them.

  Solution:

-0.3	0.2	-0.5
-0.4	-0.2	0
0.1	-0.6	-0.1

-0.4	0.1	0
0.3	-0.1	-0.5
-0.2	-0.3	0.2

0	$-\frac{7}{8}$	$-\frac{1}{4}$
$-\frac{5}{8}$	$-\frac{3}{8}$	$-\frac{1}{8}$
$-\frac{1}{2}$	$\frac{1}{8}$	$\frac{3}{4}$

- **Make −0.5.**

  Give students a whiteboard. Write down −0.5 on the board. Ask students to make −0.5 by adding, subtracting, multiplying or dividing. Choose a few of the calculations that students made and share them with the whole class.

  > TIP: If you don't have a whiteboard, you could give students a sheet of paper to write the answers on.

  STRETCH: Ask students to use negative numbers only.

  What operations can they use now?

  Why can't they multiply or divide two negative numbers to achieve −0.5?

- **How much does your name cost?**   *Problem solving*

  Provide students with a copy of the conversion table found in the photocopiable resources.

  Students choose four letters from their name (and surname).

  Use the conversion table to find their number value. Add subtract, multiply or divide the numbers that the letters correspond to achieve:

  - the smallest negative number
  - the greatest positive number.

TIP: Students could use brackets also.

TIP: Students could work individually or in pairs.

STRETCH: Students use seven letters from their name and surname and use subtraction only. What is the biggest positive number they can make? What is the smallest negative number they can make?

- FIX: Provide students with a number line so that they can visualise the calculations that they are completing.

Rounding and powers of 10

Learning objectives	Key terms
Learning objectives covered in this chapter 9Np1, 9Np2:	• n/a

- Recognise the equivalence of 0.1, $\frac{1}{10}$ and 10^{-1}; multiply and divide whole numbers and decimals by 10 to the power of any positive or negative integer.

- Round numbers to a given number of decimal places or significant figures; use to give solutions to problems with an appropriate degree of accuracy.

Prior knowledge assumptions
- Students know how to read and write positive integer powers of 10.
- Students know how to multiply and divide by 0.1.
- Students know how to round numbers to one or two decimal places.

Guidance on the hook

Purpose: The task is a problem based on understanding the effects of multiplying and dividing by 0.1, 0.01, 0.001 and 0.0001.

Use of the hook: Ask students to work in pairs. Encourage them to answer each question individually before discussing the answers together. They both check the answers using a calculator. Did they predict correctly? Did they use the same method when multiplying or dividing?

Bring the whole class back together and share answers. Discuss any possible mistakes that students may have made when predicting. Ask students to explain each other's work including any misconceptions or mistakes that some students may have made. Encourage students to explain the difficulties that someone else may have found in answering the questions. Encourage discussion.

Support students' discussion by allowing them time to think and reflect on each other's work.

> TIP: Ask students to check that they have typed the correct numbers in the calculator as quite often students complete different calculations to the ones required.

Adaptation: Ask students to work in groups. Half of the groups predict the answer, half of them use the calculator. Write an integer on the board and ask all groups to complete the calculations starting with this integer. Which of the groups was the fastest? Which group gave the most correct answers?

BEWARE: Some students may generalise too quickly. Ensure that students have completed the whole task before generalising.

Extension: Students can make up their own questions. Encourage them to make up a question they think is easy and another one that is difficult. Ask students to explain what makes the question easy/difficult. Ask students to investigate whether it is possible to multiply and divide by decimal numbers and have the same number you started with as the final answer.

Solution:

- When starting with a positive number (integer or decimal), when multiplying by 0.1, 0.01, 0.001, 0.001, the answer will always become lower. When dividing by 0.1, 0.01, 0.001, 0.001, the answer will always become higher.
- When starting with a negative number (integer or decimal), when multiplying by 0.1, 0.01, 0.001, 0.001, the answer will always become lower. When dividing by 0.1, 0.01, 0.001, 0.001, the answer will always become higher.

Starter ideas

Mental maths exercise

Round 7.062345 to one decimal place.	How many 1 cent coins make $2.20?	Round 2.0261789 to one decimal place.	Use >, <, = to complete 10^1…10.
Round 1.645345 to two decimal places.	What is the product of 0.9 and 0.1?	Round 16.013579 to two decimal places.	True or false? 3.02134 = 3 (1 d.p.)
Multiply 2.347 by 0.01.	Find the quotient of 0.16 divided by 0.01.	Divide 4.536 by 0.01.	True or false? 0.2 ÷ 0.1 = 0.02
Divide 27.3 by 0.1.	Multiply 26 by 0.01.	Divide 0.81 by 0.01.	True or false? 4.0049134 = 4.00 (2 d.p.)
True or false? 10^5 = 1 000 000	10 000 =10^a. What is a?	Which one is bigger 10 000 000 or 10^7?	Divide 3.9 by 0.01.

Start point check

Rounding in real life

Ask students to come up with examples where we use rounded information.

Possible answers:

- number of people attending a concert or sports event
- time taken to travel large distances
- time taken to cook a meal
- population of a city
- the number of sweets in a packet
- the amount of cereal in a box
- the amount of time a lightbulb lasts.

TIP: Ask students to support their answers with actual numbers and explain the rounding that they made. For example, a lightbulb lasts 2 years (rounded to the nearest whole number).

I am thinking of a number

Write on the board: 'I am thinking of a number. When I …, my answer is …. What is my number?'
Students work in small groups.

Ask one student to use one of the words in the boxes below to complete the sentence. The other students find the number.

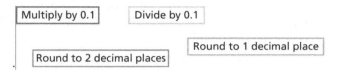

Multiply by 0.1   Divide by 0.1

Round to 2 decimal places   Round to 1 decimal place

> TIP: Follow up this task with a discussion in class about how students found the number. When multiplying or dividing, ask students to explain each other's methods.

When the number has been rounded to one or two decimal places, discuss the range that the numbers can be.

What's the question?

Separate the class into small groups. Write the following numbers on separate cards:

- 0.2 (1 d.p.)
- 0.34 (2 d.p.)
- 69.1 (1 d.p.)
- 0.01 (2 d.p.)
- 234.06 (1 d.p.)
- 199.99 (2 d.p.)
- 0.3 (1 d.p.)
- 0.45 (2 d.p.)

Ask the students to pick up a card at random and write an addition, subtraction or division question with the given answer. For example:

Write a division calculation that has an answer of 0.3 (rounded to 1 d.p.)

Then ask a few of the students to hold up their boards and read their questions.

Encourage students to solve each other's questions. Every correct answer of a calculation question is 1 point, every correct answer of a problem-solving question is 2 points. The winner is the group with the most points at the end.

> TIP: The calculations can be written on the board (rather than on cards).

> BEWARE: The emphasis of the task is on the 'rounding' rather than the calculation itself. Allow students to use a calculator if needed.

Discussion ideas

Probing questions	Teacher prompts
Convince me that: $5 \div 10^{-2} \neq 5 \div 10^{-1}$	Students can calculate both sides. Encourage them to change 10^{-1} and 10^{-2} to fractions before completing the calculations.

Probing questions	Teacher prompts
Give me an example of a calculation that gives an answer of 8 when rounded to one significant figure. And another ... and another ...	Ask students to explain the strategies they used to think of a suitable calculation.
	TIP: If students find this difficult, ask them to work backwards. For example, 8.13 is a number that can be rounded to one significant figure. An example could be: ten notebooks cost $81.30. Calculate the cost of one notebook (rounded to 1 s.f.).
True, sometimes or never true? A number rounded to a given significant figure is the same as a number rounded to a given number of decimal places.	Revisit the rules of rounding a number to one, two and three decimal places and one, two and three significant figures. For instance, 0.538 = 0.5 (to 1 d.p.) and 0.538 = 0.5 (1 s.f.), however 2.538 = 2.5 (1 d.p.) and 3 (1 s.f.)

Common errors/misconceptions

Misconception	Strategies to address
When dividing by positive or negative powers of 10, students are unsure where to start or what to do.	Converting the powers to integers or fractions usually clears up the confusion. Revisit multiplying and dividing by 10, 100 and 100 if necessary.
Students often confuse rounding to significant figures with rounding to decimal places, especially with numbers less than 1.	Give plenty of opportunities for students to round to a number of decimal places and a number of significant figures. Ask students to make a table showing examples of the same number rounded to one or two decimal places and one or two significant figures. Make sure that students know that, for example, in the number 0.076, the second zero is in the first decimal place, but the 7 is the first significant figure. Ensure students understand that the decimal places are counted after the decimal point. Significant figures are counted from the first non-zero digit.
Students may not check that their answer is of the correct order of magnitude when rounding to significant figures, dropping zeros from the end. It is common to see answers where the zeros have been left off, for example, 23 856 = 24 to 2 s.f., rather than 23 856 = 24 000 to 2 s.f.	Remind students to check that the answer makes sense. For example, if the organisers of a concert order bottles of water for the people who attend the concert and they know that there will be 23 856 people in the stadium, this number cannot be rounded to 24 people (or they should not order 24 bottles of water).
Rounding before the calculation. For example, calculate 148 ÷ 25 = 5.92 = 6 rounded to 1 significant figure. However, if rounded before = 100 ÷ 30 = 3. The answer of 3 is half of what the answer should have been.	Remind students to always round after the calculation, unless told otherwise. Discuss the importance of rounding correctly in real life. For example, a worker taking three days or six days to complete a job may affect his wages, planning, etc.

Developing conceptual understanding

9Np1 Recognise the equivalence of 0.1, $\frac{1}{10}$ and 10^{-1}; multiply and divide whole numbers and decimals by 10 to the power of any positive or negative integer.

- FIX: Students need to be comfortable with multiplying and dividing fractions and decimals by 10, 100 and 1000. To reinforce this, you can use a place value grid. For example,

$$29 \times 10^{-2} = 29 \times \frac{1}{10^2} = 29 \div 100.$$

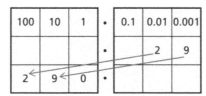

- FIX: Students need to be comfortable that dividing by $\frac{1}{10}$ is the same as multiplying by 10.

  Extend on previous knowledge by finding the missing powers. For example, if $3400 \div 10^a = 3.4$, what is the value of a?

> TIP: When teaching written methods of calculation, place value counters can provide a useful concrete (and visual) representation of the processes.

9Np2 Round numbers to a given number of decimal places or significant figures; use to give solutions to problems with an appropriate degree of accuracy.

STRETCH: Students working at greater depth could begin to investigate problem solving questions that involve rounding to a given degree of accuracy. For example, a box has dimensions of 34.8 cm, 23.6 cm, 7.98 cm. Calculate its capacity to one significant figure.

For instance, they could find numbers that lie between −2 and −3 on a number line or between −2.4 and −2.5.

STRETCH: Students working at a greater depth can estimate the answer as accurately as possible and identify if mistakes have been made when rounding. For example, is $9100 \div 7 = 13$ (rounded to 2 s.f.)?

- FIX: Students should have access to a place value grid that they can use if needed. Discuss the rules of rounding and the common mistakes students make. Clarify any misconceptions students may have.

End of chapter mental maths exercise

1. True or false? 0.056 is rounded to two significant figures.	4. Complete $600 \times 10^{-3} = \ldots$
2. Add $9.607 + 3.4$. Round the answer to two significant figures.	5. Which is greater: $680 \div 10^{-3}$ or 680×10^{-3}?
3. Divide 0.964 by 10^{-3}	6. The area of a rectangle is 178.5 cm². Its length is 16 cm. What is its width (correct to two significant figures)?

Technology recommendations

- Many scientific calculators have a button that can be used to round numbers to 1, 2 or 3 significant figures (it is sometimes marked as 'Sci'). If your students have a calculator with a button that can be used to round to different degrees of accuracy, show them how to use it.

- Search on the internet for the longest rivers in the world. Make a spreadsheet with ten of them. Round the values to one significant figure. What is the difference between the longest and shortest river in your table? Will the answer be different if you use the actual values, then round the difference to one significant figure?

  Repeat the same task but now round the values to two significant figures. Will the answers change?

Investigation/research tasks

- **What am I?**   *Problem solving*

  Let students work in pairs.

  When a number α is divided by 9, the answer is 9 when rounded to one significant figure.

  When the number α is divided by 10, the answer is 9 when rounded to one significant figure.

  What could α be if α is a whole number?

STRETCH: allow α to be a decimal number (1 d.p.)

STRETCH: ask students to make three similar questions for each other.

TIP: Allow students to use a calculator.

- **Investigation: rounding**

  A **whole number divided by 9** gives an answer of **8** when rounded to one significant figure.

  The smallest possible value that the number can be is 68 because 68 ÷ 9 = 8 (1 s.f.) and the largest possible number is 71 because 71 ÷ 9 = 8 (1 s.f.)

  The difference between 71 and 68 is 3 because 71 − 68 = 3.

  Now it is your turn to investigate. Can you find these missing numbers?

  A **whole number divided by 9** gives an answer of **7** when rounded to one significant figure.

  What is the **smallest** possible value for the original number?

  What is the **largest** possible value for the original number?

  What is the **difference** between these values?

  (Answer: 59 and 62, 3)

  A **whole number divided by 9** gives an answer of 6 when rounded to one significant figure.

  What is the **smallest** possible value for the original number?

  What is the **largest** possible value for the original number?

  What is the **difference** between these values?

  (Answer 53 and 50, 3)

STRETCH: A whole number divided by **9** gives an answer of α when rounded to one significant figure.

  What is the **smallest** possible value for the original number?

  What is the **largest** possible value for the original number?

What is the **difference** between these values?

(Answer: $9\alpha - 4$ and $9\alpha - 1$, 3)

- **Powers of 10**   *Problem solving*

  Using the grid in the photocopiable resources ask students to work in pairs or small groups and to follow these instructions. Roll the dice. Pick up a yellow card. Choose the column that corresponds to the number on the dice. Divide or multiply each of the numbers in your column by the number on the yellow card. Choose a different yellow card every time. Continue the game until all the yellow cards have been chosen. Every correct answer wins you a point. The winner is the student with the most points.

STRETCH: Round the answer to one significant figure. Can you predict whether the rounded answer will be greater or smaller than the actual answer?

TIP: Check each other's answers in your group by using a calculator.

TIP: Discuss the rules of multiplying and dividing by the powers of 10. Clarify any misconceptions that students may have.

TIP: Provide each table with a copy of the grid. Ask students to cut out the yellow and purple cards and mix them before working on the task. Grids are available in photocopiable resources.

Fractions

Learning objectives

Learning objectives covered in this chapter: 9Nf1, 9Nf2

- Consolidate writing a fraction in its simplest form by cancelling common factors.
- Add, subtract, multiply and divide fractions, interpreting division as a multiplicative inverse, and cancelling common factors before multiplying or dividing.

Key terms

- proper fraction
- improper fraction
- mixed number
- equivalent

Prior knowledge assumptions

- Students know how to add and subtract fractions with different denominators.
- Students know how to multiply a fraction by an integer.
- Students know how to divide an integer by a fraction.

Guidance on the hook

Purpose: This task reminds students how to add fractions.

Use of the hook: The aim of the task is not to simply add fractions, but notice that similarly to working with numbers, the laws of operations can also be applied when working with fractions, to make the calculations easier. Encourage students to find the easiest way to add the fractions on each side.

Students should approach the question systematically and look to find fraction pairs to make 1:

$$1 + \left(\frac{8}{9} + \frac{1}{9}\right) + \left(\frac{2}{10} + \frac{4}{5}\right) + \left(\frac{5}{6} + \frac{1}{6}\right) + \left(\frac{1}{8} + \frac{7}{8}\right) + \left(\frac{1}{7} + \frac{6}{7}\right) = 6.$$

On the right-hand side, students can add $\frac{1}{14}$, $\frac{1}{7}$ and $\frac{1}{28}$ together and $\frac{1}{4}$, $\frac{1}{6}$ and $\frac{1}{3}$ together.

$$\frac{1}{14} + \frac{1}{7} + \frac{1}{28} = \frac{2}{28} + \frac{4}{28} + \frac{1}{28} = \frac{7}{28} = \frac{1}{4}, \text{ and } \frac{1}{4} + \frac{1}{6} + \frac{1}{3} = \frac{3}{12} + \frac{2}{12} + \frac{4}{12} = \frac{9}{12} = \frac{3}{4}.$$

$1 + \frac{1}{4} + \frac{3}{4} = 2$. Students need to conclude that the scales will not balance.

Adaptation: To make the question easier, remove the brackets on the left-hand side and encourage students to group the fractions according to their denominators.

Extension: Students could design their own addition questions using fractions that add up to make 1. Encourage them to use fractions with different denominators.

> BEWARE: Some students may be confused by the calculations on both sides. Encourage students to deal with one calculation at a time before establishing whether both sides are equal or not.

Starter ideas

Mental maths starter

Write $\frac{1}{4}$ as a decimal.	Simplify $\frac{14}{20}$.	Simplify $\frac{18}{32}$.	True or false? $\frac{1}{5} = \frac{5}{20}$
What is the sum of $\frac{3}{7}$ and $\frac{2}{8}$?	Work out $\frac{7}{6} + \frac{1}{4}$	Find the difference of $\frac{3}{8}$ and $\frac{3}{16}$.	Does $\frac{3}{10} = \frac{1}{3}$?
What is $\frac{55}{100}$ in its simplest form?	What is $\frac{500}{1,000}$ in its simplest form?	What is $\frac{24}{36}$ in its simplest form?	What is $\frac{64}{80}$ in its simplest form?
What is the product of $\frac{3}{5}$ and 10?	Add $\frac{2}{3}$ and $\frac{2}{5}$.	Multiply $\frac{5}{8}$ with 10.	Divide 3 by $\frac{2}{3}$.
Mary buys five packets of biscuits. She eats $\frac{5}{7}$ of each packet every day. How many days will the biscuits last?	Which is smaller: $\frac{1}{5}$ of 3 kg or $\frac{3}{10}$ of 2 kg?	Which is larger: $\frac{48}{100}$ or $\frac{4}{10}$? How much larger?	Work out $\frac{3}{7}$ of 14 kg.

Start point check

Star fractions

Provide students with star fractions as provided in the photocopiable resources.

Ask them to write six calculations on each corner of the star so that the answer equals the fraction given in the middle of the star. Prompt for a mixture of calculations, including adding, subtracting, multiplying and dividing. Can they be imaginative with their suggestions?

> TIP: You could create a set of blank star diagrams and laminate them. Students can fill them in with marker pens.

STRETCH: students can suggest their own centre and have their partner fill in the corners of each star. The one who fills in the most calculations in the time allowed wins.

Colourful fractions

Give students a copy of the table with fractions (photocopiable resources). Ask them to colour the equivalent fractions accordingly. This will allow the students to work out any they don't know by deduction.

> TIP: One of the fractions in the table does not have an equivalent. Which one is it?

True or false?

Give each student a mini whiteboard. The first student writes down two fraction calculations on the board. For example: $\frac{3}{5} - \frac{1}{2} = \frac{2}{3}$ and $\frac{3}{5} - \frac{1}{2} = \frac{1}{10}$. The second student spots the calculation that is wrong and explains the mistake. Students take it in turns so that each student has created five true/false questions.

To make the question easier, give students calculations that have mistakes. Students find the mistakes and correct them.

> TIP: If you don't have mini whiteboards you could give students a sheet of paper to write the answers on.

Discussion ideas

Probing questions	Teacher prompts
Explain why $\frac{60}{18} = 3\frac{1}{3}$.	Prompt students to simplify the fraction fully before changing it to a mixed number.
Always, sometimes, never? Is the sum of two positive fractions always bigger than each of the fractions?	Prompt students to give examples of adding fractions with the same denominator and fractions with different denominators. Encourage students to add fractions and mixed numbers also before generalising their answer.
Without calculating, is $4\frac{1}{3} - 1\frac{1}{2} < 1\frac{1}{2}$?	Ask students to estimate. Encourage students to think of the calculations with the fractions in the same way as they do with whole numbers.
Is $1\frac{1}{3} \times 1\frac{1}{4} = 1\frac{1}{12}$?	Encourage students to use their knowledge of multiplying mixed numbers to calculate the product of the fractions on the left-hand side.
Without doing any calculations is $\frac{19}{20} \times \frac{9}{10}$ less than or greater than 1?	Students should be encouraged to think about what they already know. Each of these fractions is less than 1 and the product of two numbers less than 1 is less than 1.

Common errors/misconceptions

Misconception	Strategies to address
Following the 'do the same to the top as you have to the bottom' rule can lead to adding the same value rather multiplying.	Use familiar fractions to demonstrate that this doesn't work. If the problem is deep rooted, pictorial and concrete exercises might be needed to really understand the relationship between equivalent fractions.
Students sometimes simplify a fraction partially, but not fully, especially after repeated division by 2, leaving a fraction that could be cancelled further by using, for example, 3 or 7 as a divisor.	Present fractions that have odd numbers but familiar factors, such as $\frac{18}{24}$, which can be simplified to $\frac{9}{12}$ and furthermore to $\frac{3}{4}$. Reinforce times tables and the divisibility rules, such as when the digits add up to 9, the number has a factor of 9.

Misconception	Strategies to address
Students may insist on dividing by 2, even if the result is a fraction within the fraction.	Present fractions that have odd numbers but familiar factors such $\frac{5}{15}$. Reinforce times tables and the divisibility rules, such as when a number ends in 0 or 5 it can be divided by 5. Put emphasis on the common factors, including the HCF of the numerator and denominator.
Students occasionally divide the numerator and denominator by different numbers. For example, students may make the mistake of saying that $\frac{140}{250} = \frac{14}{25} = \frac{2}{5}$.	Ask students to represent each fraction using a bar model.
Many students simply multiply the denominators to find a common multiple, but this can result in large numbers and significant cancelling. For example, they may calculate $\frac{120}{300} \times \frac{50}{240} = \frac{6000}{72000}$ rather than $\frac{1}{6} \times \frac{1}{12} = \frac{1}{12}$.	Emphasis must be put on cancelling fractions fully before multiplying or dividing.
Some students do not convert mixed numbers to improper fractions before multiplying. Instead they multiply the fraction part and the whole number part.	Emphasis must be put on how to multiply and divide mixed numbers correctly. Ask students to use a calculator to check their answers.
Some students may cancel 'across' denominators (or just numerators). For example, some students make the mistake that $\frac{3}{20} \times \frac{6}{30} = \frac{1}{2} \times \frac{2}{3}$.	Ensure that students understand that the reason for simplifying a fraction is to make the calculations easier, whilst not changing the values of the fractions.

Developing conceptual understanding

9Nf1 Consolidate writing a fraction in its simplest form by cancelling common factors.

- FIX: Use bar models to represent how a fraction can be simplified. Ensure that students understand and can see that the value of the fraction does not change.

  For example, the diagram on the next page shows that $\frac{12}{20} = \frac{6}{10} = \frac{3}{5}$.

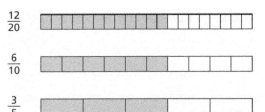

TIP: Reinforce simplifying fractions by using a calculator and changing each value to a decimal. Ask students to insert $\frac{12}{20}$, $\frac{6}{10}$ and $\frac{3}{5}$ in the calculator. They will notice that all the three fractions are equal to 0.6.

9Nf2 Add, subtract, multiply and divide fractions, interpreting division as a multiplicative inverse, and cancelling common factors before multiplying or dividing.

- Students could use fraction bars to conceptualise the addition and subtraction of mixed numbers with different denominators.

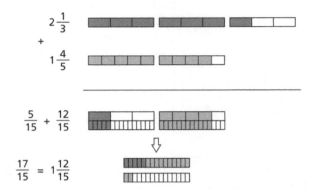

STRETCH: You could encourage students who are confident in adding and subtracting fractions to make worded problems or missing number problems that go with certain calculations, by thinking of contexts where addition and subtraction of fractions can be used.

- Students need to be proficient in multiplying with fractions before they tackle the extra complications of cancelling common factors. Check students can remember the methods required with a few straightforward questions such as $\frac{3}{4}$ of 20, $\frac{1}{3}$ of 22, $21 \div \frac{1}{3}$ and so on.

- Provide students with scenarios when multiplying or dividing fractions can be used. For example, finding the area of a rectangle when the side lengths are fractions, separating a quantity, for example $3\frac{1}{8}$ kg into cups that contain $\frac{1}{2}$ kg. Understanding that fractions are all around us will help students visualise how they can be used.

End of chapter mental maths exercise

1. Simplify $\frac{420}{350}$.	4. Halve $3\frac{3}{8}$.
2. There are 500 students in the primary school. 375 students are in Year 1. What fraction of the students are not in Year 1? Give your answer in simplified form.	5. True or false? $6\frac{2}{5} - 2\frac{1}{3} = 4\frac{1}{2}$.
3. Work out $5\frac{1}{3} + 2\frac{1}{4}$.	6. Find the area of a rectangle with side lengths of $5\frac{1}{2}$ cm and $1\frac{1}{10}$ cm.

Technology recommendations

- Use a scientific calculator to work with mixed numbers. Some students write the whole number 5, then insert the fraction $\frac{\Box}{\Box}$. Instead students need to press shift and insert when working with mixed numbers.

- Make a spreadsheet to change distances from miles to km. To change the miles to km, every distance that is in miles needs to be multiplied by $\frac{5}{8}$.

  Investigate what values the distances should be so that the answer is a whole number.

- Make another spreadsheet to change distances from km to miles. Insert five distances. What calculation do you need to do now? Why?

Investigation / research tasks

- **What is the odd one out?**

  Write a series of fractions on the board that are equivalent, apart from one of them. Can the students spot which one is the odd one out?

  Make the fractions easier or more challenging, depending on the level of the student.

  TIP: Ask students to show their simplifying calculations clearly.

- **Biggest/smallest?**

  Write four fractions on the board. Include at least one mixed number. Ask students to use one of the operations × ÷ − +) so that the answer is:

  o   the biggest that it can be

  o   the smallest that it can be.

STRETCH: ask students to use all four operations to make two different numbers. Alternatively, give students the final numbers and ask them to insert × ÷ − + to make the target number.

TIP: This activity can turn into a game. Every correct answer wins 1 point.

- **Making four problems.**

  Separate the class into three groups. Each group makes four worded problems or puzzles that have an answer less than 1, a mixed number between 1 and 2, or a mixed number greater than 2 (see photocopiable resources).

  Once students have finished, swap the problems around so that each group solves the problems one of the other two groups has made.

TIP: Encourage students to show their workings clearly.

TIP: Ask students to solve their own problems first. They could check the answer by using a calculator.

Once students have completed the problems, discuss the operations that they used.

STRETCH: Ask students to make two-step or multi-step problems.

Mental methods

Learning objectives

Learning objectives covered in this chapter: 9Nc1, 9Nc2

- Extend mental methods of calculation, working with decimals, fractions, percentages and factors, using jottings where appropriate.
- Solve word problems mentally.

Key terms

- positive
- mentally
- simplify
- derive
- highest common factor (HCF)
- lowest common multiple (LCM)

Prior knowledge assumptions:

- Students know how to use known facts to derive new ones.
- Students know how to increase or decrease a quantity by a given percentage,
- Students know how to find the HCF and LCM of two numbers,
- Students know how to change the order of numbers in addition and multiplication calculations without changing the calculation,
- Students can recall square numbers to 20 × 20 and cube numbers to 5 × 5 × 5,.

Guidance on the hook

Purpose: This hook revisits prior knowledge of finding factors of a number, ratio and direct proportion problems, calculating a percentage increase and using known facts to find new ones.

Use of the hook: Give each pair of students a copy of the secret code box from the photocopiable resources and ask them to work out the answers of each question and complete the secret code.

Adaptation: If students get stuck, or if they complete the challenge totally, review with the whole class how they can progress step by step.

Extension: The numbers used in the task can be altered to make the calculations more challenging.

TIP: Students can work individually or in pairs. This task can turn into a game by winning a point for every correct answer. Alternatively, students can compete against time.

TIP: Some students will guess the words once they know only a few letters. Encourage students to show the workings for each calculation.

BEWARE: Pay attention to the questions that students get stuck on. Provide additional practice on that particular area before moving on with the lesson.

Once students have completed the task, gather the whole class together and discuss the answers that they found.

Solution:

E = 8, A = \$1.20, S = 68%, U = 72%, N = 1200, D = 8 g

S	U	N		A	N	D		S	E	A
68	72	1200		\$1.20	1200	8 g		68%	8	\$1.20

Starter ideas

Mental maths starter

Divide 45 by 30.	Find all the factors of 30.	Find the HCF and LCM of 30 and 40.	What is 5^3?
Work out 15^2.	Decrease 180 by 20%.	Work out 11^2.	Decrease 96 by 25%.
Increase 320 by 20%.	Given that 20 × 16 = 320, calculate 21 × 16.	Calculate 18 × 9.	True or false? Given that 8 × 50 = 400, 8 × 51 = 408.
Split \$150 in the ratio 3 : 2 : 5.	130 increased by 10% equals …	If A : B = 2 : 3 and B = 60, what will A be?	6 erasers cost 92 cents. How much do 8 erasers cost?
Which is greater 4^3 or 8^2?	The ratio of boys : girls in the orchestra is 2 : 1. How many boys are there if there are 120 girls?	True or false? $\frac{8}{25} = 16\%$	True or false? 2, 3, 5, 15, 20, 30 are all factors of 30.

Start point check

Shape grid

Give students a copy of the Shape grid from the photocopiable resources. Students work in pairs. They take it in turns to choose a shape. If they choose the triangle, rectangle or circle, they complete the missing answers. If they choose the pentagon, square or the hexagon, they write three related facts based on the fact they see. For example, three facts related to 20 × 27 = 540, could be:

21 × 27 = 540 + 27 = 567

19 × 27 = 540 − 27 = 513

40 × 27 = 2 × 540 = 1080

TIP: Students take it in turns to pick up number statements for each other. One of the students says the first number fact, the other student derives three new facts based on it.

TIP: This can be run as a game with students playing in teams, with 2 points being awarded for every correct answer.

You can make this easier or more challenging by changing the number facts involved.

Correct the statement.

Write a statement on the board that is wrong, for example 'If you increase 60 by 20% the answer is 80', and ask students to find the mistake and correct it. Give each student a mini whiteboard and ask them to show you why the statement is not correct. Students can use a drawing or bar diagrams to support their answer. Explain to the students that the aim of the task is not to just say 'this is wrong' but to show why that is the case. Encourage students to discuss other mistakes that could happen with similar questions.

> TIP: If you don't have mini whiteboards, you can give students a sheet of paper to write their answers on.

> BEWARE: This question provides a good opportunity to see whether there are students who need more support with the previous learning that they will need for this lesson. Look for misconceptions that students may have and clarify them prior to continuing with the rest of the lesson.

STRETCH: Adapt the questions so that the numbers used make the calculations more challenging.

Odd one out

Write these sentences on the board and ask students to find the odd one out from each:

- 25, 36, 49, 121, 125
- 1 : 2, 2 : 3, 15 : 30, 120 : 240
- Factors of 30 are: 1, 2, 3, 4, 5, 6, 10, 15, 30
- 1, 8, 9, 27, 64, 125

Allow students to discuss in pairs and decide the correct answer. Share the results with the whole class. Ask students to explain their reasoning.

> TIP: This can be run as a game with students working in teams, with 1 point being awarded for each correctly reasoned answer.

> BEWARE: This question provides a good opportunity to see whether there are students who have forgotten the square and cube numbers, ratios or factors of a number.

Solution:

- 125 is a cube number. All the other numbers are square numbers.
- 2 : 3. All the other ratios can be simplified to 1 : 2.
- 4 is not a factor of 30.
- 9 is a square number. All the other numbers are cube numbers.

STRETCH: Ask students to make their own 'Odd one out' questions and work in pairs to test each other.

Discussion ideas

Probing questions	Teacher prompts
Convince me that $3^2 \times 0.1^2 \neq 3.1^2$.	Students can calculate the left-hand side and the right-hand side of the equation. Encourage students to write 3.1 as 3 + 0.1 rather than 3 × 0.1.
Given that 23 × 16 = 368, what is 23 × 32?	Encourage students to use the given fact. Ask: What is the same? What has changed?
True or false? To find all the factors of 60, find the factors of 6 then multiply them by 10.	You may prompt students by discussing what the factors of a number are.
How can you calculate 0.2% of a number?	Encourage students to start with the percentages that they know and use different methods to calculate 0.2%. For example, they could find 2% first, then divide by 10, or they can find 20% first, then divide the answer by 100. Alternatively, students could find 1%, then divide the answer by 5. Encourage students to be creative in their answers.
True or false? To find 12.5% of 160, divide 160 by 8.	Ask students to change 12.5% into a fraction. If 25% = $\frac{1}{4}$, what is 12.5%?
Show me that reducing $60 by 40% = $60 × 0.6	Students can use a bar model to represent the reduction of 40%.

Common errors/misconceptions

Misconception	Strategies to address
Using the known facts incorrectly. For example, some students may mistakenly think that to calculate 18^2, they can calculate 10^2 and 8^2 and add the answers: $18^2 = 10^2 + 8^2 = 100 + 64 = 164$.	Ask students to estimate. 18 is close to 20 and $20^2 = 400$. Therefore 18^2 should be close to 400. The answer of 164 is less than half of the estimation, so it cannot be correct. Revisit the laws of arithmetic with smaller numbers. For example, ask students to think about: is $4^2 = 3^2 + 1^2$?
Confusing factors and prime factors. Some students think that when finding all the factors of a number, they only need to include the prime factors. Other students include decimals and fractions, when finding factors for example they say that 2.5 and 4 are factors of 10.	Ask students to explain what a factor is. Use smaller numbers as examples.
Lacking confidence in manipulating fractions and percentages. For example, some students are unsure how to calculate $\frac{1}{5}$ of 5% of $7 mentally. They think that they need to calculate 5% of $7 first, then find $\frac{1}{5}$ of the answer.	Revisit the laws of arithmetic and encourage students to apply them to percentages and fractions in the same way as they do for numbers.

Developing conceptual understanding

9Nc1 Extend mental methods of calculation, working with decimals, fractions, percentages and factors, using jottings where appropriate.

- FIX: Students need to be comfortable working with decimals, fractions and percentages so that they are able to manipulate them. Ask students not to rush but take their time and explore the calculations given. They need to look for the most efficient way to answer the question rather than just answer the question.

- FIX: When dividing big numbers, encourage students to write the division as a fraction and simplify fully before dividing using a written method. Encourage students to use the mathematics they have learned to simplify calculations where possible. For example,

  $5952 \div 124 = \dfrac{5952}{124} = \dfrac{2976}{62} = \dfrac{1488}{62} = \dfrac{744}{31}$. When you can't simplify any further, divide using a written method.

  $$31\overline{)744}^{\,12} \quad \begin{array}{c} 24 \end{array}$$

  STRETCH: Students working at a greater depth can use number facts to find missing number questions. For example, given that $25 \times 0.4 = 10$, find two possible decimal numbers that have a product of 10.

  $\ldots \times \ldots = 10$

- FIX: When calculating with fractions and percentages, students can use bar models to help visualise the answers better. For example, when increasing \$35 by 20%, students can calculate 120% of \$35.

100% = \$35				
20% \$7	20% \$7	20% \$7	20% \$7	20% \$7

120% = \$42	
100% = \$35	20% \$7

  STRETCH: Students working at a greater depth can use number facts to find missing number questions. Students working at a greater depth can use fraction and percentage facts to find missing number questions. For example, $\dfrac{5}{8} \times 16\%$ of $27 = \ldots\%$ of 27.

9Nc2 Solve word problems mentally.

- FIX: Use a bar model to represent ratios, making it clear which part is missing or what you need to find.

- FIX: Be systematic in your approach. Find out the information as you go along. Encourage students to ask: What do I know? What can I find with this information?

STRETCH: Students working at a greater depth can solve multi-step questions which involve percentages, fractions and decimals.

STRETCH: Students working at a greater depth can apply their knowledge of numbers to solve questions involving algebra, data and shapes.

End of chapter mental maths exercise

1. Work out 16^2.	5. Work out 120% of 90.
2. Calculate 6.25×1.8.	6. If $5x = 75$ and $8y = 60$, find the value of $15x + 4y$.
3. Work out $456 \div 12$.	
4. Work out $\dfrac{3}{20}$ of 40% of 60.	7. If 20% of a packet of cereal = 140 g, how much does the whole box of cereal weigh?

Technology recommendations

- Use a calculator without the percentage button to work out percentage increases and decreases by calculating the multiplier first.
- Use calculators to carry out inverse operations to check answers to mental calculations.
- Make a spreadsheet which starts with known percentages facts. Manipulate these number facts to achieve new ones. Record all the results in a table. What facts do you need to know to calculate decimal percentages, for example 0.1%, 0.2%, 0.5%? 2.5%?

Investigation/research tasks

- **Match the cards**   *Problem solving*

  Use the fact that $125 \times 8 = 1000$ to divide or multiply the numbers in the circles and create equal statements. Give students a copy of the calculations from the photocopiable resources. Ask them to cut them out, mix them and then rearrange them to make equal statements.

BEWARE: Prompt students to check the answers are correct rather than rush through them.

STRETCH: For each number statement written, ask students to make two new number statements.

- FIX: Change the numbers or use smaller numbers to make the calculations easier.

  Solutions:

$25 \times 0.8 = 20$	$10 \div 80 = 0.125$	$1.25 \times 32 = 40$	$0.4 \times 12.5 = 5$	$60 \div 16 = 3.75$

- **Investigation: Continue the question**   *Problem solving*

  Give students a copy of these calculations from the photocopiable resources. Ask them to make questions based on the calculation given.

TIP: Students could work in pairs. They solve each other's questions.

TIP: This activity can change into a game by awarding points for every correct answer.

TIP: You can write the questions on the board and ask students to copy them in their notebooks.

STRETCH: Ask students to create their own 'True or false' questions based on the fact given.

- **Investigation: Make a problem** *Problem solving*

    Separate the class into four groups. Ask each group to create a problem based on the lesson today. Encourage students to be creative. Each problem must have two or more steps.

TIP: Provide students with a list of words that they may wish to use. For example:				
20% full	5.5% increase	2.5% shorter	angles in a hexagon	$\frac{3}{4}$ of the distance

When students finish writing the questions, ask each group to solve the other groups' questions. Share the questions with the whole class and encourage discussion about the methods used to solve them.

TIP: Ask students to use a bar model to solve or illustrate each question.

STRETCH: Ask students to create questions that can be solved in two or more ways.

STRETCH: Ask students to create questions that could have multiple answers.

Algebraic expressions

Learning objectives

Learning objectives covered in this chapter: 9Ae1, 9Ae2, 9Ae3, 9Ae4

- Know the origins of the word *algebra* and its links to the work of the Arab mathematician Al'Khwarizmi.
- Use index notation for positive integer powers; apply the index laws for multiplication and division to simple algebraic expressions.
- Construct algebraic expressions.
- Simplify or transform algebraic expressions by taking out single-term common factors.

Key terms

- index law for multiplication
- index law for division
- expanding brackets
- factorising

Prior knowledge assumptions

- Students can use index notation for small positive integer powers.
- Students can simplify expressions.
- Students can construct linear expressions.
- Students can multiply a single term over a bracket.
- Students can find the highest common factor of two numbers.

Guidance on the hook

Purpose: The purpose of this hook is to explore the idea of multiples of numbers and expressions to help students when they need to factorise an expression by taking a common factor outside a bracket.

Use of the hook: Recap multiples briefly with the class. For example, 15*a* is a multiple of 5 and *a* but is not a multiple of 10 or *b*.

The hook could be played as a game. Split the students into pairs. On their turn, a student takes one of the expressions and writes it in the correct place in the Venn diagram.

A player could score 1 point for an expression placed outside the circles, 3 points for an expression in the overlap, or 2 points for an expression in the other two sections.

Once they have sorted the expressions in the Venn diagram, the students could then design a different Venn diagram for sorting the expressions, for example.

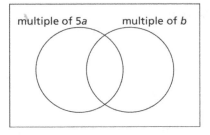

Adaptation: You could give students a simpler set of eight expressions, for example:

6	15a	2a	30
10	ab	20a	9b

Extension: Students could create their own set of expressions and their own Venn diagram.

Starter ideas

Mental maths starter

Simplify $t \times t \times t$.	Simplify $a \times a \times a \times a$.	Simplify $e \times e$.	Simplify $y \times y \times y \times y \times y$.
Simplify $2a + 3b - 4a + b$.	Simplify $5 - e + 1 - 3e$.	Simplify $4x - y - 6x + 2y$.	Simplify $2w + 6u + w - 9u$.
Expand $t(2t + 3)$.	Expand $2u(u + 4)$.	Expand $3n(2n + m)$.	Expand $a(2a - 3b)$.
Find the highest common factor of 18 and 24.	Find the highest common factor of 12 and 36.	Find the highest common factor of 30 and 45.	Find the highest common factor of 36 and 63.
I buy 5 books costing n dollars each. How much change do I get from 50 dollars?	I buy y metres of string. I cut off m pieces, each 2 metres long. How much string do I have left?	Potatoes cost a dollars per kilogram. Carrots cost b dollars per kilogram. Find the total cost of 3 kg of potatoes and 2 kg of carrots.	I drink x millilitres of juice every morning and y millilitres of juice every evening. How much juice do I drink in five days?

Start point check: Odd one out

This activity is available as a photocopiable resource. Find the expression that is the odd one out in each set. Give a reason for your answer.

Missing factor:

Give students mini-whiteboards.

Set the class questions like the following:

$2p^2 = 2p \times \ldots\ldots$

$8mn = 4m \times \ldots\ldots$

$12w^2 = \ldots\ldots \times 3w$

$24t^2u = 8t \times \ldots\ldots$

Ask students to show you on their mini-whiteboards the missing factor.

Discussion ideas

Probing questions	Teacher prompts
$r^n \times r^m = r^{12}$. What could be the values of n and m? $p^n \times p^n = p^{16}$. What is the value of n? $q^{10} \div q^m = q^3$. What is the value of m?	Encourage students to convince you that their answers are correct.
Draw me a shape with an area of $2mn + m^2$. What about a shape with an area equal to $4t^2 + 6t$?	Prompt students to think of shapes that have an L-shape. What about rectangles with that area?
Which rectangle is the odd one out? 	Prompt students to think about the area of each rectangle. Can students find another rectangle with the same area as rectangle D?
These two rectangles have equal areas. Find the missing length. 	If students struggle, set the problem out algebraically: $3a(\ldots + \ldots) = 6a^2 + 9a$
Find the missing terms: $8mn + 10m = 2m(4n + ?)$ $10n^2 + ? = 5n(? + 3)$ $8uv + ? = ?\,(4v + 5)$	Encourage students to check their answers by expanding out the brackets.

Common errors/misconceptions

Misconception	Strategies to address
Confusing m^3 or $m \times m \times m$ with $3m$	Use sorting cards in the photocopiable resources to address this misconception.
Thinking that: • $p^n \times p^m$ simplifies to p^{nm}, and • $p^n \div p^m$ simplifies to p^{n+m}	When discussing $p^2 \times p^4$, remind students that p^2 represents $p \times p$ and p^4 represents $p \times p \times p \times p$. So $p^2 \times p^4$ has a total of six ps multiplied.

Misconception	Strategies to address
	When simplifying expressions like $\dfrac{p^5}{p^2}$, write the expressions in the numerator and denominator in full and then cancel out ps to leave p^3.
Simplifying $y \times y^4$ as $y^{0+4} = y^4$ instead of $y^{1+4} = y^5$.	Convince students by writing the product in full: $y \times y^4 = y \times (y \times y \times y \times y) = y^5$
Factorising expressions like $2a^2 + a$ as $a(2a + 0)$.	Encourage students to write in the invisible coefficient 1: $$2a^2 + a = 2a^2 + \mathbf{1}a = a(2a + 1)$$ Encourage students to expand out the brackets to check their factorisation.
When factorising, taking the highest common factor (HCF) out of the first term only. For example, $10t + 15 = 5(2t + 15)$	Encourage students to write both terms as a product involving the HCF. For example, $10t + 15 = 5 \times 2t + 5 \times 3 = 5(2t + 3)$

Developing conceptual understanding

9Ae2 Use index notation for positive integer powers; apply the index laws for multiplication and division to simple algebraic expressions.

- FIX: When beginning to work on the index laws, encourage students to write out expressions in full.

  For example:
  $a^3 \times a^4 = (a \times a \times a) \times (a \times a \times a \times a) = a^7$
  Or
  $$\frac{a^5}{a^2} = \frac{a \times a \times a \times \cancel{a} \times \cancel{a}}{\cancel{a} \times \cancel{a}} = a^3$$
  This will help students to remember the rules.

STRETCH: Students could create expressions that simplify, for example, to p^3. For example, $\dfrac{p \times p^6}{p^4}$.

> BEWARE: Be aware that negative indices are beyond the scope of Stage 9.

9Ae3 Construct algebraic expressions.

- FIX: When forming an algebraic expression, it can help to replace all the letters by numbers and then consider how all the numbers should be combined.

  Example:

Algebraic problem	Translate into this numerical problem
A ball has mass m kg.	A ball has mass **2** kg.
6 balls are packed into a box.	6 balls are packed into a box.
The empty box has mass n kg.	The empty box has mass **1** kg.
Find the total mass of p boxes of balls.	Find the total mass of **8** boxes of balls.

Encourage students to substitute the values for each letter into their algebraic expression to check it gives the same answer as the numerical problem.

9Ae4 Simplify or transform algebraic expressions by taking out single-term common factors.

- FIX: Build up factorisation skills steadily in stages. Begin by looking at factorising where only a number can be taken out (for example $10y + 25$). This can be done by considering grouping:

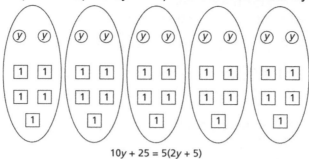

$$10y + 25 = 5(2y + 5)$$

Then consider situations where a single letter can be taken out as a factor (for example, $m^2 + 2m$). Finally, consider situations where both a number and letters can be removed (for example, $6y^2 + 8y$ or $12ab + 8a$).

- FIX: Consider the use of a grid method to help with the factorising.

  For example, to factorise $6y^2 + 8y$:

	$3y$	$+$	4
$2y$	$6y^2$	$+$	$8y$

  $6y^2 + 8y = 2y(3y + 4)$

  write highest common factor here

STRETCH: Students working at a greater depth could try to factorise expressions containing three or more terms.

For example, factorise $6xy + 15x^2 + 21xz$

End of chapter mental maths exercise

1. Simplify $v \times v \times v \times v \times v \times v \times v \times v$.
2. Simplify $a^2 \times a^4$.
3. Find the missing power: $p^{15} \div p^? = p^5$.
4. Find an expression for the shaded area.

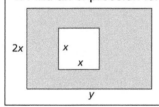

5. Find the highest common factor of $24ab$ and $16a^2$.
6. Factorise $12m + 18$.
7. Factorise $14g^2 - 7g$.
8. Complete this statement:

   $40t^2 - \ldots = \ldots\ldots (5t - 2)$.

Technology recommendations

- Set up a spreadsheet to find the powers of 2, 3 and 4. Continue your spreadsheet up until 2^{10}, 3^{10} and 4^{10}.

	A	B	C	D	E
1		Power of 2	Power of 3	Power of 4	Sum
2	1	=2^A2	=3^A2	=4^A2	=sum(B2 : D2)
3	2	=2^A3	=3^A3	=4^A3	
4	3				
5	4				
6	5				

Use your spreadsheet to comment on the value of $2^n + 3^n + 4^n$ for different values of n.

Set up a new spreadsheet to find the value of $2^n + 3^n + 4^n + 5^n$ for different values of n. What do you notice?

> TIP: Encourage students to focus on the value of the final digit in each sum. Students may need to widen the width of the columns if the numbers become too big to fit in.

STRETCH: Investigate whether $2^n + 3^n + 4^n$ is a multiple of 3 for different values of n.

Will $2^{102} + 3^{102} + 4^{102}$ be a multiple of 3?

- **Use internet research**

  Ask students to research the mathematician Al'Khwarizmi and find out why he is sometimes known as the 'father of algebra'.

  Students could also find out about Diophantus, another ancient mathematician who was important in developing the foundations of algebra.

  Students could present their findings on a poster.

Investigation/research tasks

- **Index laws**   *Problem solving*

  Students could try to discover the index laws for multiplication and division for themselves:

  o   Write $5^2 \times 5^3$ as $5 \times 5 \times 5 \times 5 \times 5$ and then simplify this as a single power of 5.
      Then try to simplify $7^4 \times 7^3$ and $9^4 \times 9^5$.
      Write down your own rule for multiplying together powers.
      Use your rule to simplify $6^7 \times 6^3$.
      Can you use your rule to simplify $2^4 \times 3^2$?

  o   Write $\dfrac{6^7}{6^2}$ as $\dfrac{6 \times 6 \times 6 \times 6 \times 6 \times 6 \times 6}{6 \times 6}$. Simplify this to give a single power of 6.

      Then simplify $\dfrac{2^9}{2^3}$ and $\dfrac{5^{10}}{5^5}$.

      Write down your own rule for dividing powers.

      Use your own rule to simplify $\dfrac{3^{11}}{3^7}$.

      Can you use your rule to simplify $\dfrac{6^8}{3^2}$?

- **Last digits**   *Problem solving*

  Here are the first four powers of 3 and the last digit of each power:

		Last digit
$3^1 =$	3	3
$3^2 =$	9	9
$3^3 =$	27	7
$3^4 =$	81	1

Continue the table up to 3^{12}. What do you notice about the pattern in the last digits? Predict the last digits of 3^{13}, 3^{14}, 3^{15} and 3^{16}.

Predict the last digits of 3^{41} and 3^{60}. Give a reason for each answer.

Students should discover that the last digits repeat:

TIP: To predict the last digits of 3^{41} and 3^{60}, students could think about how 41 and 60 relate to multiples of 4.

STRETCH: Investigate the last digits of powers of other numbers.

- **Bracket expansions**   *Problem solving*
  Complete this statement in as many ways as possible:

$$12p^2 + 16p = \ldots(\ldots + \ldots)$$

Repeat for $20m^2n - 30mn^2$

$$20m^2n - 30mn^2 = \ldots(\ldots + \ldots)$$

BEWARE: Prompt students to avoid using decimals or fractions.

STRETCH: Students could try to find brackets that expand to give $16y^4 - 40y^3$.

- **Number tricks**   *Problem solving*
  Here is a number puzzle.
  - Think of a number.
  - Multiply it by 2.
  - Add 10.
  - Multiply it by 3.
  - Add 12.
  - Divide by 6.
  - Subtract the number you first thought of.
  - Write down your final answer.

Explore the final answer for different starting numbers. What do you notice?
Use algebra to explain why the number puzzle always gives the same answer.

Repeat with this different number puzzle.
  - Think of a number.
  - Multiply it by 2.
  - Add 8.
  - Multiply it by 2.
  - Subtract 12.
  - Divide by 4.
  - Subtract the number you first thought of.
  - Write down your final answer.

TIP: Encourage students to write the expression at each stage of the puzzle.

Think of a number.	n
Multiply it by 2.	$2n$
Add 10.	$2n + 10$
Multiply it by 3.	$3(2n + 10) = 6n + 30$
Add 12.	$6n + 30 + 12 = 6n + 42$
Divide by 6.	$\dfrac{6n + 42}{6} = n + 7$
Subtract the number you first thought of.	$n + 7 - n = 7$
Write down your final answer.	7

STRETCH: Students could make up their own number puzzle which always gives the same answer.

Sequences

Learning objectives

Learning objectives covered in this chapter: 9As1, 9As2
- Generate terms of a sequence using term-to-term and position-to-term rules.
- Derive an expression to describe the nth term of an arithmetic sequence.

Key terms
- linear sequence
- arithmetic sequence

Prior knowledge assumptions
- Students can generate a sequence using a simple term-to-term rule.
- Students can generate a sequence using a simple position-to-term rule.
- Students can find a position-to-term rule for a linear sequence.
- Students can find an expression for the nth term for a sequence of patterns.

Guidance on the hook

Purpose: The purpose of this hook is to construct the first few rows of Pascal's triangle and to explore some of the patterns that are hidden within it.

Use of the hook: Give students a sheet of isometric paper to help them draw their own version of Pascal's triangle. The activity is best done with students first working on their own before sharing ideas in small groups and then in whole-class discussion.

Students should first complete the first eight rows of Pascal's triangle and shade all cells containing an odd number. You could also give students a copy of the larger Pascal's triangle (available as a photocopiable resource) and ask students to shade all the odd numbers on that.

Show the whole class pictures from the internet showing the odd numbers shaded on Pascal's triangle produced with many rows. How do their Pascal triangles relate to these diagrams?

In pairs, students should then explore the number patterns in the diagonals of Pascal's triangle. How would the sequences 1, 3, 6, 10, 15, … and 1, 4, 10, 20, 35, … continue? Can students spot any links between the terms in the sequence 1, 3, 6, 10, 15, … and the terms in 1, 4, 10, 20, 35, …?

Then encourage students to explore the sequence formed by considering the sum of the numbers in each row. What is the term-to-term rule for this sequence? What would be the sum of the numbers in the next two rows of Pascal's triangle?

> TIP: 1, 3, 6, 10, 15, … is the sequence of triangular numbers and 1, 4, 10, 20, 35, … are the tetrahedral numbers. The nth tetrahedral number is the sum of the first n triangular numbers.
> The numbers in each row of Pascal's triangle sum to make powers of 2.

Adaptation: You could give students a photocopy of the first eight rows of Pascal's triangle – available as a photocopiable resource.

Extension: Students could research the Sierpinski triangle and consider how the pattern of odd numbers in Pascal's triangle relates to the Sierpinski triangle.

Students could shade in all the multiples of 3 in Pascal's triangle.

Starter ideas

Mental maths starter

A sequence begins 3.8, 5.2, 6.6, … Find the next two terms.	A sequence begins 11.3, 9.7, 8.1, … Find the next two terms.	A sequence begins – 8.2, –6.7, –5.2, … Find the next two terms.	A sequence begins 1.2, 1.45, 1.7, … Find the next two terms.
The term-to-term rule of a sequence is 'subtract 0.8'. The first term is 6.3. Find the fourth term.	The term-to-term rule of a sequence is 'add 0.7'. The first term is 3.2. Find the fourth term.	The term-to-term rule of a sequence is 'subtract 1.2'. The first term is 8.9. Find the fifth term.	The term-to-term rule of a sequence is 'subtract 2.4'. The first term is 7.6. Find the third term.
Find the missing second term in this linear sequence: $1\frac{1}{2} \ldots 6\frac{1}{2}$	Find the missing second term in this linear sequence: $3\frac{1}{2} \ldots 6$	Find the missing second term in this linear sequence: $4\frac{1}{3} \ldots 7$	Find the missing second term in this linear sequence: $3\frac{3}{10} \ldots 7\frac{7}{10}$
The position-to-term rule for a sequence is 'multiply by 3 and subtract 10'. Find the second term.	The position-to-term rule for a sequence is 'multiply by 8 and add 11'. Find the ninth term.	The position-to-term rule for a sequence is 'divide by 2 and add 6'. Find the eighth term.	The position-to-term rule for a sequence is 'divide by 2 and subtract 7'. Find the sixth term.
Find the position-to-term rule for the sequence that begins 6, 12, 18, 24, …	Find the position-to-term rule for the sequence that begins 4, 8, 12, 16, …	Find the position-to-term rule for the sequence that begins 7, 14, 21, 28, …	Find the position-to-term rule for the sequence that begins −9, 18, 27, 36, …

Start point check: Target board

3	11	20	36
24	40	−10	33
−4	23	41	−8
17	44	32	4

Which numbers in the board appear in these sequences?

Sequence A: First term 11, term-to-term rule 'add 7'

Sequence B: First term 45, term-to-term rule 'subtract 11'

Sequence C: First term −8, term-to-term rule 'add 3'

Sequence D: Position-to-term rule 'multiply by 6'

Sequence E: Position-to-term rule 'multiply by 4 and add 5'

Sequence F: Position-to-term rule 'multiply by 9 and subtract 6'

STRETCH: Some of the numbers in the target board do not appear in sequences A–F. Find a sequence that these unused numbers will all fit into.

What's next?

Split the class into small groups (about three students per group).

Ask each group to come up with a possible next term in each of these sequences.

After about 8–10 minutes, ask each group for their answers.

A group scores 5 points for each answer that no other team thought of. Otherwise they score nothing.

Sequence A: 5   10   ?

Sequence B: 7   8   ?

Sequence C: 16   8   ?

Sequence D: 45   30   ?

Sequence E: 0.5   2   ?

Sequence F: 9   12   ?

Discussion ideas

Probing questions	Teacher prompts
Explain why the sequence 3, 6, 12, 24, … is not a linear sequence. What is the term-to-term rule for the sequence 3, 6, 12, 24, …? What are the next two terms? Give me another sequence that has the same term-to-term rule? And another?	Highlight to students that another name for a linear sequence is an arithmetic sequence. Note that the terms in the sequence are increasing, but the increase is not the same each time.
The term-to-term rule of a sequence is 'divide by 3'. If the third term is 6, what are the first five terms?	Point out to students that to work backwards from the third term, they will need to 'multiply by 3'.
Give me the first five terms of any sequence where the term-to-term rule is: • 'multiply by −1' • 'multiply by −2'.	Point out that the terms in all these sequences alternate in sign.
The term-to-term rule of a sequence is 'multiply by 3 and then add 4'. How is the sequence generated by this rule that starts with 2 different from the one that starts with −2? Find me another combination of term-to-term rule and starting value that produces a sequence that stays constant.	Encourage students to explore other starting values for this term-to-term rule so that they appreciate that the sequence beginning with −2 is alone in remaining constant.

Probing questions	Teacher prompts
The nth term of a sequence is $5n + 3$. Convince me that the terms of the sequence go up in 5s. Give me the nth term of another sequence whose terms go up in 5s. And another.	Encourage students to substitute $n = 1$, $n = 2$, $n = 3$, … into the nth term formula to see the difference between the terms. Relate rules of the form $5n + c$ to the 5 times table.
Always, sometimes, never? For sequences with nth term of the form $an + b$, where a and b are integers: • the first term is positive • the sequence is increasing • the sequence is linear • the second term is twice the first term.	Encourage students to give reasons for their choice. If a statement is sometimes true, prompt students to come up with an example when it is true and another example when it is false.
A sequence is generated by the nth term formula $30 - 7n$. Is the sequence increasing or decreasing? How can you tell? What is the first term? How do you know?	Encourage students to think of the sequence generated by $30 - 7n$ as the sequence that is formed by subtracting each number in the 7 times table from 30.
Here are 2 sequences: 6, 12, 18, 24, 30, … 29, 23, 17, 11, 5, … What is the sum of the two first terms? The second terms? The third terms? How does this help you to find the nth term for the sequence 29, 23, 17, 11, 5, …? What is the nth term of the sequence that begins 19, 15, 11, 7, …?	Remind students that the nth term for the 6 times table is $6n$. For the sequence 19, 15, 11, 7, …, prompt students to add on terms from the 4 times table.

Common errors/misconceptions

Misconception	Strategies to address
Thinking that the term-to-term rule 'multiply by 2' generates the sequence of even numbers.	Consider lots of sequences that can be generated by the term-to-term rule 'multiply by 2', for example: 1, 2, 4, 8, … 0.75, 1.5, 3, 6, … −5, −10, −20, −40, … Point out that these sequences are not linear and can contain negative and fractional terms.
Only writing down part of the nth term rule. For example, for the sequence beginning 2, 10, 18, …, giving the rule as $8n$.	Point out to students that the nth term rule has two parts: • One part is the bit that relates to the times table the sequence is produced from. • The other part is the adjustment from the times table to get the sequence.

Misconception	Strategies to address
Thinking that the nth term of a linear sequence has the form: [difference between terms]n + [first term]	Generate sequences from several different nth term rules (such as $5n + 7$, $6n + 2$, $3n - 5$, $45 - 2n$). Note that the first term in the sequence is not one of the coefficients in the formula. You could point out that the constant term in the formula could be thought of as the imaginary term that appears before the first term.
Forgetting the minus sign when giving the nth term rule for decreasing sequences. For example, giving the nth term for the sequence 33, 31, 29, … as $35 + 2n$ instead of $35 - 2n$.	Encourage students to always check their formulae by substituting in $n = 1$ and $n = 2$ to check they give the first two terms of the sequence.

Developing conceptual understanding

9As1 Generate terms of a sequence using term-to-term and position-to-term rules.

- FIX: Look at sequences generated by a range of different term-to-term rules, such as:
    - 'add 11'
    - 'multiply by 5'
    - 'divide by 2'
    - 'multiply by −3'
    - 'multiply by 2 and add 3'
    - 'divide by 2 and subtract 1'.

Note that some sequences can be increasing, some decreasing and some have signs that alternate between positive and negative. Encourage students to appreciate that not all sequences are linear.

- FIX: Develop understanding for nth term rules by getting students to generate the sequences produced from different rules.

> TIP: Use the matching cards available as a photocopiable resource to pair a rule with a term from the corresponding sequence.

STRETCH: Students working at greater depth could make up some term-to-term rules that match the first two terms of a sequence.

For example, a sequence begins 16, 4, … What could the term-to-term rule be?

9As2 Derive an expression to describe the nth term of an arithmetic sequence.

- FIX When finding the nth term of an increasing sequence, encourage students to adopt a step-by-step approach.

For example: 11, 18, 25, 32, …

○ Decide on the times table it is based on.	7 times table
○ Write down the first few terms in this times table.	7, 14, 21, 28, …
○ Decide on the adjustment needed to get the sequence.	Add 4 to each term
○ Write down the nth term.	$7n + 4$

STRETCH: Students working at greater depth could begin to consider the nth term of sequences that contains fractions or decimals.

For example, find the nth term of 2.5, 3, 3.5, 4, … or $\dfrac{7}{10}, \dfrac{9}{10}, \dfrac{11}{10}, \ldots$

End of chapter mental maths exercise

1. The term-to-term rule for a sequence is 'multiply by 6'. Find the third term if the first term is 5.

2. The term-to-term rule for a sequence is 'multiply by 2 and subtract 1'. The second term is 9. What was the first term?

3. The position-to-term rule for a sequence is 'multiply by –3 and then add 17'. Find the fifth term.

4. The nth term of a sequence is given by the formula $7n + 4$. Find the fourth term.

5. The nth term for a sequence is $5n - 3$. Find the sum of the first two terms.

6. Write down the nth term formula for the sequence that begins 1, 5, 9, 13, …

Technology recommendations

- **Golden ratio**

  The Fibonacci sequence begins 1, 1, 2, 3, 5, …

  Each term in the Fibonacci is the sum of the two terms that come before it.

	A	B	C
1	Position in sequence	Fibonacci sequence	Divide terms
2	1	1	
3	2	1	=B3/B2
4	3	=B2 + B3	
5	4		
6	5		

Enter the numbers from 1 to 20 in column A.

Copy the formula from cell B4 down column B to generate the first 20 terms in the sequence.

Copy the formula from cell C3 down column C. What do you notice about the numbers in Column C?

TIP: The numbers in column C should converge to the **golden ratio** 1.61803… Encourage students to research the golden ratio on the internet. How does it relate to art, architecture, the human body and nature? Ask students to produce a poster to show what they have found out.

STRETCH: Explore this alternative way to find the golden ratio.

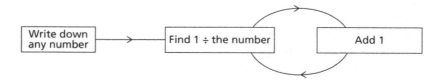

Example: Starting number 5

Stage 1: $1 \div 5 = 0.2$ \hspace{2cm} $0.2 + 1 = 1.2$

Stage 2: $1 \div 1.2 = 0.8333…$ \hspace{1cm} $0.8333… + 1 = 1.8333…$

Stage 3: $1 \div 1.8333… = 0.54545…$ \hspace{0.5cm} $0.54545… + 1 = 1.54545…$

Try to create a spreadsheet to perform the calculations for you.

- The term-to-term rule for a sequence is 'divide by 4'.

  The first term in the sequence is 30.

  Set up a spreadsheet to find the first 12 terms in the sequence.

	A	B	C
1	Position in sequence	Sequence	Sum of terms
2	1	30	=B2
3	2	=B$\frac{2}{4}$	=C2+B3
4	3	=B$\frac{3}{4}$	=C3+B4
5	4		
6	5		

  What do you notice about the numbers in the sequence?

  Use column C to calculate the sums of terms in the sequence (first term, sum of first two terms, sum of first three terms, etc.). What do you notice about the numbers in column C?

Investigation/research tasks

- **Fibonacci sequence in Pascal's triangle**   *Problem solving*

  Find the sum of the numbers along each of the diagonals in Pascal's triangle, as shown in the diagram.

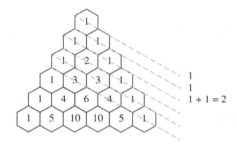

  These sums should form the Fibonacci sequence 1, 1, 2, 3, 5, 8, …

  Each term in the Fibonacci sequence is the sum of the two previous terms.

  Continue the sequence to get the first 15 terms.

  Take any three consecutive terms in the Fibonacci sequence, such as 2, 3, 5. Square the middle term ($3^2 = 9$) and multiply the other two terms together ($2 \times 5 = 10$). Repeat for other sets of three consecutive terms. What do you notice?

  STRETCH: Take any four consecutive terms in the Fibonacci sequence, such as 2, 3, 5, 8. Find the product of the first and fourth of these terms ($2 \times 8 = 16$). Then find the product of the other two terms ($3 \times 5 = 15$). Repeat with other sets of four consecutive terms from the sequence. What do you notice?

- **Triangular numbers**   *Problem solving*

  The diagram shows the first three patterns in a sequence.

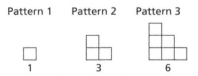

Pattern 1   Pattern 2   Pattern 3
1   3   6

Draw Patterns 4 and 5.

These patterns produce the sequence of triangular numbers: 1, 3, 6, 10, 15, … Find the first 10 triangular numbers.

Find the sum of pairs of consecutive triangular numbers. For example: 3 + 6 = 9

What is special about all these sums?

STRETCH: Find a way for finding any triangular number directly from its position number. Use your method to find the 100th triangular number.

STRETCH: Explain your result about the sums of consecutive triangular numbers.

- **Number chains**   *Problem solving*

  A chain of numbers is produced using these rules:

    If even, divide by 2.
    If odd, add 1.
    Stop when you get to 1.

  Example: The chain starting with 9 is 9 → 10 → 5 → 6 → 3 → 4 → 2 → 1

  This chain has a length of eight.

  Find the chain that starts with 11.

  Find the chains for other numbers less than 20. Do all the chains eventually reach 1? Which starting number less than 20 has the longest chain?

  Find all the chains that have a length of five. What is the largest number you can find that has a chain length of five?

  Find all the chains that have other lengths. What is the largest number that has each of these lengths?

  TIP: Encourage students to work systematically and to record their results neatly.

STRETCH: Explore chains of numbers produced by other rules, such as:

  If even, divide by 2.
  If odd, multiply by 3 and then add 1.
  Stop when you get to 1.

3D shapes

Learning objectives

Learning objectives covered in this chapter: 9Gs3, 9Gs4, 9Gs5

- Draw 3D shapes on isometric paper.
- Analyse 3D shapes through plans and elevations.
- Identify reflection symmetry in 3D shapes.

Key terms

- isometric paper
- plan view
- front elevation
- side elevation
- plane of symmetry

Prior knowledge assumptions

- Students can identify the number of faces, edges and vertices of 3D shapes.
- Students can remember that 3D objects can be represented by nets.
- Students can identify all the symmetries of 2D shapes.

Guidance on the hook

Purpose: The purpose of this hook is to introduce the idea of reflecting a three-dimensional shape in a mirror line and to develop spatial skills in readiness for the work in the chapter.

Use of the hook: Give each student five cubes. Arrange students into pairs.

Student 1 in each pair should arrange their cubes to make a 3D shape. Student 2 then reflects the 3D shape in an imaginary mirror line that is placed between the two players.

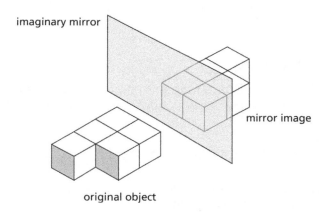

The two players then swap roles.

Encourage students to find a way of recording on paper what the original and reflected shapes looked like.

Adaptation: You could give each pair of students a real mirror so that they can see what the reflected shape looks like.

Extension: Students working at a greater depth could work with a greater number of cubes. They could also reflect the initial object in a pair of mirror lines.

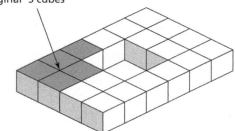

Starter ideas

Mental maths starter

Write down the number of faces of a cuboid.	Write down the number of faces of a triangular-based pyramid.	Write down the number of faces of a triangular prism.	Write down the number of faces of a square-based pyramid.
How many more vertices does a cube have than a tetrahedron?	What is the number of vertices on a prism with a cross-section that is a pentagon?	What is the total of the number of edges on a cube and the number of edges on a tetrahedron?	For a triangular prism, what is the difference between the number of edges and the number of vertices?
Which 3D object is this the net of?	Which 3D object is this the net of?	Which 3D object is this the net of?	Which 3D shape is this the net of?
What is the order of rotational symmetry for an equilateral triangle?	What is the order of rotational symmetry for a parallelogram?	What is the order of rotational symmetry for a regular hexagon?	What is the order of rotational symmetry for a rectangle?
How many lines of symmetry does a kite have?	How many lines of symmetry does an isosceles triangle have?	How many lines of symmetry does a rhombus have?	How many lines of symmetry does a regular octagon have?

Start point check: Target board

Give students a copy of the Target Board from the photocopiable resource and provide the following instructions. From the Target board, choose me an example of a letter with:
- o no line symmetry
- o two lines of symmetry
- o two lines of symmetry but no rotational symmetry
- o rotational symmetry of order 2
- o rotational symmetry of order 2 and no lines of symmetry
- o no rotational symmetry and no line symmetry.

TIP: The Target board is available in the photocopiable resources.

Show me …

Give each student six cubes.

Ask students to use all six cubes to make objects with different plan views.

For example, show me an object with these plan views:

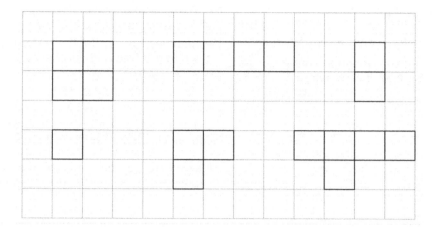

Discussion ideas

Probing questions	Teacher prompts
How many cubes are each of these objects made from?	Prompt students to appreciate that we cannot be absolutely sure as some cubes could be hidden. Where could hidden cubes be? What if both objects were prisms? Could the number of cubes be counted then?
Here are the plan and elevations of a prism made from cubes. plan front elevation side elevation How many cubes is the prism made from? What is the least number of cubes that are needed to make it into a cuboid?	How many cubes are needed to make the cross-sectional shape? How many cubes back does the prism extend? What will the size of the cuboid be?
Here are the plan views of four 3D objects. What could each object be?	Could some of the diagrams represent more than one possible object? Why do you think we combine plan views with front and side elevations?

Probing questions	Teacher prompts
Always, sometimes, never? • A pyramid has at least one plane of symmetry. • A prism with a trapezium-shaped cross section has exactly one plane of symmetry. • A hemisphere has no planes of symmetry.	Encourage students to give reasons for their answers. If students believe a statement is sometimes true, prompt them to give an example of when it is true and another example of when it is false.
An object is made from five cubes. By adding a sixth cube, is it possible to make an object with: • no planes of symmetry • one plane of symmetry • two planes of symmetry • three planes of symmetry?	Build the object from cubes if students have difficulty in visualising the situation. If the object can be made, prompt students to explain where the sixth cube would need to be placed. If the object cannot be made, encourage students to try to give a reason why.

Common errors/misconceptions

Misconception	Strategies to address
When using isometric paper, drawing the hidden lines. For example, drawing a cuboid as: 	Begin by getting students to draw a single cube and then cuboids of different sizes. Once students are happy drawing cuboids, extend to drawing more complex 3D shapes.
Drawing lines in the wrong direction on isometric paper. For example: 	Emphasise that horizontal lines are not drawn on isometric paper. Give students different representations of cuboids drawn on isometric paper. Ask students to discuss in groups which diagrams show isometric paper being used correctly. (See the photocopiable resources for a possible set of cuboids that could be given to students.)

Misconception	Strategies to address
Not drawing a view from the correct direction.	Show students some real-life examples of plans and elevations. For example, architectural drawings of houses.
Not spotting all planes of symmetry. For example, only identifying planes of symmetry that are vertical or horizontal.	Use models of 3D shapes to help students to visualise more easily where the planes are. Use modelling clay to cut a shape in half along a plane of symmetry.

Developing conceptual understanding

9Gs3 Draw 3D shapes on isometric paper.

- FIX: Give each student about eight cubes and ask them to construct an object from them. Students should then draw their object on isometric paper.

Ask students to swap their drawings with a partner to see whether they can use the drawing to build the original object.

TIP: Make sure students have their isometric paper the right way up. There should be lines/ dots running vertically up the page.

TIP: When drawing an object on isometric paper, encourage students to work from a starting vertex. Students may find it easiest to begin with a vertex on the left of the shape and then work down and across.

- FIX: Students could develop their skills at using isometric paper by writing their name in capitals in 3D.

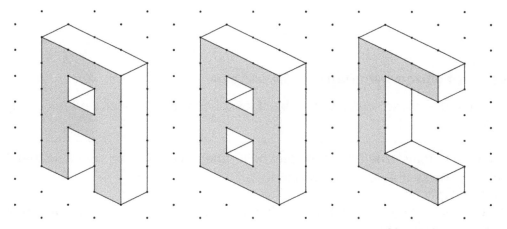

STRETCH: Students working at greater depth could try to draw what an object could look like when two objects are placed on top of each other.

For example, students could find possible objects when these two objects are placed on top of each other:

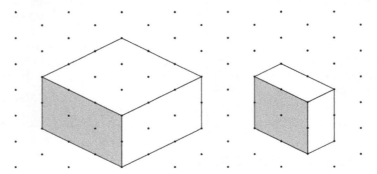

9Gs4 Analyse 3D shapes through plans and elevations.

- FIX: Students could begin by drawing the plan and elevation of 3D objects, such as a cuboid, triangular prism, cone and pyramid. They could then progress onto more complex shapes.

TIP: If students are struggling to draw the plans and elevations, give them models of the shapes so that they can look at them from different directions.

STRETCH: Students working at a greater depth could try to draw plans and elevations that involve drawing hidden edges.

For example, drawing the plan of this 3D object:

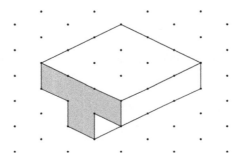

9Gs5 Identify reflection symmetry in 3D shapes.

- FIX: You could use modelling clay (or a block of cheese) to demonstrate the concept of planes of symmetry.

TIP: Some students may benefit from models of 3D shapes or building cubes so that they can see more clearly where the planes of symmetry are.

STRETCH: Students working at a greater depth could try to draw shapes that have a given number of planes of symmetry.

For example, draw two pyramids with four planes of symmetry.

End of chapter mental maths exercise

1. Here is a prism:

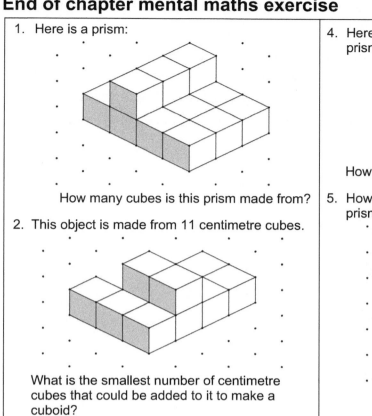

   How many cubes is this prism made from?

2. This object is made from 11 centimetre cubes.

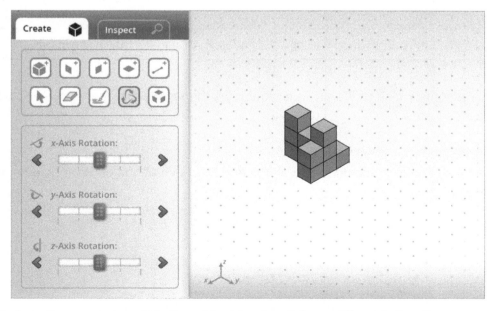

   What is the smallest number of centimetre cubes that could be added to it to make a cuboid?

3. Sketch the plan view of a cylinder that is standing on one of its circular faces.

4. Here are the plan and front elevations of a prism.

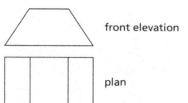

   front elevation

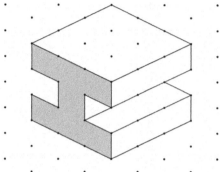

   plan

   How many faces does the prism have?

5. How many planes of symmetry does this prism have?

6. Two congruent cubes are stuck together so that one cube is directly on top of the second.

   How many planes of symmetry does the new object have?

Technology recommendations

- Use an isometric drawing tool website to demonstrate the use of isometric paper:
  https://www.nctm.org/Classroom-Resources/Illuminations/Interactives/Isometric-Drawing-Tool/

The tool also allows you to rotate the object to view it from different directions.

As well as being used for whole-class demonstrations, students could use the tool on their own to build their own objects and to promote understanding.

- Use an interactive website to introduce plans and elevations. The following website has activities at four levels that are designed to introduce students to the idea of viewing objects from different directions: http://www.transum.org/Maths/Activity/Plans_and_Elevations/

  Students could work through the activities on their own or work through them in pairs.

Investigation/research tasks

- **Five-cube problem**   *Problem solving*

  Find all the different ways of arranging five cubes. The cubes can stick together.

  These two arrangements are congruent so only count once.

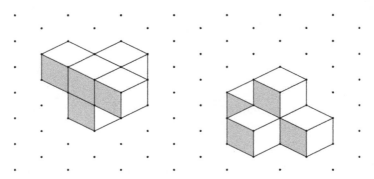

  Record all of your arrangements on isometric paper.

  Find the number of planes of symmetry of each arrangement.

BEWARE: The cubes should be joined so that the entire face of one cube connects with the entire face of another.

TIP: Give all students some interlocking cubes to help them find different arrangements.

TIP: There are 29 different arrangements – 12 flat shapes and 17 that are not flat.

STRETCH: Investigate which of the arrangements has the smallest surface area and which has the greatest surface area.

- **What's the object?**   *Problem solving*

  The diagrams show the plans, side elevations and front elevations of three objects made from four cubes.

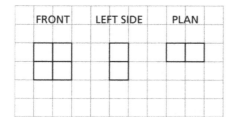 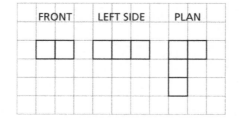

FRONT	LEFT SIDE	PLAN

Make each of the objects with cubes and draw them on isometric paper.

- **Planes of symmetry of a cube**   *Problem solving*

  Find all the planes of symmetry for a cube.

  Draw each possible plane on a diagram.

TIP: A cube has a total of nine planes of symmetry.

- **Impossible isometric drawings**   *Research*

  Here is an isometric drawing.

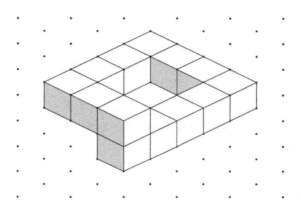

It shows an impossible object.

Research on the internet other impossible objects and make a display.

STRETCH: Students could draw their own impossible object on isometric paper.

Transformations and tessellations

Learning objectives	Key terms
Learning objectives covered in this chapter: 9Gp1, 9Gp2 • Tessellate triangles and quadrilaterals and relate to angle sums and half-turn rotations; know which regular polygons tessellate, and explain why others will not. • Use the coordinate grid to solve problems involving translations, rotations, reflections and enlargements.	• tessellate • regular tessellation • transformation • translation • reflection • rotation • enlargement • object • image

Prior knowledge assumptions
- Students know the names of polygons with different numbers of sides.
- Students know the sum of the angles in a triangle and in a quadrilateral.
- Students can translate, rotate, reflect and enlarge shapes.

Guidance on the hook

Purpose: The purpose of this hook is to introduce the idea of tessellations by considering simple tiling patterns in a familiar context.

Use of the hook: Give students a piece of centimetre-squared paper. Students will also need a ruler, pencil and coloured pencils.

Ask students to draw a rectangle measuring 12 cm by 6 cm to represent the patio. The tiles that are to cover the patio should be drawn to a size of 2 cm by 1 cm. Tiles at the edge of the patio can be cut to fit.

Emphasise that the tiles should be placed to make a repeating pattern.

Encourage students to colour their design, making sure that the colouring maintains the repeating pattern.

Finished designs could be made into a display.

Adaptation: Students could cut out 2 cm by 1 cm tiles from coloured paper and then stick these onto the rectangular paper. The size of the rectangular pattern could be altered.

Extension: Students working at a greater depth could try to tile the patio using a different shaped tile for example:

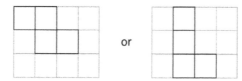

or

Starter ideas

Mental maths starter

Write down the name of a polygon with five sides.	How many sides has a heptagon?	Write down the name of a polygon with 10 sides.	Work out the total of the number of sides on an octagon and the number of sides on a hexagon.
Two angles in a triangle are 85° and 40°. Find the size of the third angle.	A triangle has angles of 90° and 48°. Work out the size of the third angle.	Two of the angles in an isosceles triangle are 62°. Work out the size of the third angle.	One of the angles in an isosceles triangle is 102°. Work out the size of one of the other angles.
A quadrilateral has angles measuring 100°, 120° and 50°. Work out the size of the fourth angle.	A quadrilateral has two right-angles and an angle of 75°. Work out the size of the fourth angle.	The acute angles in a parallelogram measure 40°. Work out the size of each obtuse angle.	A quadrilateral has two angles of 105° and an angle of 80°. Work out the size of the fourth angle.
A translation moves a shape three squares right and two squares up. Describe the translation that will take the image back to the original shape.	A translation moves a shape seven squares left and one square up. Describe the translation that will take the image back to the original shape.	A translation moves a shape five squares right and three squares down. Describe the translation that will take the image back to the original shape.	A translation moves a shape four squares left and one square down. Describe the translation that will take the image back to the original shape.
The shortest side of a shape measures 3.5 cm. The shape is enlarged by a scale factor of 3. Write down the length of the smallest side of the image.	A shape is enlarged by a scale factor of 4. The longest side of the image is 8.6 cm. Work out the length of the longest side of the original shape.	The shortest side of a shape measures 3.4 cm. The shape is enlarged by a scale factor of 5. Write down the length of the smallest side of the image.	A triangle has sides of lengths 2 cm, 3.5 cm and 4.5 cm. The triangle is enlarged by a scale factor of 2. Work out the perimeter of the image.

Start point check: Mini whiteboards

Give each student a mini whiteboard and ask them to show you:

- a nonagon
- an isosceles triangle with an angle of 50° (mark on the sizes of all the other angles)
- a rhombus with an angle of 65° (mark on the sizes of all the other angles)
- a quadrilateral with a reflex angle
- a quadrilateral that would look the same if it was rotated by 90° in a clockwise direction
- a pentagon that would look the same if it was reflected in a horizontal line.

> TIP: If you do not have any mini whiteboards you could ask students to reveal their answers to you on A4 paper.

Remember me …

Show students a geometrical image (such as the image shown here) for two minutes and ask students to remember it. (The image could be projected onto the wall or shown on an interactive whiteboard.)

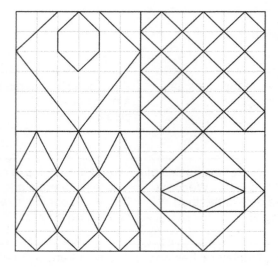

Give out pieces of centimetre-squared paper and then give students four minutes to recreate the image.

> TIP: If you do not have a projector or interactive whiteboard, you could fix photocopies of the image to the wall.

Discussion ideas

Probing questions	Teacher prompts
Show me two shapes that will tessellate. Now show me another two.	Prompt students to show a tessellation for each of their shapes. Encourage students to draw different types of shapes.
Convince me that a regular octagon does not tessellate.	Prompt students to see what happens when trying to fit regular octagons around a point.
Always, sometimes never? • A parallelogram will tessellate. • A triangle will tessellate. • An octagon will tessellate.	Prompt students to appreciate that two triangular shapes will fit together to make a parallelogram which can tessellate. Prompt students to consider octagons such as:

Probing questions	Teacher prompts
What's the same and what's different? • enlargement of R scale factor 2, centre (-6, 2) and • enlargement of R scale factor 3, centre (-5, 3)	Prompt students to think about both the size and the location of the image of R under the two enlargements.
What happens to the coordinates of a point when it is reflected in the x-axis? What happens to the coordinates when the point is reflected in the y-axis?	Prompt students to consider points in different quadrants. Encourage students to write down the coordinates of the starting point and the coordinates of the image.

Common errors/misconceptions

Misconception	Strategies to address
Believing that any regular polygon can be made to tessellate.	Give students opportunities to try to tessellate a range of different regular shapes, some of which tessellate and some of which do not.
Joining shapes together to fill a space but without showing a repeating pattern.	Colouring all shapes the same way round in the same colour can help students to see a repeating pattern. Make sure students show enough shapes in their diagrams so that the repeating pattern is evident.
When reflecting a shape in a diagonal line, students sometimes do not consider the distance in a direction perpendicular to the line.	Use tracing paper to help get the image in the correct position.
Thinking that the centre of rotation or enlargement is always the origin.	Give students plenty of opportunities to rotate and enlarge for a variety of different centres. Encourage students to always mark the centre on the grid.

Misconception	Strategies to address
When finding the image of a point P under an enlargement, students may make the mistake of measuring the distance to the image from the original point P rather than measuring from the centre.	Encourage students to check that their enlarged shape has actually been enlarged by the correct scale factor.

Developing conceptual understanding

9Gp1 Tessellate triangles and quadrilaterals and relate to angle sums and half-turn rotations; know which regular polygons tessellate, and explain why others will not.

- FIX: Give students tiles of various triangles and quadrilaterals. Students should use these tiles to try to produce a tessellation (see photocopiable resources).

TIP: If students are experiencing difficulty producing a tessellation, encourage them to try using the original tile and a rotation of the original tile through 180°.

- FIX: Students could use dynamic geometry software to explore tessellations of regular polygons. Students could attempt to create tessellations of regular polygons with between 5 and 10 sides so that they can explore which regular polygons tessellate and which will not.

TIP: Encourage students to see that three regular pentagons fit around a point but these leave a gap which is too small for another pentagon to fit into.

BEWARE: Knowing the interior angles of regular polygons is not covered until Chapter 19.

STRETCH: Students working at a greater depth could explore semi-regular tessellations, such as a tessellation involving octagons and squares:

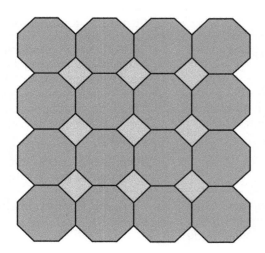

9Gp2 Use the coordinate grid to solve problems involving translations, rotations, reflections and enlargements.

- FIX: Students could be encouraged to using tracing paper to reflect a shape in a mirror line:
  - o Trace the original shape and the mirror line.
  - o Flip the tracing paper over and position the tracing paper so that the traced mirror line is on top of the actual mirror line.
  - o The tracing paper will now show the position of the image.

> TIP: This method for finding the position of a reflected shape is particularly useful when the mirror line is not vertical or horizontal.

- FIX: Tracing paper is particularly useful when rotating a shape using a given centre:
  - o Trace the original shape.
  - o Put the point of a pencil on the centre and turn the tracing paper through the desired angle.
  - o The tracing paper will now show the position of the image.
- FIX: Enlargements on a grid can be best done by counting grid squares:
  - o Count the number of squares horizontally and vertically from the centre to a vertex.
  - o Multiply these distances by the scale factor.
  - o Find the image of the vertex by counting the new number of squares from the centre.

STRETCH: Students working at a greater depth could try enlarging a shape with a fractional scale factor.

End of chapter mental maths exercise

1. An arrow is drawn on a coordinate grid.

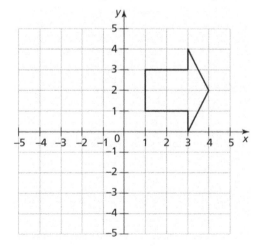

   The arrow points to the right. In which direction will the arrow point after if it is reflected in the line $y = 1$?

2. The arrow from Question 1 is rotated by 90° anticlockwise, centre the origin. In which direction will the arrow now point?

3. A square has sides that each measure 0.8 cm. The square is enlarged by a scale factor of 3. Find the perimeter of the image.

4. Draw a regular polygon that will tessellate.

5. Draw a regular polygon that will not tessellate.

Technology recommendations

- Use a tessellation creator tool to demonstrate tessellations:
  https://www.nctm.org/Classroom-Resources/Illuminations/Interactives/Tessellation-Creator/

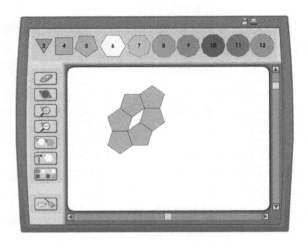

The tool could also be used by students to discover for themselves which regular polygons will tessellate.

Interactive whiteboards are also an immensely valuable tool to use when demonstrating tessellations.

- Use dynamic geometry software to motivate the learning of transformations. Ask students to use the software to:
  - o reflect a shape in an axis
  - o rotate a shape about a given point
  - o enlarge a shape using a given centre
  - o translate a shape.

Investigation/research tasks

- **Tessellating triangles**   *Problem solving*

Draw a tessellation of these right-angled triangles.

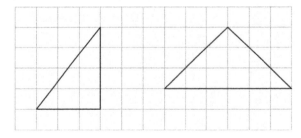

Do all right-angled triangles tessellate?

Draw a tessellation of these isosceles triangles:

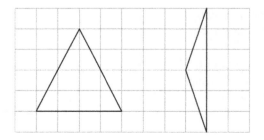

Do all isosceles triangles tessellate?

Draw a tessellation of these scalene triangles.

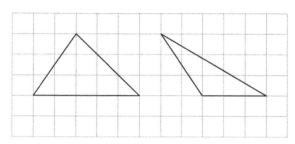

Do all triangles tessellate?

TIP: Photocopy a sheet containing lots of each type of triangle (photocopiable resources). Students could then cut these out and use them as tiles to produce a tessellation. They could then stick each of their tessellations onto a sheet of paper.

STRETCH: Encourage students to see if they can give any explanations about why triangles tessellate.

- **Tessellating pentominoes**   *Problem solving*

  A pentomino is a shape made from five squares connected edge-to-edge.

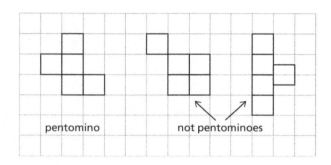

pentomino   not pentominoes

Find all the different pentominoes. Check that each of your pentominoes is not a reflection or rotation of another.

Investigate which of your pentominoes will tessellate. Remember to draw enough shapes in your tessellation to show the repeating pattern.

TIP: Students may benefit from cutting out each of their pentominoes so that they can check that they are all different. Students should find that there are 12 different pentominoes and that they all can tessellate.

BEWARE: Students may try to fit pentominoes together without showing a repeating pattern. Make sure that students are aware that a repeating pattern needs to be seen.

STRETCH: Ask students to find examples of hexominoes (formed by connecting six squares) that do not tessellate.

• Escher tessellations

Students could research the tessellations of Escher on the internet.
Students could then try to draw their own Escher-style tessellation.

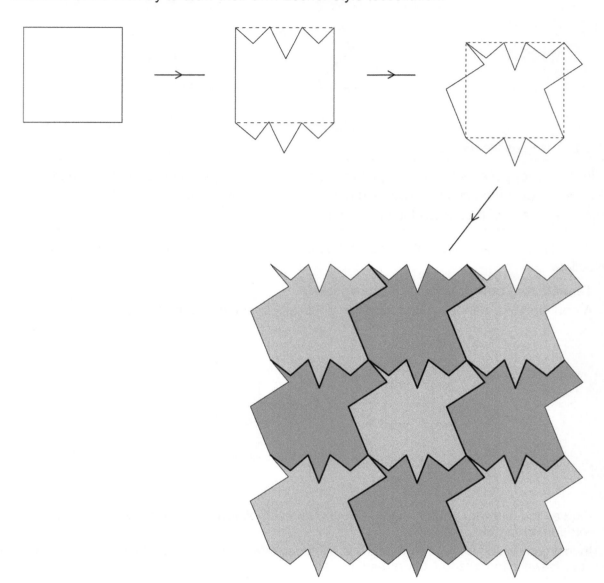

Measures

Learning objectives

Learning objectives covered in this chapter: 9Ml1, 9Ma1

- Solve problems involving measurements in a variety of contexts.

- Convert between metric units of area, e.g. mm^2 and cm^2, cm^2 and m^2 and volume, e.g. mm^3 and cm^3, cm^3 and m^3; know and use the relationship $1\ cm^3 = 1\ ml$.

Key terms

- 10 mm = 1 cm
- 100 cm = 1 m
- 1000 m = 1 km
- 1000 mg = 1 g
- 1000 g = 1 kg
- 1000 kg = 1 t (tonne)
- 1000 ml = 1 l

Prior knowledge assumptions

- Students should know how to use suitable metric units.
- Students should be able to convert between metric measures.
- Students should be familiar with multiplying and dividing by powers of 10.

Guidance on the hook

Purpose: This task places the concept of area in an everyday context for the students. It develops the skill of estimating area using the students' immediate surroundings.

Use of the hook: Begin by asking students to discuss in groups how the areas of different items can be estimated (for example, the area of the wall, window, desk top, classroom floor, hall floor, playground, sports field, farmer's field) and what units could be used. (Is there more than one unit that could be used, and which ones are appropriate/not appropriate?)

Begin the hook activity and include discussing the calculations needed to estimate the area of the floor. Discuss whole amounts, fraction, decimal parts of the area, etc.

Adaptation: For lower-attaining pupils, smaller areas could be investigated first. For example, estimating the area of a desk top using the area of a book cover.

Extension: Students could repeat the hook activity for larger areas. For example, estimating the area of a sports field.

TIP: An alternative approach to the hook is for a student-led approach in groups, finding the areas of different items.

BEWARE: The hook activity could need a lot of time.

Starter ideas

Mental maths starter

Estimate the length of 'this desk top' in cm.	Use a suitable unit to find the area of 'this piece of small card'.	Estimate the mass of 'this ball' in g.	What is the capacity of 'this tin'?

What is the area of a table top 3.5 m long and 0.25 m wide?	What is the total mass of four 65.5 g balls?	Find the volume of a cuboid 8 mm long, 16 mm wide and 40 mm high	Find the total capacity of twelve 26 ml small spoons.
Calculate 5 mm + 30 cm	Calculate 2250 m − 1.5 km + 30 m	Calculate 50 g + 0.55 kg	Calculate 6 l − 1.5 l + 350 ml
How many mm are in 2.67 cm?	Find the difference between 2.3 m and 543 cm.	What is total mass of two 345 g bags of flour and three 4.3 kg bags of flour?	How many 145 ml cups equal the capacity of a 7.25 l bucket?
Calculate 2.35 × 100	Calculate 0.0064 × 1000	Calculate 9000 ÷ 10 000	Calculate 704 ÷ 100 000

Start point check

Matching – multiplication and division by powers of ten   *Problem solving*

Give students a set of cards (see photocopiable resources).

Ask students to work in pairs to match the cards, completing any blank cards. Explain that if a question needs to be written, it should be a multiplication or division involving powers of ten. Students check each other's solutions, justifying to each other why new questions work.

- FIX: Limit the number of cards that need matching to any students who are struggling; do not include blanks.

STRETCH: Pairs of students can create their own set of cards, including blanks, for another pair to match (see photocopiable resources). Students check each other's solutions, justifying to each other why new questions work.

Card matching – conversion of metric units   *Problem solving*

Give students a set of cards (see photocopiable resources).

Ask students to work in pairs to match the cards, completing any blank cards. Explain that one card needs units to be added to it. (Students can use any units except units of area or volume.) Students check each other's solutions, justifying to each other why new questions work.

- FIX: Limit the number of cards that need matching to any students who are struggling; do not include blanks.

STRETCH: Pairs of students can create their own set of cards, including blanks, for another pair to match (see photocopiable resources). Students check each other's solutions, justifying to each other why new questions work.

> TIP: For an alternative start point activity, conversion of metric units and multiplication and division by powers of ten could be reinforced through a spiral activity. For example:
>
> Write '10' in the middle of the board. Gradually add calculations using multiplication and division by powers of 10, as in the example below, using suggestions from the students:

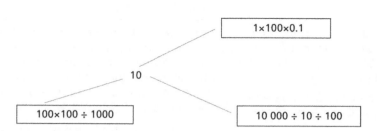

Write '6 cm' in the middle of the board. Gradually add equivalent conversions, as in the example below, using suggestions from the students:

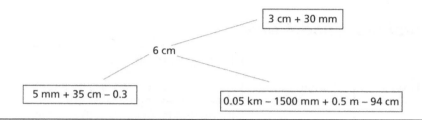

Discussion ideas

Probing questions	Teacher prompts
What would happen if an area was measured in both mm^2 and cm^2?	Suggest to the students that they try an example to support their thinking, with any necessary drawings. • FIX: Suggest that a drawing could be made of a cm^2 divided into mm^2 to help with the conversion.
A field of area 5000 m^2 consists of barley, except for track of length 50 m and width 375 cm. Explain why the area of barley is less than 5000 m^2.	Encourage the students to draw bar models/diagrams to help with the problem and to consider the different steps needed for the explanation. *Problem solving* • FIX: Suggest that the area of the track is found first.
A recipe consists of three ingredients in the ratio 5 : 2 : 3. Enzo has the ingredients in the ratio 250 g : 100 g : 0.4 kg Convince Enzo that he can't make the recipe without modifying his ingredients.	Ask the students to write out their explanation on paper and then explain it to a partner. Ask them to use full, complete mathematical sentences. *Problem solving* TIP: Use think, pair, share as an approach when using this question. • FIX: Encourage the conversion of 0.4 kg to grams as a first step.
A piece of cloth has an area of 2.25 m^2. How could you determine that there is enough cloth for exactly 900 squares, each with an area of 25 cm^2?	Encourage the students to draw bar models/diagrams to help with the problem. Ask them to write out their explanation on paper and then explain it to a partner. Ask them to use full, complete mathematical sentences. *Problem solving* TIP: Ask students to demonstrate their answers to the rest of the class.

Probing questions	Teacher prompts
A $2.50 litre of paint will cover 16 m². John's restaurant is a rectangle 9 m long and 7 m wide. The walls are 250 cm high. John wants to paint the walls and the ceiling. How can John be sure that $40 will be enough money to buy all the paint that is needed?	Encourage the students to draw bar models/diagrams to help with the problem. Ask them to write out the steps needed to solve the problem on paper and then explain it to a partner. Ask them to use full, complete mathematical sentences. *Problem solving* • FIX: Provide hint/support cards/other forms of scaffolding that suggest steps that can be used to tackle the problem.

Common errors/misconceptions

Misconception	Strategies to address
Students find it difficult to visualise the size of areas/volumes.	Reinforce understanding by students drawing/creating units of area/volume and then using them, that is, using cm² tiles/m² made from canes to find an area.
Students convert between area/volume measures using linear conversions.	Reinforce understanding (by using diagrams, that is, squares/cubes) to show the relationships between units.
Students not understanding whether a step needed, when solving a problem, is division or multiplication.	Reinforce understanding by students considering the answer and whether multiplication or division will achieve it.

Developing conceptual understanding

9MI1 Solve problems involving measurements in a variety of contexts.

• FIX: Problems can be scaffolded by the use of hint/support cards that students can refer to when solving them.

STRETCH: Ask students to work in pairs to create their own questions, based on those in Exercise 1. Solutions to the questions can be found by sharing with others. Students should be encouraged to explain and justify their solutions.   *Problem solving*

9Ma1 Convert between metric units of area, e.g. mm² and cm², cm² and m² and volume, e.g. mm³ and cm³, cm³ and m³; know and use the relationship 1 cm³ = 1 ml.

• FIX: To support students in remembering what the conversion factor is, suggest that the multiplication of the linear units is considered. For example, for converting cm² to m² and vice versa, remember 100 cm × 100 cm = 1 m².

• FIX: To support students in remembering what the conversion factor is, use look and say. Students repeat a sentence. For example:

'To convert mm³ to cm³ you multiply by 1000.'

Ask students to repeat the phrase to another student.

STRETCH: Converting between, for example mm² and m², mm³ and m³, could be used to extend the understanding for students who have mastered the objective.

STRETCH: Ask students to work in pairs to create their own questions, based on those in Exercise 2, questions 3, 4 and 6. Solutions to the questions can be found by sharing with others. Students should be encouraged to explain and justify their solutions. *Problem solving*

End of chapter mental maths exercise

1. A snail travelled 10.5 mm in 65 seconds.

   How many minutes and seconds would it take to travel 5.25 cm?

2. A metal sheet is 90 cm long and 45 mm wide.

   Each 10 cm^2 has a mass of 50 g.

   What is the total mass of the metal sheet in kg?

3. Alfie, Pier and Andrea buy 3 tonnes of gravel.

   They share the gravel in the ratio 3 : 2 : 5 (Alfie : Pierre : Andrea).

   How many kg of gravel do they each receive?

4. Enzo's bath tap drips 15 ml every second.

   How long will it take for a 4.5 l bucket to become completely full? Give your answer in two units.

5. State whether the following are true or false. If they are false, correct any errors.

   a) 40 000 mm^2 = 40 cm^2

   b) 20 m^2 = 0.002 cm^2

   c) 300 cm^3 = 0.0003 m^2

6. A shipping container is 4 m long, 2.5 m wide and 2.5 m high.

   It costs \$5 to rent $\frac{1}{10}$ of the container.

   How much does it cost to rent 5 000 000 cm^3?

7. A tank holds 1000 l of oil. The last 40 l cannot be used.

   A boiler uses 40 ml of oil every time it starts.

   How many times can the boiler burn before the oil cannot be used?

Technology recommendations

• Ask students to investigate the history and use of metric units in different countries, industries etc. For example:

http://www.britannica.com/science/measurement-system/The-metric-system-of-measurement

9Ma1 Convert between metric units of area, e.g. mm^2 and cm^2, cm^2 and m^2 and volume, e.g. mm^3 and cm^3, cm^3 and m^3; know and use the relationship 1 cm^3 = 1 ml.

• Ask students to use spreadsheets to model the conversion between units. For example:

	Conversion of metric units of area	
mm^2	cm^2	m^2
12	0.12	0.000012
1000	10	0.001
20	0.2	0.00002
35	0.35	0.000035
4590	45.9	0.00459

	Conversion of metric units of area	
mm^2	cm^2	m^2
12	$=D\frac{4}{100}$	$=E\frac{4}{10000}$
1000	$=D\frac{5}{100}$	$=E\frac{5}{10000}$
20	$=D\frac{6}{100}$	$=E\frac{6}{10000}$
35	$=D\frac{7}{100}$	$=E\frac{7}{10000}$
4590	$=D\frac{8}{100}$	$=E\frac{8}{10000}$

Investigation/research tasks

- **Present students with the following information**:   *Problem solving*

Cube   Cuboid

Ask students to investigate the surface area and volume of the two shapes, choosing their own units for the dimensions.

Ask the students to convert the dimensions of the shapes into other units and then convert the areas and volumes without using calculations.

- FIX: For students who are less confident with surface area, the nets of the shapes could be drawn/found from boxes to support understanding.

STRETCH: For students who are confident with the learning objective, other shapes such as a cone and sphere (with their formulae) could be investigated.

> TIP: Encourage students to turn their images to help them if necessary – it is often easier to estimate an angle where one of the lines is either horizontal or vertical.

- **Present students with the following information:**   *Problem solving*

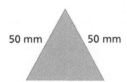

50 mm   50 mm

Ask students to find the area of each shape (using any measuring that is necessary).

Ask students to draw each shape on a coordinate grid, enlarging each shape using their own scale factor and centre of enlargement.

Ask students to convert the dimensions of the shapes into other units, and then convert the areas and the enlarged areas without using calculations.

- FIX: Students who are less confident with measuring can be given alternative dimensions (as integers) for the square and rectangle and be given the height of the triangle.

TIP: Students might need reminding of the formula for the area of a triangle.

TIP: When tasks are completed ask students to check the solutions.

STRETCH: Ask students to collect data from within the local area (for example, from the local sports centre) for creating their own questions, similar to Exercise 1 and Exercise 2, questions 3, 4 and 6.

TIP: Give students angles in increasing size to begin with to help them use their previous answer to help them estimate the next angle.

Data collection and averages

Learning objectives	Key terms
Learning objectives covered in this chapter 9Dc1, 9Dc2, 9Dc3, 9Dc4, 9Dp1	• primary data • secondary data

- Suggest a question to explore using statistical methods; identify the sets of data needed, how to collect them, sample sizes and degree of accuracy.
- Identify primary or secondary sources of suitable data.
- Design, trial and refine data collection sheets.
- Collect and tabulate discrete and continuous data, choosing suitable equal class intervals where appropriate.
- Calculate statistics and select those most appropriate to the problem.

Prior knowledge assumptions
- Students can calculate the mean, median and mode for a set of data and identify the modal class for a grouped frequency table.
- Students understand when to use each type of average.
- Students can identify sets of discrete and continuous data.
- Students can complete a frequency table so that it has equal class intervals.

Guidance on the hook

Purpose: This activity tests students on their ability to calculate statistics for a set of data, with a problem-solving approach where the statistic is given and students need to deduce the missing piece of data.

Use of the hook: Students are given the first seven scores in a game, and then asked to work out the eighth score, given a statistic (mean, median or range) for the first eight scores. There are five questions which students could work on individually or in pairs.

Solutions:

- If the mean is 11, the eighth score is 14.
- If the range is 9, the eighth score is 5 or 16.
- If the median is 10, the eighth score is 9 or any number less than 7.
- If the mean is 9.5, the eighth score is 2.
- If the median is 11, the eighth score is 11.

TIP: Students may find it helpful to write the known scores in order of size, especially when thinking about the median.

Extension: Students can try making up their own questions of this type.

Starter ideas

Mental maths starter

Find the median of the numbers 5, 1, 8, 3, 10.	Find the median of the numbers 77, 68, 55, 86, 93.	Find the median of the numbers 10, 50, 20, 60.	Find the median of the numbers 50, 42, 35, 65.
Find the mean of the numbers 5, 4, 9.	Find the mean of the numbers 2, 8, 8.	Find the mean of the numbers 12, 10, 15, 7.	Find the mean of the numbers 25, 23, 22, 10.
List the possible values of x if it is an integer in the range $0 < x < 5$.	List the possible values of x if it is an integer in the range $9 \leq x < 14$.	List the possible values of x if it is an integer in the range $12 < x \leq 18$.	List the possible values of x if it is an integer in the range $8 \leq x \leq 10$.
Which numbered value is the median of 11 data values?	Which numbered value is the median of 55 data values?	Which two numbered values are used to find the median of 20 data values?	Which two numbered values are used to find the median of 46 data values?
Three numbers have mode 6 and mean 7. What are the three numbers?	Three numbers have mean 10 and mode 11. What are the three numbers?	Three numbers have mean 20 and mode 20. What are the three numbers?	Three numbers have mean 6 and mode 4. What are the three numbers?

Start point check: Planning a school investigation

In small groups, students discuss how to investigate a question relating to students at their school, choosing from topics such as: internet use, mobile phone use, time spent watching television, time spent studying at home, time spent playing sport. Points for discussion could include:

- What do you want to find out?
- Who will you ask? (Just one class, or a year group, or the whole school?)
- What questions will you ask?
- How will you record the responses? (Audio recording of interviews, questionnaires on paper, or an online survey?)
- Will you group the data into classes, and if so, what class intervals will you use?

Either share ideas afterwards in a whole-class discussion, or ask each group to write a summary of their ideas. Discuss and correct any misconceptions.

Activity: Creating mnemonics for terms relating to data

Students often find it difficult to remember mathematical terms, particularly the correct name for each of the three types of average. Either in small groups or as a whole-class discussion, ask students to share ideas for mnemonics (memory aids) to help them remember key terms relating to data collection and analysis. Possible terms to include are:

Terms introduced prior to this chapter	Terms introduced in this chapter
mean	primary data
median	secondary data
mode	
range	
continuous data	
discrete data	
frequency diagram	

TIP: If students have not worked with mnemonics before, share some examples first. Some examples from other areas of mathematics are given below:

- acute angle – these belong to the smallest class of angle, and they are cute angles because they are so little!
- x- and y-axes (which is which) – the tail of the y hangs vertically, like the y-axis
- diameter – if you draw a diameter across a circle, it dies, because you have cut it in half!

TIP: Examples of mnemonics for some of the data-related terms above are:

- mean – this is the only type of average that always requires calculation, and the calculation can be difficult to do without a calculator, so it would be particularly 'mean' to ask a student to calculate the mean
- median – this sounds similar to the word 'medium'; when we arrange things in order of size, we put them in the order small-medium-large; medium is in the middle (like the median, which is the middle of a set of numbers when they are written in order of size)
- mode – the mode is the most common number
- secondary data – secondary data was collected by someone else, so you are the second person to handle it.

Discussion ideas

Probing questions	Teacher prompts
Why is it a good idea to collect a small amount of data and then use it to refine your data collection sheet, before collecting the rest of your data?	What sort of things might you learn about your data collection methods from collecting a small sample? In what ways might a questionnaire work more or less well?
	Exercise 2 of the Student's Book chapter includes questions about the design of data collection sheets (see photocopiable resources).
Why do we sometimes group data into classes, and sometimes not? Describe situations where you think it is appropriate to use groups, and situations where you think it is not.	Can you think of examples where we might or might not use grouped data? Could this depend on either or both of: the nature of the data; what we are hoping to learn from the data?
	If students are finding it difficult to think of examples, they could look at the Student's Book chapter for ideas.
	In the investigation called Effect of class interval on frequency diagrams (below), students can compare frequency diagrams created using the same data but with different class intervals, to see how this affects the usefulness and clarity of the diagrams.

Probing questions	Teacher prompts
What ages, *a* years, are included in each range? $5 < a \le 10$ $5 \le a < 10$ $5 \le a \le 10$ Which of these formats could be suitable for the class intervals of a grouped frequency table showing: discrete data consisting of integers only; continuous data?	Are the meanings of these class intervals affected by whether the data is discrete or continuous? For each of these class intervals, what would be the next class interval above the one shown, for discrete data consisting of integers only? What is the problem with using class intervals of the form $5 \le a \le 10$ with continuous data?
Comment on any problems with each of the frequency table designs below, and say how you would improve them. | Height of adult human (*h* cm)	Frequency
$0 < h < 10$	
$10 < h < 20$	
$20 < h < 30$	
$30 < h < 40$	
$40 < h < 50$	
$h > 50$	| | Age of student (*a* years)	Frequency
$0 \le s \le 4$	
$4 \le a \le 8$	
$8 \le a \le 12$			What are typical heights of adults? With class intervals of this format, in which class would a data value of 40 cm belong? In the second table, in which class does an age of 4 years belong?
When is it better to use the median than the mean?	Give students specific examples to work with. For example, in an organisation, nine people are paid $5 per hour and one person is paid $100 per hour. What are the mean and median amounts paid per hour? Which better represents the 'typical' pay per hour in this organisation?
With what type of data is the mode the only type of average that can be used?	When is it not possible to calculate a mean or find a median (because there are no numbers to work with)? Prompt students to think about categoric data. (For example, for data on people's favourite colour or animal, the mode can be stated as the most popular colour or animal type, whereas there is no meaning to the mean or median).

Common errors/misconceptions

Misconception	Strategies to address
Thinking that the highest possible degree of accuracy should always be used when collecting data.	Give examples of unnecessarily high degrees of accuracy, and ask students to think of more. Some examples are: including in school records the time of day (hour and minute) when each student was born; asking for people's ages to two decimal places; measuring people's heights to the nearest millimetre for their medical records; asking people's annual salaries to the nearest cent in a survey of pay in different professions. An example in which a relatively high degree of accuracy is desirable is in the records of winning times for the 100 m sprint in international tournaments, which may differ by only hundredths of a second.
Thinking that primary data sources are always 'better' than secondary data sources; or alternatively, thinking that 'primary' means 'basic' or 'simple' in this context.	Show students plenty of examples of primary and secondary data sources. Exercise 1 of the Student's Book chapter gives students practice in differentiating between primary and secondary sources (see photocopiable resources).
Not thinking critically about secondary sources of data.	Encourage students to check where secondary data comes from before they decide whether to use it: who collected it, and why? What methods were used in collecting and processing the data? When searching online, students quite often choose the first website that appears in the search results. With some search engines the first few sites to appear are advertisements, where companies have paid for their websites to appear when certain search terms are used. Point out that the most suitable website does not always appear on the first page of the search results. It may help to model this kind of thinking for students. Choose, or ask students to choose, a type of data to search for. Display your search on the board and speak your thought processes aloud as you sift through the results.
Having gaps or overlaps when grouping data.	Ask the student where they would place a data item that would be in the gap or overlap. Ask how they would organise their groups so that every possible data item will belong to one, and only one, of the class intervals.
Thinking that any type of average is appropriate for any set of data.	Have a class discussion about the advantages and disadvantages of the three types of average in different situations. Exercise 4 of the Student's Book chapter includes several questions in which students are asked to choose a suitable average for a set of data and explain their choice (see photocopiable resources).

Developing conceptual understanding

9Dc1 Suggest a question to explore using statistical methods; identify the sets of data needed, how to collect them, sample sizes and degree of accuracy.

- Ask students to talk about how they have used these skills in other subjects, such as geography and science. Ask them to share examples of data sources they used.

- FIX: It may not be easy for students to express a question in such a way that it can be answered using data collection and analysis. They may start with a vague question, such as 'Do students spend a lot of time on the internet?' or 'What subjects do people like?' and then need some help with refining the question and deciding exactly how to collect relevant data.

9Dc2 Identify primary or secondary sources of suitable data.

- FIX: Do not assume that the meanings of 'primary' and 'secondary' will be obvious to students in this context. If they are familiar with the terms 'primary school' and 'secondary school' then this may lead students to assume that primary data is basic or simple in some sense, and secondary data is more advanced. Check that students have a clear understanding of the terms, and discuss examples of primary and secondary data sources.

9Dc3 Design, trial and refine data collection sheets.

- FIX: Students may find data collection more challenging if it relates to topics that they know little about. Choose topics that are relevant to students, or topics that particularly interest them.

- Show examples of poor design in data collection sheets, for example, leading questions ('Why do you like maths?'), confusing question wording ('Do you not have breakfast in the morning? Yes/No'), or limited options ('What is your favourite sport? Football/Baseball/Gymnastics'; 'How many hours do you spend on the internet each week? Less than one hour/More than one hour'). Ask students to comment and suggest improvements.

9Dc4 collect and tabulate discrete and continuous data, choosing suitable equal class intervals where appropriate.

- FIX: Check that students understand notation of the forms $5 < x \leq 10$ and $5 \leq x < 10$.

- FIX: Students may need help to understand the difference between $5 < x \leq 10$, $5 \leq x < 10$, $5 \leq x \leq 10$, and 5–10, and when it might be appropriate to use each of these in a grouped frequency table. (If students confuse < and > (or $\leq$ and $\geq$), point out that the 'wide' side of the symbol is next to the larger number, while the small point is next to the smaller number.) Note that in some sources, a class interval of the form 5–10 is used with continuous data to mean $4.5 \leq x < 10.5$.

STRETCH: Students could be introduced to the idea that class intervals do not have to be equal, and discuss when it might be appropriate to use unequal class intervals. To go further, you could discuss histograms with unequal class intervals, and why they might look misleading if the bar heights represented frequencies (instead of having the bar areas represent frequency, as is usual in practice).

9Dp1 calculate statistics and select those most appropriate to the problem.

- FIX: Students sometimes find it difficult to remember how to estimate the mean from a grouped frequency table. It can help if they understand the method instead of simply trying to memorise it. When demonstrating the method, you could use the discussion points below.

  o How can we find a mean when we don't know any of the actual data values? What would be our 'best guess' of the data values in any particular class? Prompt students to think about why it makes more sense to choose the mid-point than any other value within a class interval.

  o How would we find the mean if we had the original list of raw data values? How can we add up all of the estimated data values for one row of the grouped frequency table?

  o How can we add up all of the estimated data values for the whole table?

  o How can we set out the above calculations in a clear, organised way? (Suggest adding additional columns to the grouped frequency table.)

  o When we have added up all of the estimated data values, what final step do we take to find the mean?

STRETCH: Students could try estimating the median value (rather than just finding the class interval that contains the median) from a grouped frequency table or a frequency diagram by interpolation. For example, consider the grouped frequency table below.

Age of person surveyed (a years)	Frequency
$20 \leq a < 30$	12
$30 \leq a < 40$	10
$40 \leq a < 50$	7
$50 \leq a < 60$	22

The total frequency is 51, so the median data value is the 26th and lies in the $40 \leq a < 50$ class. This class contains the 23rd to 29th data values, and the 26th value is the middle one of these. So a reasonable estimate of the median value is the middle of the class interval, 45 years.

End of chapter mental maths exercise

1. Three numbers have median 15, mean 14 and range 5. What are the three numbers?

2. A set of data consists of ten data values in the class interval $0 \leq x < 6$, and 20 data values in the class interval $6 \leq x < 12$.

   a. State the modal class.

   b. State the class interval that contains the median.

   c. Calculate an estimate of the mean.

   d. Write down an estimate of the range.

3. A grouped frequency table showing people's ages, A years (to the nearest whole number), has $0 \leq A < 5$ as its first class interval. The class intervals all have equal width.

   a. Write down the class interval that includes age 67 years.

   b. Write down the class interval that includes age 25 years.

   c. The highest age in the data set was 95 years. Write down the class interval for the last row of the table.

Technology recommendations

- Use online sources to collect secondary data (usually in the form of downloadable spreadsheet files), such as: https://www.gapminder.org/data/, https://data.oecd.org/, https://www.clio-infra.eu/, https://data.worldbank.org/, and https://data.humdata.org/.

- Use Excel, or a similar spreadsheet program, to produce a grouped frequency table from a list of data values. This is particularly useful when working with large datasets. A simple way to do this in Excel is to use the COUNTIF function, which counts the number of cells within a given range of cells that contain values that meet a given condition. The function takes two inputs: the first is the range of cells containing the data, and the second, in double quotation marks, is the condition.

  First, enter the raw data in one column (it does not have to be in size order). Elsewhere on the page, write labels for the frequency table rows and columns. Then if the data values are in cells A2:A101, for example, you can find the frequency for the range $20 < x \leq 30$ by typing:

  =countif($A$2:$A$101,"<=30")−countif($A$2:$A$101,"<=20")

  into the cell where you wish to display that frequency. Prompt students to think about why this subtraction gives the correct number of results.

- Investigate ways to use online technology to carry out a survey, using a website such as https://docs.google.com/forms, https://www.surveymonkey.com, or https://surveyplanet.com/.

Investigation/research tasks

- **Effect of class interval on frequency diagrams**

  Give students a set of raw data and give different class intervals to different students. Each student should create a grouped frequency table using the class interval they have been given, and then use this to draw a frequency diagram of the data.

  Share the frequency diagrams with the class and discuss whether some class intervals were more appropriate than others, and whether the choice of class interval might depend on the purpose for which the data was collected.

> TIP: Students could use a spreadsheet program to plot their frequency diagrams. See Technology recommendations, above, for a method of creating a grouped frequency diagram from a list of raw data in the Excel spreadsheet program.

> TIP: If you do not have a readily available set of data to use for this activity, you could collect heights in centimetres of students at your school. Ask the class to suggest how to collect the data.

- **Secondary data trawl**

  Ask students, individually or in pairs, to research what sets of secondary data they can find on the internet and in books. Can they think of any reasons (for example, reliability, ease of measurement, ease of collection, privacy issues) why data on some topics is easy to find and plentiful, whereas for some topics there seems to be little or no readily available data?

  Look into some of the sources students have found, and discuss how the data was collected and processed. Discuss data quality, and the possibility of bias.

  > TIP: Collate the results of this research, and give it to students as a list which could help them find an idea for the Data collection and analysis project, below.

- **Data collection and analysis project**

  Carry out a data collection and analysis project in which you complete each of the points below.

  1. Choose a question that you will try to answer by collecting data and using it to plot a frequency diagram and find averages.
  2. Decide whether it is more appropriate to collect primary or secondary data.
  3. Choose an appropriate degree of accuracy needed for the data values.
     Collect the data.
  4. Choose a suitable class interval and create a grouped frequency table for your data.
  5. Use your grouped frequency table to find the classes in which the mode and median lie, and estimate the mean.
  6. Draw a frequency diagram to display your data.
  7. Comment on what your frequency diagram shows.

  Ask students to create a poster about their investigation. They could write about their method, display their table and frequency diagram, and write comments about what their results show.

Square roots, cube roots and calculation

Learning objectives

Learning objectives covered in this chapter: 9Ni2, 9Np3

- Estimate square roots and cube roots.
- Use the order of operations, including brackets and powers.

Key terms

- square root
- cube root
- positive integer power
- index

Prior knowledge assumptions

- Students know how to calculate square numbers and square roots, cube numbers and cube roots mentally, for example, they know the value of $\sqrt{9}$ and $\sqrt[3]{64}$.
- Students know how to use known square roots and cube roots to find related ones, for example, they know the value of $\sqrt[3]{8000}$.
- Students know how to use the order of operations, including brackets, with more complex calculations, for example, they can calculate $7 - (1 + 2)^2 \times 3$.

Guidance on the hook

Purpose: This hook encourages students to explore using the order of operations when calculating.

Use of the hook: Introduce students to the context of the hook. Discuss as a class what the task requires. Encourage students to discuss the different answers that they can get if they follow or do not follow the correct order of operations. Ask students to record the correct answers that the mistakes that may happen.

Adaptation: You could give the students the numbers used in each set and ask them to rearrange them to achieve each target.

Extension: You can change the numbers to make the calculations more challenging. You could ask students to make their own puzzle questions. Share answers with the whole class.

> BEWARE: Look out for students who are unsure how to use the calculator to find square roots. Ensure students are confident that squaring and calculating the square root are inverse operations.

Starter ideas

Mental maths starter

What is $\sqrt{121}$?	What is $\sqrt[3]{27}$?	Write a square number that is 2 more than a prime number.	What is the cube root of 125?
What is $\sqrt[3]{64}$?	Which is bigger: 3^3 or 6^2?	What is $\sqrt[3]{27} + \sqrt{16}$?	Is 12^2 greater than 5^3?
Write the square number that comes after 64.	Write a cube number between 110 and 130	Does $66 \div (11 \times 2) = 66 \div 11 \times 2$?	Calculate $(60 - 14) - 3 \times 9$
What is $\sqrt[3]{125}$?	How many square numbers are there between 20 and 50?	How many cube numbers are there which are less than 100?	What is $5 \times (13 - 7) + 3$?
What is $121 \div (2^3 + 2^2)$?	What is $(50 - 1) \div (5 + 2)$?	Is $2^3 \times 1^2 > 8$?	Calculate $13^2 - (100 - 27)$

Start point check

Making 25

Using +, −, ×, ÷ and brackets, and using each of the numbers 2, 4, 6 and 8 once only, make the number 25.

TIP: You are allowed to use fractions, however $\dfrac{4}{8}$ counts as 4 ÷ 8.

Extension: Ask students to make ten different numbers.

Follow up this task with a discussion in the class about how students completed their calculations. Ask a student to explain their method. Ask if anyone had a different strategy. What are the pros and cons of each?

Possible solutions:

$$\left(\frac{2}{8} + 6\right) \times 4 = 25$$

True or false?

Write a statement on the board for everyone to see (also in photocopiable resources). Ask students to check whether it is true or false. If the statement is false, they need to correct it.

List of statements:

a) $105 - (6 + 4)^2 \div 2 = 55$

b) $25 - 6 + 5 \times 2 = 48$

c) $5 \times (8 + 4 \div 4) = 24$

d) $25 + 3 \times 4 \div (4 - 3) = 37$

Possible solutions:

a) False

b) False: $25 - 6 + 5 \times 2 = 19$

c) False: $5 \times (8 + 4 \div 4) = 29$

d) True

> TIP: Read the question aloud for students to complete. Are they true or false?

> TIP: Use different calculations to make the questions easier or more challenging.

STRETCH: Ask students to make their own questions. Encourage them to use square and cube numbers if possible.

What's different?

Read these pairs of numbers aloud for students to hear and ask them to write down one thing that is different about them. Encourage them to think of powers and roots. For example, when comparing 8 and 16, we could say that 8 is a cube number and 16 is a square number because $8 = 2^3$ and $16 = 4^2$.

a) 121 and 125

b) 27 and 100

c) $\sqrt{49}$ and $\sqrt{8}$

d) $\sqrt[3]{8}$, $\sqrt[3]{25}$

STRETCH: Ask students to create a similar task for their partner using squares up to 20×20 and cube numbers up to 5^3.

> BEWARE: Pay attention to the students who are unsure what square and cube root numbers are. Explain or clarify any misconception students may have, otherwise they will be stuck later on in the lesson.

Solution:

a) 121 is a square number and 125 is a cube number. $121 = 11^2$ and $125 = 5^3$.

b) 27 is a cube number and 64 is a square number. $27 = 3^3$ and $100 = 10^2$.

c) $\sqrt{49}$ is an integer because $\sqrt{49}$ and $\sqrt{8}$ is not an integer.

d) $\sqrt[3]{25}$ is not an integer. $\sqrt[3]{8}$ is an integer because $\sqrt[3]{8} = 2$

Discussion ideas

Probing questions	Teacher prompts
Can you estimate which is bigger: $\sqrt{100} + \sqrt{6}$ or $\sqrt{90} + \sqrt{16}$?	Ask students to estimate the values of $\sqrt{6}$ and $\sqrt{90}$. Encourage students to use a number line to compare the numbers.
Is there a time you do the additions or subtractions before multiplying or dividing?	Ask students to calculate $18 + 2 \times 5$ and $(18 + 2) \times 5$. Remind students that if there is a bracket in place, they need to complete the calculation inside the bracket before the rest of the calculations.
Why does a square root have a positive and a negative answer, but a cube root has only got one answer?	What operation is the inverse of calculating the square root of a number? Encourage students to check their answers by calculating the square and the cube of each number.
Always, sometimes or never true? For two positive integers, the square root of a number is greater than its cube root.	Prompt students to consider the square root and cube root of 1. To extend, ask students to use a calculator and compare the square root and the cube root of fractions.

Common errors/misconceptions

Misconception	Strategies to address
Calculating in the wrong order, usually from left to right, rather than prioritising brackets, powers/indices, then multiplication and division, then addition and subtraction.	Asking students to use a scientific calculator to check answers will help them realise that they are making errors. Reinforce the order of operation throughout the lesson.
Students sometimes follow the BIDMAS rules too literally, for example: working out $8^2 - 3 \times 4$ as $64 - 3 \times 4 = 64 - 12 = 52$ whereas doing several parts 'at once', as $8^2 - 3 \times 4 = 64 - 12$, saves time and increases fluency.	Encourage students to square and multiply at the same time if they feel confident in their calculations. Highlight the fact that students who rush when calculating will often make mistakes, hence checking the calculations is very important.
Students may not realise that finding a power (2 or 3) and finding the corresponding root are inverse operations.	Encourage discussion of inverse operations. Students will be able to estimate roots accurately and check their answers by doing an appropriate inverse calculation.
Using brackets when not needed – for example $(1 + 2 - 3) + 5^2 = 25$ is correct. However there is no need for a bracket in this calculation.	Encourage students to explore the different ways that a calculation can be completed. The more practice the students have in calculating, testing, exploring and making mistakes, the deeper their learning will be.

Developing conceptual understanding

9Ni2 Estimate square roots and cube roots.

- FIX: Put the sequence $\sqrt{1}$, $\sqrt{4}$, $\sqrt{9}$, $\sqrt{16}$, $\sqrt{25}$, ... $\sqrt{100}$ on the board:

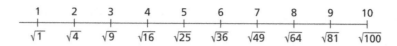

Ask students to estimate where $\sqrt{50}$ should be. Encourage students to use a number line to show the position of $\sqrt{50}$:

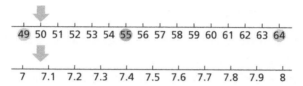

- FIX: Put the sequence $\sqrt[3]{1}$, $\sqrt[3]{8}$, $\sqrt[3]{27}$, $\sqrt[3]{64}$, $\sqrt[3]{125}$ on the number line:

Ask students to predict where the $\sqrt[3]{10}$ will be.

Can they estimate its value?

Repeat for other values and allow students to use a calculator to check their estimations.

> TIP: Ensure that students have access to these square root and cube root number lines. This will help the students visualise where other numbers could be and estimate accordingly.

STRETCH: Can you make ' Guess my number ...' questions? For example, 'I am thinking of a number. Its square root is between ... and ... Its cube root is between ... and ... What is my number?'

9Np3 Use the order of operations, including brackets and powers.

- It is important that students understand that the order of operation is a convention used internationally so that the mathematical operations happen in the same way around the world.
- FIX: Give students four different numbers, for example 1, 2, 3, 4, and use them with any of the usual four rules of arithmetic (+, −, × and ÷) as well as brackets and squaring, to make different numbers.
- FIX: Give students different calculations and ask them to put brackets around the calculation to achieve different results. For example:
  $3 + 5^2 \times 4 + 2 = 3 + 100 + 2 = 105$
  $(3 + 5^2) \times 4 + 2 = 28 \times 4 + 2 = 114$

STRETCH: Students working at a greater depth could begin to find all the possible answers to a given calculation by depending on where two sets of brackets were placed. For example, $(3 + 5^2) \times (4 + 2) = 28 \times 6 = 168$.

STRETCH: Ask students to make similar questions. They could work in pairs to solve each other's questions, then use a calculator to check each other's answers.

End of chapter mental maths exercise

1. What is $(6^2 + 18) \div 3^3$?
2. True or false? $4^2 - 2^2 = 3 \times (2^3 - 2^2)$
3. Add a bracket to make this calculation correct: $2^2 \times 3 + 5 \times 4 = 92$
4. Use two consecutive integers to make this correct: $\ldots < \sqrt{95} < \ldots$
5. Write a number with one decimal place that is a good approximation for $\sqrt[3]{300}$.
6. Calculate $(80 + 2^3) \div (3^2 - 5)$.
7. Estimate the value of $\sqrt{200} + \sqrt[3]{100}$.

Technology recommendations

- Use a calculator to find square roots and cube roots.

  Make sure that students know the correct key sequence for their own calculators. This can vary between different models. They can practise by making sure they can get the correct answers for square roots and cube roots that they already know.

  Emphasise that, in most cases, when finding roots students will need to round the calculator answer.

- Use a calculator to find the square root and the cube root of a number when the calculator doesn't have a square root and a cube root button/function? For example, how can you find the $\sqrt{200}$ and $\sqrt[3]{200}$?

  What inverse operations will you use?

  What degree of accuracy will you round your answer to?

  (Carry out inverse operations to check answers to mental or written calculations.)

Investigation/research tasks

- **What could the number be?**

  Provide students with a whiteboard.

  Ask them to write an integer on their board that has a square root between 1 and 2, 2 and 3, 3 and 4.

  Repeat for cube roots.

  Make a table to record the results.

TIP: Provide a table for students (see photocopiable resources) and ask them to work in groups to complete it.

- FIX: Students should have access to the first 20 square numbers and the first five cube numbers.

STRETCH: Repeat for square roots and cube roots between 6 and 7, 7 and 8 and 8 and 9.

	Between 1 and 2	Between 2 and 3	Between 3 and 4
$\sqrt{\Box}$			
$\sqrt[3]{\Box}$			

- **1991**   *Problem solving*

  Using the digits of 1991 and the operations +, −, ×, ÷ $\sqrt{\Box}$ and brackets make the first 20 numbers 1, 2, 3, 4 … 20.

- FIX: Ask students to make as many different numbers as possible.

STRETCH: Use a target number that can be achieved by using all the numbers and two brackets.

- **Making 0**   *Problem solving*

  Using +, −, ×, ÷ and brackets, and using each of the numbers 2, 4, 6 and 8 once only, make the number 0.

TIP: Square roots and cube roots are allowed.

  Possible solution:

  $\sqrt{4}$ + $\sqrt[3]{8}$ − 6 = 0 or (6 + 4) − (8 + 2) = 0

- FIX: Students can make a table to show their results.

STRETCH: Make your own question, ensuring you use powers also.

Indices

Learning objectives	Key terms
Learning objectives covered in this chapter: 9Ni3 • Use positive, negative and zero indices and the index laws for multiplication and division of positive integer powers.	• positive integer power • index • indices • negative powers

Prior knowledge assumptions:

• Square roots, cube numbers and cube roots mentally.
• Students know how to use indices to show powers.

Guidance on the hook

Purpose: This hook is a cross figure which provides an opportunity for students to work with square and cube numbers.

Use of the hook: Introduce students to the context of the hook. Discuss as a class what the task requires. Encourage students to be systematic in their approach.

Adaptation: Students can work in pairs or individually. Provide students with copies of the cross figure. Discuss the order of operations. Make the questions easier or harder (whilst keeping the answers the same) according to the students' needs.

Extension: Can students make their own cross figure? What calculations can they use?

Possible solution:

²3	¹6		³4	⁴9
⁵1	2	0		9
	5		⁶8	
⁷2		⁸1	4	⁹4
¹⁰5	5		¹¹1	7

TIP: This question can be turned into a game by asking students to work in groups and compete against time. Who can complete the cross figure first?

BEWARE: Students should notice that their answer is correct when the answers across and down match with each other.

Starter ideas

Mental maths exercise

What is $\sqrt{900}$?	What is $\sqrt[3]{27000}$?	Write $5 \times 5 \times 5 \times 5 \times 5$ using power notation.	What is $\sqrt[3]{125}$?
What is $\sqrt{6400}$?	True or false $\sqrt[3]{6400} = 40$?	Write $3 \times 3 \times 3 \times 3 \times 3$ using power notation.	What is 12^2?
Write the square number that comes after 45.	Write a cube number between 60 and 70.	What is $54 \div (11 - 8)^2$?	True or false? $3^3 \times 3^2 \times 3 = 243$
Which is bigger: $\sqrt[3]{125000}$ or? $\sqrt{400}$	Work out 36^2.	How many cube numbers are there less than 50?	What is $5 \times (13 - 7)$?
Write $2 \times 2 \times 2 \times 2$ as 2 to the power of …	What is $7^2 \div (3^2 - 2)$?	Which is bigger: 4^3 or 7^2?	Calculate 13^2.

Start point check

Four powers

Using $\times$ and $\div$, and 4^1, 3^2, 2^2 and 1^4, how many integers can you make? For example, $144 = 4^1 \times 3^2 \div 4^2 \div 1^4$.

Follow up this task with a discussion in the class about how students completed their calculations. Ask a student to explain their method. Clarify any misconceptions or mistakes that students may have made.

STRETCH: Ask students to use + and − also. How many different numbers can they make?

BEWARE: Some students might not be confident in working with powers and may simplify the calculations by multiplying or adding the powers incorrectly. For example, look for students who think that $4^1 \times 3^2 = 12^3$. Clarify any misconceptions that students may have.

Possible solutions:

- $144 = 4^1 \times 3^2 \div 2^3 \div 1^4$
- $288 = 41 \times 32 \times 23 \times 14$
- $18 = 3^2 \times 2^3 \times 1^4 \div 4^1$

TIP: You could allow students to use brackets also. Will the answers change?

Power snap

Use the 'Power Snap' game (see photocopiable resources) to recap prior knowledge.

Cut out the cards. Mix them up. Students play in pairs to find the matching cards. Collect all the matching cards you can make. The winner is the pair that has collected the most cards.

TIP: Encourage students to write down all the matching cards they make.

Pick up a number

Write the numbers 8, 25, 32 and 100 on four pieces of paper. Fold each piece of paper so that you are not able to see the numbers. Pick up a number at random. Write the number using powers and roots only. Students need to find three different ways to write 32 by using powers and roots only and any of the operations they prefer. For example, $32 = 2^5$ or $32 = 3^3 + \sqrt{25}$ or $32 = 5^2 + 2^3 - 1^4$.

Encourage students to be creative and make different number statements.

> TIP: Students can work in pairs or groups of four.

Follow up the task with a discussion in class about the different ways that a number can be expressed.

STRETCH: Adapt the numbers used in the task according to the students' needs.

Discussion ideas

Probing questions	Teacher prompts
Is $2^{-1} + 8^{-1} = 10^{-1}$?	Change the negative powers to fractions. Without calculating, can $\dfrac{1}{2} + \dfrac{1}{8} = \dfrac{1}{10}$? Ask students to calculate the left-hand side and the right-hand side and compare the answers.
Why is $9^0 > 81^{-1}$ if $9 < 81$?	Encourage students to check their answers by calculating both sides of the statement. Encourage students to generalise if possible about the powers of 0 and negative powers.
Convince me that $3^2 + 3^2 + 3^2 = 3^3$.	Prompt students to consider the addition of $3^2 + 3^2 + 3^2$ and use multiplication to write it instead. Prompt students to think of the power of 1 and how every number can be written as a power of 1. Discuss the multiplication of powers and the rules that students have learned in this lesson.

Common errors/ misconceptions

Misconception	Strategies to address
A negative power means a negative number.	Ask students quick 'True or false' questions throughout the lesson for more practice. For example, is $2^{-1} = -2$? Asking students to use a scientific calculator to check answers will help them realise that they are making errors.
Any number to the power of zero equals 0.	Checking answers with a calculator will flag up incorrect answers. Discuss the division of a number by itself. Ask students to calculate $5^2 \div 5^2$. Use the rules that students have learned, to write $5^2 \div 5^2$ as 5^0.

Misconception	Strategies to address
When multiplying powers of the same number, some students multiply the powers, for example: $3^1 \times 3^4 = 3^4$.	Write the calculations on both sides without the power. Is $3 \times 3 \times 3 \times 3 \times 3 = 3 \times 3 \times 3 \times 3$?
When adding numbers, some students add the powers. For example, they make the mistake of calculating $3^1 + 3^3 = 3^4$.	Write the calculation on each side without the powers. For example, $3 + 3 \times 3 \times 3 = 3 + 27 = 30$, which is different from 3^4 (or 81). Discuss the order of operation when adding and multiplying.
Mixing the power rules, for example $2^2 \times 2^3 = 4^5$?	Calculate each side of the statement. Revisit the way a product can be written in index form. Revisit the rules that students have learned in this lesson.

Developing conceptual understanding

9Ni3: Use positive, negative and zero indices and the index laws for multiplication and division of positive integer powers.

- Students understand that a negative power does not mean a negative number. They are confident in changing a negative power to a fraction.

- FIX: Put the numbers 2^{-1}, 3^{-1}, 5^{-1} and 1^{-1} on the board. Ask students to put these numbers in order starting with the smallest.

> TIP: Write each negative power as a fraction.

STRETCH: Use what you know about the power rules to make true and false statements. Work in pairs to correct each other's statements that are wrong. Correct them.

- FIX: Ask students to work in groups and make a poster called the 'Power rules'. Encourage students to write all the rules clearly using different colours and pictures.

STRETCH: Ask students to make a poster with all the mistakes that they, or their friends, may have made when working with powers.

Share all the ideas with the whole class and encourage discussion.

> TIP: Students can gather all the ideas from the discussion and write a list of misconceptions and mistakes that happen when working with powers. This list could be placed on the wall so that all students have access to it.

End of chapter mental maths exercise

1. Write as a power of 2: $8 \times 8 \times 64$.
2. True or false?
3. $3^{-r} = -81$.
4. Write as a power of 3: $9 \times 3^3 \times 81$.
5. Simplify $7^{-i} \times 7^3 \times 7^0$.
6. Which is bigger: 8^0 or 11^0?
7. Place these numbers in order starting with the smallest: 3^3, 3^{-4}, 3^0, 3^2, 3^{-1}.
8. Calculate $2^{-4} \times 3^{-4}$.
9. Calculate $5^2 \div 5^0$.
10. Which is bigger: $9^2 \div 9^3$ or 9^1?

Technology recommendations

- Use a scientific calculator to work with negative powers. Ensure students know how to use the correct button on the calculator to insert negative powers and 0 as the power.

- Use a basic calculator to calculate negative powers, and highlight the importance of using the correct calculator in lessons. Give half the class a scientific calculator and the other half a basic one. Ask them to quickly calculate 3^{-4}. When using the basic calculator, students need to be confident about what a negative power means. Ask students to notice the amount of time that it takes to work with negative powers using a basic calculator.

Investigation/research tasks

- In the lesson, students looked at the positive powers of 3 and noticed that the numbers end in 1, 3, 9 or 7. Ask students to investigate the negative powers of 3. Do they follow a pattern also?

Power	3^{-1}	3^{-2}	3^{-3}	3^{-4}	3^{-5}
Value					

- Research the use of negative powers in real-life contexts on the internet. Students could come up with examples such as in biology, science, astronomy. Discuss all the findings with the whole class.

- Ask students to write two questions involving negative powers within the contexts that they have researched. Ask students to work in pairs and solve each other's questions.

- Research the history of negative powers. Students could produce a presentation to explain why negative powers were first introduced and how they have been integrated over time. Highlight the importance of using positive and negative powers in real life.

Percentages

Learning objectives

Learning objectives covered in this chapter: 9Nf3, 9Nf4

- Solve problems involving percentage changes, choosing the correct numbers to take as 100% or as a whole, including simple problems involving personal or household finance, e.g. simple interest, discount, profit, loss and tax.
- Recognise when fractions or percentages are needed to compare different quantities.

Key terms
- profit
- loss
- sales tax
- tax
- income tax
- simple interest

Prior knowledge assumptions
- Students know how to how to increase or decrease a quantity by a given percentage.
- Students know how to calculate % of a quantity, for example, they can find 20% of 80 kg.
- Students know how to write a number as a percentage of another.

Guidance on the hook

Purpose: To revisit equivalent fractions, decimals and percentages.

Use of the hook: Students need to look at the numbers on each domino and notice that the numbers next to each other are equal, for example $\frac{1}{2}$ = 50%, 40% = 0.4. Lead a discussion with the whole class about the different methods that students can use to convert percentages to fractions to decimals. Bring the class together after a few minutes and discuss the answers and the methods used.

Adaptation: If students get stuck, or if they complete the challenge totally, review with the whole class how they can progress step by step.

Extension: The percentages given can be altered to make the calculations a little more challenging.

TIP: You could time how long the task lasts and repeat it at the start of several lessons for more practice with fractions, decimals and percentages.

BEWARE: Some students may be confused by the numbers on both sides of the domino. Encourage students to deal with one calculation at a time before establishing what the link between the numbers is.

Possible solution:

0.8	25%	$\frac{1}{4}$
80%	B	0.5
$\frac{3}{5}$	0.6	50%

$\frac{9}{10}$	30%	$\frac{3}{10}$
90%	C	10%
75%	$\frac{3}{4}$	$\frac{1}{10}$

Starter ideas

Mental maths starter

Find 45% of 120.	Find 20% of 80.	Find 25% of 168.	Increase $68 by 30%.
Increase 120 by 30%.	Write 15 kg as a percentage of 20 kg.	Increase 200 by 35%.	Write 48 as a percentage of 60.
Write as a %: $42 out of $100.	Write as a %: 7 g out of 50 g.	Write as a %: 140 marks out of 420 marks.	Write as a %: 23 students out of 92 students.
True or false? $\frac{1}{8}$ = 12.5%.	Write 45% as a fraction in simplified form.	Without calculating, which is bigger $\frac{7}{8}$ or 70%?	Increase 75 ml by 20%.
Work out 32% of 80 m.	Work out 22% of 750 m.	Increase 210 km by 55%.	Write 150 as a percentage of 250.

Start point check

Increase and decrease

Students work in pairs. Give each pair a set of Increase/Decrease cards (see photocopiable resources). Lay out the cards on the table with each card face down.

The players take it in turns to turn up a card. If they pick up an orange card, they increase the amount on the card by the given percentage. If they pick up a white card, they decrease the amount by the given percentage.

Every correct answer wins the card.

Continue the game until there are no more cards to win.

The winning player is the one with the most cards.

What is the question?

Give each student a mini whiteboard.

Write down a simple percentage on the board, for example: 10%, 20%, 25%, 30%, 40%, 50%, 75%

Ask the students to write two numbers, so that one of them is the given percentage of the other one. (For example, if you write 20%, the numbers could be 20 and 100 or 2 and 10 or 1 and 5.) Ask students to make a number statement with these numbers (for example, 20 g out of 100 g, or 2 litres out of 10 litres). Choose a few of the number statements created and share them with the whole class.

TIP: If you don't have mini whiteboards, you can give students a sheet of paper to write the answers on.

- FIX: Students can start by writing the equivalent fraction to the percentage given, then work backwards to find the possible numbers.

STRETCH: Change the percentages given to make the question more challenging.

Discussion ideas

Probing questions	Teacher prompts
True or false? To find the percentage profit, simply find the profit you made.	Rather than tell students what is right or wrong, ask them to look back in the lesson so that they can establish for themselves the steps needed to calculate the percentage profit.
Tom sold 50 ice creams on Monday. On Tuesday the number of ice creams sold increased by 120%.	Prompt students to give possible examples of percentage increases greater than 100% (for example, the price of something increased by 120% or the sale of tickets increased by 120%).
True or false? 50 ml out of 1 litre ≠ 50%	Students could represent this as bar model and actually calculate the answer. This may be a good opportunity to revisit measurements and how many ml there are in 1 litre.
A bank pays 5% simple interest per year. Show me that if you leave $1000 in the bank for three years you will receive more interest than if you leave the same amount in the bank for two years.	Encourage students to start with $1000 and check for themselves the interest after one year, two years and three years.

Common errors/misconceptions

Misconception	Strategies to address
When calculating a percentage profit, students compare the profit with the new amount, not the original one.	Ask students to check the answer by calculating the percentage increase. If students compare the increase to the new amount they will achieve a different percentage as their answer.
Students sometimes make mistakes when calculating the highest proportion. They compare the actual amounts rather than the percentages of the whole amount that these amounts represent.	Give students plenty of opportunities to calculate different proportions of given quantities. Use a bar model to compare the answers. For example, 400 g of sugar out of 1000 g is a lower proportion of sugar than 8 g of sugar out of 10 g. | 200g	200g	200g	200g	200g | | 2g	2g	2g	2g	2g	

Misconception	Strategies to address
When calculating a percentage profit, students compare the profit with the new amount, not the original one.	Ask students to check the answer by calculating the percentage increase. If students compare the increase to the new amount they will achieve a different percentage as their answer.
Students sometimes make mistakes when calculating the highest proportion. They compare the actual amounts rather than the percentages of the whole amount that these amounts represent.	Give students plenty of opportunities to calculate different proportions of given quantities. Use a bar model to compare the answers. For example, 400 g of sugar out of 1000 g is a lower proportion of sugar than 8 g of sugar out of 10 g. 200g 200g 200g 200g 200g 2g 2g 2g 2g 2g
When comparing two quantities, students may not compare like for like. For example, they may think that 90 g out of 10 kg equals 90%.	When making comparisons, students need to ensure that they are using the same data from each set, and when they aren't, convert it as needed.
When increasing a quantity by a given percentage, students may find the percentage increase or decrease, but they do not add it or subtract it from the original amount.	Ask students to think about the question. What does 'increase/decrease' mean? What happens to the number when it is increased or decreased? Does the answer make sense?

Developing conceptual understanding

9Nf3 Solve problems involving percentage changes, choosing the correct numbers to take as 100% or as a whole, including simple problems involving personal or household finance, e.g. simple interest, discount, profit, loss and tax.

- FIX: Use bar models to represent the percentage profit. For example, if the cost price = $90 and the sale price = $120, there is $30 profit:

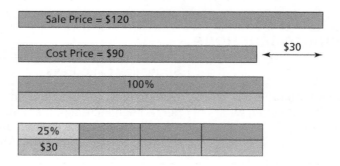

STRETCH: Students who have mastered this objective could develop their knowledge by considering the original amount if the final amount and the percentage increase or decrease is given.

9Nf4 Recognise when fractions or percentages are needed to compare different quantities.

- FIX: Write a number as a fraction of the other one. Change it to a percentage by multiplying the fraction by 100.

- FIX: Use bar models to compare different amounts.

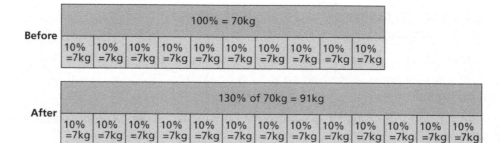

STRETCH: Students working at a greater depth can try to solve reverse percentage increase or decrease problems. For example, if after an increase of 30%, the amount is 91 kg, what is the original amount?

End of chapter mental maths exercise

1. Which is bigger: 29 out of 62 or 47%?
2. Write this list in order, starting with the largest: $\frac{6}{11}$, 52%, 0.49, $\frac{1}{2}$
3. The sale price of an item is $45. The cost of the item is $36. What is the % profit?
4. Complete the missing numbers: 48 marks out of 150 marks = $\frac{\Box}{150}$ = ...%

5. Calculate the sale price of a jacket costing $80 on a 45% sale.
6. Use >, < or = to make this statement true: 1.15 ... 180 out of 150.
7. What is the percentage reduction if the original price is $90 and the original price is $110?

Technology recommendations

- Use the % key on a scientific calculator to calculate the final number after a percentage increase or decrease. For example, to calculate a 23% reduction on a bill of $160, subtract 23% from 100% (100% − 23% = 77%) then insert 77 (%) button × 160. In some calculators, to get the % , you need to press:

$$\boxed{\text{SHIFT}} \quad \boxed{(} \quad (\%)$$

When using multipliers, students can change a % to a decimal by writing the percentage in the calculator, followed by:

$$\boxed{\text{S} \leftrightarrow \text{D}}$$

In the example above the multiplier will be 0.67.

- Use the internet to investigate the number of dry days (no rain) in your country for the past ten years. Make a table with your results and calculate the proportion of the time that the weather was dry. Do your results show a pattern? Why do you think this information may be useful?

Investigation/research tasks

- **Shopping**   *Problem solving*

  Ask students to work in groups of five or six. Each group is in charge of a shop. The shop could be a stationery shop, a clothes shop or a bookshop. Students need to fix the prices of each item being sold.

  Provide students with the cost of ten items. What will the prices be if the shopkeeper wants to achieve 20% profit on each item?

  Ask students to have a sales day, where each item is reduced by 20%. What will the new prices be?

- FIX: Use whole numbers or numbers that are easy to work with for the prices of the items.

- FIX: Encourage students to use a calculator to check their answers.

STRETCH: Adapt the numbers used in the question to make the calculations more challenging.

> TIP: Don't let students just guess the answer. Ensure they can explain why they used multiplication or division.

STRETCH: Ask students to write 'spot the mistake' questions. They need to write four questions with their answers given, however one of the answers must be wrong. Encourage students to work in pairs, spot each other's 'mistakes' and correct the answers.

- **Which one is the biggest?**

  Before starting this task, ask students to cut across the lines and separate the blue cards, and the white cards, as found in the photocopiable resources.

  Students work in pairs or small groups. They take it in turns to pick up a white card and a blue card. Students say which of the cards represents the biggest proportion. Students use calculators to check each other's answers. Every correct answer is 1 point. The winner is the player who has the most points by the time all the cards are used.

- FIX: Ask students to say the equivalent percentage or decimal to each card picked up.

STRETCH: Ask students to play the same game, but make the numbers used more challenging. For example, you can use numbers that do not simplify or decimal percentages.

- **$150**   *Problem solving*

  Students have $150. They roll the dice twice to make a two-digit number. This is the amount that they spent. Subtract this amount from $150.

  Ask students to calculate the percentage of the money spent. Every correct answer is 1 point.

  Repeat until you are left with an amount of $10 or less.

  The winner is the one who wins the most points by the end of the game.

> TIP: allow students to use a calculator.

STRETCH: Ask students to use their knowledge of fractions and proportion to calculate each percentage spent.

Calculating with decimals

Learning objectives

Learning objectives covered in this chapter: 9Nc3 9Nc4 9Nc5

- Consolidate use of the rules of arithmetic and inverse operations to simplify calculations.
- Multiply by decimals, understanding where to position the decimal point by considering equivalent calculations; divide by decimals by transforming to division by an integer.
- Recognise the effects of multiplying and dividing by numbers between 0 and 1.

Key terms

- multiply numerators
- multiply denominators
- inverse fraction
- fraction inverted

Prior knowledge assumptions

- Students know how to multiply and divide integers and decimals by decimals.
- Students know how to use the laws of arithmetic and inverse operations to simplify calculations with integers and fractions.

Guidance on the hook

Purpose: The purpose of this hook is not only to revisit adding and multiplying decimals by integers, but also to encourage students to use the laws of arithmetic and question more, rather than simply multiply and add decimals.

Use of the hook: Provide students with a printout of the task and ask them to think about the questions. This can be done very effectively as a think, pair, share activity (individual students should think about their answers, then discuss as a pair with another student and then ideas can be shared as a class). When students are giving their answers, ensure that you ask them to explain their methods.

> BEWARE: Some students may want to generalise after checking that 'the rule' works for one of the triangles. Encourage them to explore their idea further by testing it with other triangles before generalising.

Adaptation: Some students may be confused by the triangle pictures. Rather than telling students what to do, you could ask them to rearrange the numbers to make different sums. When looking at the first triangle, allow students to use a calculator to check the sums that they can make.

Extension: Ask students to make three similar triangle puzzles themselves. They can then solve each other's puzzles.

> TIP: It may be helpful to have all the triangle puzzles laminated. Students should have a piece of paper where they can record the number statements that they make. Ensure students have access to a number line or place value grid for more support.

Starter ideas

Mental maths starter

Calculate 2.25 + 3.6.	Multiply 5 by 0.87.	Calculate the product of 2.3 and 7.	Without calculating, is 12 × 0.1 < 12?
Calculate 2.37 − 1.8.	Find the product of 8 and 0.87.	Calculate $25 \times \dfrac{1}{3} + 14 \times \dfrac{1}{3}$.	What number is 1.56 less than 5?
Find the sum of 1.68 and 1.89.	Write two new facts based on: 4.16 − 2.5 = 1.66.	Without calculating, is the answer of 2.25 × 4 greater than 9?	True or false? $11 \times \dfrac{2}{5} + 11 \times \dfrac{3}{5} = 11$
Find the difference between 2.6 and 1.87.	Write two new facts based on: 0.16 × 2 = 0.32.	Write two new facts based on: 0.67 + 0.2 = 0.87.	Is $13 \times \dfrac{1}{8} + 11 \times \dfrac{1}{8} = 3$?
Multiply 7.8 by 0.6.	Is the product of 12 and 0.25 = 3?	Calculate the sum of 2.25 and 0.67.	What is the product of 0.8 and 7.2?

Start point check

Choosing numbers

Give students the board from the photocopiable resources and ask them to choose two numbers:

- that have the product of 0.64
- that are numbers equivalent to 3.27 × 0.9.

Then choose:

- three numbers from the board that have a total of 111
- a number equivalent to the sum of 88.31 and 5.69
- a number equivalent to the product of 0.45 and 0.8
- a number equivalent to $\dfrac{4}{7} \times 20 + \dfrac{4}{7} \times 15$
- four numbers that have a total of 15.

TIP: Prior to starting the task, remind students to give all the answers in simplified form.

What is the question?

Write a decimal number on the board. Ask students to make an addition, subtraction, multiplication or division question that has as its answer the decimal number you wrote.

- FIX: Ask students to use one operation only.

STRETCH: Students can use two or more operations, including brackets.

TIP: Students can work in pairs. They can use a calculator to check each other's answers.

STRETCH: Ask students to write a worded problem to go with each calculation.

True or false?

Divide the classroom into two groups. Each group makes up two questions that have the same answer. One of them is correct, the other one is not. Students need to find out which one is correct.

> BEWARE: Some students will just guess the answer. Ask students to look at the calculation and think about the value that the digit represents. Students will need to use their knowledge of working with decimals and inverse operations to manipulate the questions and check the answers.

Discussion ideas

Probing questions	Teacher prompts
Convince me that $8.07 + 11.6 + 6.93 - 5.6$ $= 8.07 + 693 + 11.6 - 5.6$.	Encourage students to think of different ways to explain this. Try to encourage students to discuss the commutative law of addition and when it is useful to use it, as well as using a place value grid to support their answers.
Convince me that $1.36 - 0.8 + 1.2 + 0.64 \neq 0$.	Write the calculation on the board. Students can work out the calculation on the left-hand side by adding and subtracting the decimals given. Discuss why some students may make the mistake of thinking that the answer could be 0.
Without calculating, explain why 5.68×3.4 is not equal to 19.72?	Prompt students by asking how many digits there are after the decimal point in each of the numbers on the left-hand side and how many digits they expect to be after the decimal point in the answer.
Always, sometimes or never true? When dividing an integer by a decimal number, the answer is always bigger than the original number.	Prompt students to use examples of dividing by a decimal number less than 1, between 1 and 2, greater than 2 and greater than 1 before generalising.

Common errors/misconceptions

Misconception	Strategies to address
When multiplying decimals, students often forget to insert the decimal point. Or they place the decimal point in the wrong place.	Give students plenty of opportunities to practise multiplying decimals. Ensure that the decimal numbers that they are multiplying vary. Talk through the methods and strategies that students use and discuss them with the whole class, including the mistakes that students make.
Students fail to recognise or use the laws of arithmetic to make the calculations easier, for example when calculating $\frac{1}{3}$ of 20% of \$51, they calculate $\frac{1}{3}$ of 20% first, then multiply \$51 by the answer.	Ask students to look for ways to make the calculations easier, rather than simply calculating. Discuss the laws of arithmetic with the whole class and ensure students have access to them. This could be by writing them on the board or placing a poster of them on the wall.

Misconception	Strategies to address
When dividing decimal numbers by decimals, students think that the answer must be a decimal too, though there is no reason for it to be so. For example, students think that $75.2 \div 1.6 = 4.7$ $$\begin{array}{r} 47 \\ 16\overline{)7\ 5^{11}2} \end{array}$$	Remind students to check whether the answer makes sense by using reverse operations. Students can round the numbers to estimate. For example, 75.2 can be rounded to 75, 1.6 can be rounded to 2 and 4.7 can be rounded to 5. Can 75 divided by 2 equal 5?

Developing conceptual understanding

9Nc3 Consolidate use of the rules of arithmetic and inverse operations to simplify calculations.

- FIX: Pupils can use place value grid to conceptualise commutative and associative law. For example, when calculating $3.205 + 42.38 + 0.075$ students could add $3.225 + 0.075 = 3.3$ first, then add 42.38 to the answer: $3.3 + 42.38 = 45.68$. Highlight the importance of not simply calculating but finding the most efficient way to calculate.

- FIX: Ask students to use inverse operations to check their answers.

- FIX: Ask students to estimate to check whether the answer makes sense.

- FIX: Highlight the common factors to visualise them better. For example, $(7.69 \times 13.4) - (7.69 \times 3.4) = 7.69 \times (13.4 - 4.4) = 7.69 \times 10 = 76.9$.

STRETCH: Use calculations with two or more operations.

> TIP: Allow students time to explore the different ways that the calculations can be made. Ensure that students understand they should not rush to calculate answers. Instead, they need to think carefully about the strategies and approaches they should use.

9Nc4: Multiply by decimals, understanding where to position the decimal point by considering equivalent calculations; divide by decimals by transforming to division by an integer.

- FIX: Provide a decimal grid so that students can visualise the calculations better. When you multiply decimal numbers, use the place values of the decimals to work out the equivalent calculation. For example, when multiplying 16.8 by 3.8, multiply 168 by 38, then divide the result by 100.

- FIX: Divide decimal numbers by transforming the calculation to division by integer. For example, when dividing 2.61 by 0.3, multiply both 2.61 and 0.3 by 10. $2.61 \div 0.3$ is the same as $26.1 \div 3$.

STRETCH: Use missing number questions. For example, $3.75 \div \ldots = 12.5$.

9Nc5: Recognise the effects of multiplying and dividing by numbers between 0 and 1.

- FIX: Use estimation to check the answer makes sense.

- FIX: Use equivalent decimals and fractions to check the calculations. For example, when a number is multiplied by a fraction less than 1, the answer will be less than the original number. So, 50 × 0.8 will have an answer less than 50 because $\frac{8}{10}$ of 50 is less than 50.

- FIX: When dividing any number by a number between 0 and 1, change the decimal to a fraction. For example: $20 \div 0.5 = 20 \div \frac{1}{2} = 40$. Use bar models to visualise why when dividing by a decimal number between 0 and 1, the answer is greater than the original number. In the example above, there are 40 halves in 20.

End of chapter mental maths exercise

1. Work out 6.137 + 5.14 + 0.36 −0.137.	5. Calculate the product of 0.89 and 4.5.
2. Calculate $2.5 \times \frac{1}{8} + 2.5 \times \frac{7}{8}$.	6. Divide 8.904 by 0.02.
3. Use >, < or =: 87.3 ÷ 0.1 … 87.3	7. Calculate 6.52 − 1.6 + 0.48+ 3.6
4. True or false? 0.62 × 1.1 = 6.82	8. Calculate (0.73 × 4.8) + (0.27 × 4.8)

Technology recommendations

- Use a calculator to explore how to multiply and divide decimals. When using a scientific calculator, students need to ensure they know how to change an answer which is given as a fraction to a decimal number.

- Use the internet to research the prices of different packets of nuts. Ensure all the packets are less than 1 kg. Calculate the prices per kilogram. Record the results in a spreadsheet.

Investigation/research tasks

- **Quick ways of calculating**   *Problem solving*

  Continue to use the laws of arithmetic to support efficient and accurate mental and written calculations, and calculations with a calculator. For example, use mental or informal written methods to calculate:

  a) 0.284 × 0.25
  b) 7.22 ÷ 0.25
  c) $\frac{5}{18} \times 25 + \frac{5}{18} \times 11$
  d) 2036 × 5.03 − 36 × 5.03

  STRETCH: Think of a quick way to calculate $1\frac{17}{26} \times 850 - \frac{2}{13} \times 850$ mentally.

  Possible solutions:

  a) 0.284 × 0.25 = 0.284 × 100 ÷ 4 = 284 ÷ 4 = 71
  b) 7.22 ÷ 0.25 = (7.22 × 4) ÷ (0.25 × 4) = 28.88 ÷ 1 = 28.8
  c) $\frac{5}{18} \times 36 = 5 \times 2 = 10$
  d) 2000 × 5.03 = 10 060

  Ask students to think of a quick way to multiply 15 by 8.

Ask students to think of quick way to divide 625 by 25. Check the answers with a calculator.

- **Long multiplication**

    Put this multiplication on the board:

    $\frac{1}{3}$ of 20% of $51

    Ask students to think of the easiest way to complete it.

    Encourage students to notice numbers that are multiples of the same number or fractions that can be simplified.

    Put these multiplications on the board and ask students to complete them.

    - $\frac{\square}{20} \times 25\% \times \ldots = 10$

    - $\frac{5}{\square} \times \% \times 180 = 2$

    - $\frac{5}{\square} \times 13 \times 20\% \times \ldots = 80$

STRETCH: Ask students to make up three similar questions. Share all the questions with the whole class and discuss the strategies that can be used.

BEWARE: You may need to prompt students to think about the final values that they need to achieve and ask them to work backwards to find the missing values.

Possible solutions:

$\frac{1}{20} \times 25\% \times 800 = 10$

$\frac{5}{9} \times 2\% \times 180 = 2$

$\frac{5}{13} \times 13 \times 20\% \times 80 = 80$

- **Brain versus calculator**

    Separate the class into two halves. Give half of the students a calculator.

    Write on the board multiplication and division questions with decimals. For example, 3.67 × 0.8 or 3.89 ÷ 0.79.

    - ○ Ask students to predict whether the answer will be greater or smaller than the original number. Which group was faster?
    - ○ Which group gave the correct answer?
    - ○ Discuss whether the calculator is needed to predict the answer.

> TIP: Ensure you include divisions and multiplications with decimal numbers less than 1 and greater than 1.

- o Encourage generalising where possible.
- o To extend, you could write a calculation on the board. Ask students to write a different calculation on their boards, including decimal numbers, that has an answer that is greater or smaller than the one on the board.
- o Beware of any misconceptions that students may still have. Clarify them.

Simple algebraic fractions

Learning objectives

Learning objectives covered in this chapter: 9Ae5

- Add and subtract simple algebraic fractions.

Key terms

- denominator
- numerator
- simplify
- algebraic fraction

Prior knowledge assumptions

- Students know how to add and subtract fractions.
- Students know how to collect like terms.

Guidance on the hook

Purpose: To revise adding and subtracting fractions with different denominators.

Use of the hook: Ask students to solve this problem: You have three loaves of bread to be split among five people. How would you split the loaves of bread so that each person gets the same amount? Get students to discuss this problem.

Most students will say to cut each loaf into five equal pieces and to give each person three of these pieces. Students need to imagine how this would have been done in ancient Egypt, for example:

- Would there be a sharp knife to cut the bread and would the bread cut nicely or crumble?
- Would the bread need to be cut and divided up in the desert or in a field?

Explain to students, using diagrams, that cutting each loaf in half and then cutting the remaining piece may be more practical in these situations.

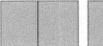

Ask students what fractions they can see in this picture, that is, $\frac{1}{2} + \frac{1}{10} = \frac{3}{5}$.

> TIP: You may also want to ask students to consider the problem where four loaves of bread are split between five people before starting the hook.

Introduce Egyptian fractions and explain what a unit fraction is (that is, the fraction must be in the form $\frac{1}{n}$). Show students how this links to the examples above and ask them to try the examples in the Student's Book.

Adaptation: Ask students to write their fractions in hieroglyph.

Extension: Students can explore further by investigating whether it is possible to write any fraction as the sum of two unit fractions.

Starter ideas

Mental maths starter

Work out $\frac{1}{3} + \frac{1}{4}$.	Work out $\frac{3}{5} - \frac{1}{4}$.	Work out $\frac{2}{7} + \frac{3}{5}$.	Work out $\frac{5}{6} - \frac{3}{8}$.
Simplify $4x - x$.	Simplify $5x - 2x$.	Simplify $x + 6x$.	Simplify $5x - x + 2x$.
Write this fraction in its simplest form: $\frac{3}{12}$.	Write this fraction in its simplest form: $\frac{12}{18}$.	Write this fraction in its simplest form: $\frac{25}{35}$.	Write this fraction in its simplest form: $\frac{21}{28}$.
Simplify $3x \times 2$.	Simplify $4y \times 3$.	Simplify $x \times x$.	Simplify $3x \times 4y$.
Expand $3(x - 1)$.	Expand $4(x + 2)$.	Expand $5(2x - 3)$.	Expand $x(x + 1)$.

Start point check

Target board

Give each student a copy of the target board from the photocopiable resources. Choose two fractions from this board (photocopiable resources) and ask students to add or subtract the fractions. You could change the difficulty by starting with choosing fractions with the same denominator, then fractions where one of the denominators is a multiple of the other, then where both denominators are different.

Ask students to add or subtract three fractions. You could also ask the students to give you the answer in decimals or as an improper fraction.

STRETCH: Give students a fraction and ask them to give you two fractions from the board which will add to this fraction.

Simplifying fractions game

Give each student a copy of the grid from the photocopiable resources. Students should fill in their grid with any of these fractions:

$$\frac{2}{3}, \ \frac{3}{4}, \ \frac{2}{5}, \ \frac{3}{5}, \ \frac{5}{6}, \ \frac{2}{7}, \ \frac{3}{8}, \ \frac{5}{8}, \ \frac{2}{9}, \ \frac{4}{9}, \ \frac{5}{9}, \ \frac{8}{9}$$

In a random order, read out the fractions from the grid on the next page. Students need to simplify the fraction and then cross out the answer if they have it in their grid. The winner is the first person to cross out all of their answers.

$\frac{22}{77}$	$\frac{25}{40}$	$\frac{9}{24}$	$\frac{32}{36}$
$\frac{36}{60}$	$\frac{14}{21}$	$\frac{12}{27}$	$\frac{24}{32}$
$\frac{30}{54}$	$\frac{40}{48}$	$\frac{12}{30}$	$\frac{18}{81}$

Discussion ideas

Probing questions	Teacher prompts
Give me two fractions which add to $\dfrac{5}{2x}$.	Write the suggestions on the board. Encourage students to give fractions in their simplest form.
What is next in this sequence? $\dfrac{1}{x}, \dfrac{1}{2x}, \dfrac{3}{2x}, \dfrac{2}{x}, \dots$ Explain why.	Prompt the students to write the fractions with the same denominator.
Explain why $\dfrac{3d-1}{2} - \dfrac{d-5}{6}$ does not equal $\dfrac{4d-4}{3}$.	Students may need reminding that when subtracting the second fraction they are subtracting $(d-5)$, which is the same as subtracting d and then adding 5.

Common errors/misconceptions

Misconception	Strategies to address
$\dfrac{x}{2} + \dfrac{x}{2} = \dfrac{2x}{4}$	Use of addition/subtraction of numerical fractions. Use of diagrams for addition/subtraction of algebraic fractions, such as those given in the Student's Book.
$\dfrac{3}{x} + \dfrac{5}{x} = \dfrac{8}{2x}$	Use of diagrams for addition/subtraction of algebraic fractions, such as those given in the Student's Book.
$\dfrac{2x-3}{2} - \dfrac{x-3}{2} = \dfrac{x-6}{2}$	Ask students what the answer to this would be: $$\dfrac{x-3}{2} - \dfrac{x-3}{2}$$ Students should notice that the answer is 0, as you are subtracting two identical expressions. Ask the students to consider why the answer is not: $$\dfrac{-6}{2} = -3$$

Developing conceptual understanding

9Ae5 Add and subtract simple algebraic fractions.

* Start by revisiting adding and subtracting numerical fractions.
* FIX: Replace the numerator of one or more of the fractions with an algebraic expression.
* FIX: Use of diagrams or pictures may be helpful. For example:

STRETCH: Addition/subtraction of algebraic fractions where the denominators and/or numerators are of the form $ax \pm b$.

STRETCH: Apply these skills to questions involving algebraic fractions, such as perimeter or angle questions.

STRETCH: Students may be able to apply this knowledge to allow them to multiply or divide algebraic fractions.

End of chapter mental maths exercise

1. $\dfrac{1}{x} + \dfrac{3}{x}$

2. $\dfrac{5}{2x} - \dfrac{1}{x}$

3. $\dfrac{1}{x} + \dfrac{2}{3x}$

4. $\dfrac{x}{3} + \dfrac{x}{4}$

5. $\dfrac{x}{5} - \dfrac{2x}{3}$

6. $\dfrac{5x}{7} - \dfrac{4x}{5}$

7. $\dfrac{2}{x} + \dfrac{1}{xy}$

8. $\dfrac{x-1}{2} + \dfrac{x+3}{3}$

Technology recommendations

- Use the internet to research the greedy algorithm.

  Fibonacci first described the greedy algorithm to write fractions using unit fractions. Students should be able to answer the following questions:

  o What is the greedy algorithm?

  o How it is used?

  o How do you use the greedy algorithm to write $\dfrac{\square}{\square}$ using unit fractions?

  Students could produce a poster or presentation about the greedy algorithm.

Investigation/research tasks

- **Fractions and Cuisenaire rods**

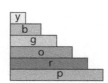

  Express each rod as a fraction of all the other rods.

  $y = \dfrac{\square}{\square}$ b?

  $y = \dfrac{\square}{\square}$ g?

  $\dfrac{2}{3}\,\square = b$

  $\dfrac{3}{5}\,\square = g$

STRETCH: $\frac{1}{5}(b + g) = \boxed{}$ $\qquad$ $\frac{5}{9}(p + g) = \boxed{}$ $\qquad$ $\frac{\boxed{}}{8}(r + o) = \boxed{}$

> TIP: Students could use strips of paper, coloured appropriately to help them visualise these. For example:

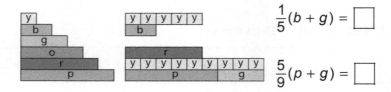

$\frac{1}{5}(b + g) = \boxed{}$

$\frac{5}{9}(p + g) = \boxed{}$

- **ABC**

   Use this prompt to start a discussion: $\qquad \frac{1}{a} + \frac{1}{b} = \frac{1}{c}$

   Ask students to calculate values of *a*, *b* and *c*.

> TIP: Encourage students to use trial and error for values of *a* and *b*, to see if these give you a unit fraction.

Formulae

Learning objectives

Learning objectives covered in this chapter: 9Ae6, 9Ae7
- Derive formulae and, in simple cases, change the subject; use formulae from mathematics and other subjects.
- Substitute positive and negative numbers into expressions and formulae.

Key terms
- variable
- formula
- change the subject

Prior knowledge assumptions
- Students know how to derive and use simple formulae.
- Students can substitute positive and negative integers into formulae and expressions.

Guidance on the hook

Purpose: This hook provides students with the opportunity to revise substituting integers into expressions.

Use of the hook: Students will need a dice, two counters and a copy of the race track from the photocopiable resources. Start by explaining the rules as shown on the race track game. Students should then play this game in pairs.

TIP: You may want to check student understanding by asking students, 'If I throw a … , how many spaces would I move if I was on square … to start'.

Adaptation: This game could be played in small groups if you used additional counters.

Extension: Students could use a dice/spinner/random number generator to generate integers between −10 and 10 and substitute these values into the expressions on the rack track.

Starter ideas

Mental maths starter

What is the value of $3x - 2$ if $x = 4$?	What is the value of $2x + 7$ if $x = -3$?	What is the value of $5 - 4x$ if $x = 2$?	What is the value of $1 - 3x$ if $x = -7$?
$(-8)^2$	9^2	13^2	$(-7)^2$
What is the value of x^2 if $x = 5$?	What is the value of x^2 if $x = -4$?	What is the value of x^3 if $x = -2$?	What is the value of $2x^2$ if $x = 3$?
Simplify $3x \times 5x$.	Simplify $2x + 8x$.	Simplify $4x \times 7y$.	Simplify $9x - y + 5x - 4y$.
What is the formula for the area of a square with side length x?	What is the formula for the perimeter of a square with side length x?	What is the formula for the circumference of a circle with radius r?	What is the formula for the area of a circle with radius r?
0.1×7	0.03×8	$2.4 \div 6$	$(0.5)^2$

Start point check

The answer is …

Write down four or more questions which have an answer of 20x.

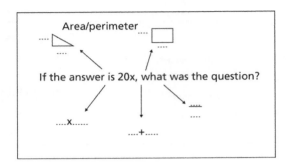

> TIP: You may need to prompt students to consider simplifying an expression/algebraic fraction, the perimeter/area of a shape, etc.

This could be played as a game where students could get a point for each unique and correct answer.

Target board

Give students a value of x. Ask them which expressions from the right-hand target board match the values on the left-hand target board. For example, if $x = 1$, $-3x = -3$, $4x - 9 = -5$, $x^3 = 1$, etc.

-5	7	1	12
2	-3	8	-9
-11	13	-7	5
6	15	0	-10

$5 - 2x$	$-3x$	$3x + 1$	$4x - 9$
x^3	$4x + 5$	x^2	$7 - 3x$
$2 - x^2$	$-2x^2$	$1 - 3x$	$5x^2$
$(2x)^2$	$8 + x^2$	$2x^3$	$4x - 3$

> TIP: It would be useful to have students jot their findings on mini whiteboards.

This could be adapted to a game, where students get 1 point for every matching expression and number they have written down which is correct.

STRETCH: You could use values which are fractions or decimals. However you would need to be careful that these did match a value from the target board on the left-hand side.

Discussion ideas

Probing questions	Teacher prompts
Are these expressions equivalent? $\frac{1}{2}(a + b) \times h$, $\frac{h}{2}(a + b)$, $\frac{(a + b) \times h}{2}$	Encourage students to substitute values of a, b and h into the three expressions. Once they have established that these all give the same solution, encourage students to manipulate one expression slightly until it looks like one of the other two expressions.

Probing questions	Teacher prompts
Which is the odd one out? $ab = c$, $\dfrac{a}{b} = c$, $a = \dfrac{c}{b}$, $b = \dfrac{c}{a}$	Encourage students to try to rearrange the equations so that they are in the same format.
A shape made from rectangle has a perimeter of $11x - 4$. Label the sides of the shape. STRETCH: You could also add the criterion that the shape must also have an area of $2x^2 - x$.	Encourage students to trial different drawing different shapes on mini whiteboards. Ask the students to label the sides and then calculate the perimeter. You may want to tell the students that the shape is a T-shape.

Common errors/misconceptions

Misconception	Strategies to address
Substituting a negative value for x into an expression where you need to subtract the negative value. For example, substituting a negative value of x into the expression $4 - x$.	Encourage students to write down all the steps in their working. For example: if $x = -5$ then $4 - x = 4 - (-5) = 4 + 5 = 9$.
Forgetting that when you square a negative number the answer is positive.	Remind students that $(-3)^2 = -3 \times -3 = 9$.
Using a calculator to evaluate the square of a negative number.	Encourage students to use brackets to input these into a calculator. For example, if you are substituting $x = -3$ in to $3x^2 - 1$, type $3 \times (-3)^2 - 1$ into the calculator.
When substituting into an expression of the form ax^n, students sometimes apply the power to ax not to x. For example, substitute $x = 4$ in to $2x^2$. Some students will interpret this as: $2 \times 4^2 = 8^2 = 64$ not $2 \times 4^2 = 2 \times 16 = 32$.	Remind students of the order of operations BIDMAS and remind them that they must apply the indices or power before they multiply. It can also be worthwhile reminding students what $2x^2$ means: $2x^2 = 2 \times x \times x$. So, in the example where $x = 4$, $2x^2 = 2 \times 4 \times 4$.
If students are asked to change the subject of the equation $a = 2b + 3$, to make b the subject, many students think that the order of operations must apply and think that they need to rearrange by first dividing by 2 and then subtracting 3.	Tell students that when rearranging a formula to make another variable the subject they should apply BIDMAS in reverse order.

Developing conceptual understanding

9Ae6 Derive formulae and, in simple cases, change the subject; use formulae from mathematics and other subjects.

* FIX: Students could initially work on describing the relationships between variables in words, before replacing the descriptions with letters. For example, to calculate the area of a trapezium you add together the lengths of the parallel sides a and b, you then multiply by the height, h, between the two parallel lines and half the answer before writing this as an equation.

STRETCH: Encourage students to consider the different formats that a formula can be written in. For example:

The formula for the area A of a trapezium can be written: $A = \dfrac{(a + b) \times h}{2}$, or $A = \dfrac{1}{2}(a + b) \times h$ or $A = \dfrac{h}{2}(a + b)$.

- FIX: Students use function machines to help them change the subject of the equation and could work backwards to rearrange to make the correct variable the subject of the equation.

STRETCH: Students working at a greater depth could begin to rearrange formulae involving squaring or powers.

BEWARE: When students are rearranging formulae such as $e = mc^2$ to make c the subject, they will need guidance to ensure that they record both the positive and negative root.

- FIX: Ask students to square both 4 and −4. They should realise that both give 16. Ask them then to find $\sqrt{16}$. Most students will forget that this can be both 4 and −4.

9Ae7 Substitute positive and negative numbers into expressions and formulae.

- FIX: You could use algebra tiles to represent a formula visually. When substituting, students can replace each element of the formula with its known value before calculating.

For example, here is a representation of $s = ut + \dfrac{1}{2}at^2$

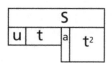

Students can practise substituting positive and negative integers in the target board starter.

End of chapter mental maths exercise

1. Substitute $x = -5$ into $4x^2$.
2. Substitute $p = 4$, $q = -0.5$ into $3p^2 - q$.
3. Substitute $a = 0.5$, $b = 0.1$ into $8a - b^2$.
4. Write down a formula for the perimeter of the shape shown below.

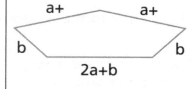

5. Make a the subject of this equation:

   $b = 4a - 5$

6. Make y the subject of this equation:

   $x = \dfrac{y}{3} + 2$

7. Make d the subject of this equation:

   $p = \dfrac{d - 3}{x}$

8. Make x the subject of this equation

   $y = \dfrac{2x + 5}{3}$

Technology recommendations

- Use scientific and basic calculators to give students experience of correctly evaluating the substituted values. This could be done alongside traditional pen and paper methods.
- Use a spreadsheet when substituting values into a formula. For example, students could create a table and use formulae to calculate the results.

	A	B	C
1	X	Y	
2	−3	−0.2	
3			
4	$\frac{y}{3} + 2$		
5	$x^2 y$		
6	$7y - x^2$		
7	$x^2 - 2y$		

	A	B
1	X	Y
2	−3	−0.2
3		
4	$\frac{y}{3} + 2$	=B2/3+2
5	$x^2 y$	=A2^2*B2
6	$7y - x^2$	=7*B2-A2^2
7	$x^2 - 2y$	=A2^2-2*B2

Solution:

- Use the internet to research different scientific formulae and their uses. Students could produce a poster or presentation with their findings.

Investigation/research tasks

Euler's formula

Euler's formula says that the number of faces of a 3D solid, F, plus the number of vertices, V, is equal to the number of edges, E, plus 2.

Investigate whether this works for all 3D shapes.

TIP: Before students start work, ask them to write a list of the 3D shapes they wish to investigate. Encourage students to write the F, V, E and +2 in a table and record for each shape whether Euler's formula works.

Inequalities

Learning objectives

Learning objectives covered in this chapter: 9Ae11

- Understand and use inequality signs (<, >, ≤, ≥); construct and solve linear inequalities in one variable; represent the solution set on a number line.

Key terms

- less than
- greater than
- less than or equal to
- greater than or equal to

Prior knowledge assumptions

- Students know how to use inequality symbols.
- Students can solve linear equations with unknowns on either or both sides.

Guidance on the hook

Purpose: This is a game to be played in pairs to remind students of inequality symbols.

Use of the hook: Students will need a dice and two copies of the grids from the photocopiable resources. Start by explaining the rules as shown in the Student's Book. Students should then play this game in pairs.

Adaptation: You could use an 8- or 10-sided dice.

Extension: Students could use a dice/spinner/random number generator to generate integers between −10 and 10 to extend the game into comparing the size of negative numbers.

TIP: You could show students how to use their calculator to generate random numbers.

BEWARE: Do check understanding of comparing the size of negative numbers. For instance, many students will think that −6 is greater than −4.

TIP: Students could use vertical number lines to help them compare the size of negative numbers.

Starter ideas

Mental maths starter

Put these in order, smallest to largest: −17, −19, −15	Put these in order, smallest to largest: −3.5, −3.2, −4	Put these in order, smallest to largest: 0.1, 0.15, 0.062	Put these in order, smallest to largest: −15, −0.98, 1.2
Solve $15x = 3$.	Solve $21 - x = 7$.	Solve $\dfrac{x}{4} = 5$.	Solve $12 + x = 5$.

Use < or >:
    −4 … 8
	Use < or >:
	    −17 … −21
		Use < or >:
		    −8 … −7.5
			Use < or >:
			    −0.1 … − 0.15

Solve $4x + 1 = 29$.	Solve $5x - 2 = 38$.	Solve $7 - 5x = -18$.	Solve $6x - 7 = -43$.
Solve $6(x - 5) = 42$.	Solve $3(x + 3) = -6$.	Solve $4(3 - 2x) = 16$.	Solve $7(4x - 5) = 35$.

Start point check

Solving equation card sort

Give students a cut-out copy of the card sort from the photocopiable resources. Students then need to match the correct value of x with the equation. Students should do this by solving the equation, not by substitution.

TIP: This can be completed in pairs or small groups.

BEWARE: There are several cards with the same answer to further challenge students to match the correct cards.

I think of a number

Give each student a mini whiteboard.

Describe a number, n to the students and ask them to write an expression for it on their whiteboard and then to reveal their expressions at the end.

For example:

I think of a number, n. I double my number and add 4 to it. Write an expression to show this.

You could also describe a number as an inequality in words and ask students to tell you what possible numbers you could be thinking of.

For example:

I think of a number, n. When I double it and subtract 4, I get a number greater than 10 but less than 20. What could my number, n, be?

Discussion ideas

Probing questions	Teacher prompts
Sometimes, always, never? $x \geq 4x$	Encourage students to trial different values of x. You may need to prompt student to trial decimals and negative numbers.
Same or different? $7 \geq 3x + 13x + 1 \leq 7$	Encourage students to rearrange one of the inequalities so that both inequalities are written in the same format.
A number is rounded to 5 to the nearest whole number. This can be written as the inequality: $4.5 \leq x \leq 5.5$ True or false?	Encourage students to consider what numbers can be rounded to 5. You could ask whether 4.45 would round to 5, when rounded to the nearest whole number. Ask students to consider; when does the number given round down. When does it round to the next whole number?
A student's age is 8. This can be written as the inequality: $8 \leq x < 9$ True or false?	Encourage students to consider how someone's age is described. For example, someone is 8 from the day they turn 8 until the day before they turn 9.

Common errors/misconceptions

Misconception	Strategies to address
Students do not recognise that these are equivalent: $x \leq 2$ and $2 \geq x$.	Ask students to give you the integer values which satisfy these inequalities. Students will then see that the inequalities are equivalent.
When dividing an inequality by a negative number, students do not realise that they need to reverse the inequality symbol.	Avoid this issue by instead adding the amount to each side of the inequality. For example, $$-5x > 25$$ Add $5x$ to both sides $$0 > 5x + 25$$ Subtract 25 from both sides $$-25 > 5x$$ Divide by 5 $$-5 > x$$
When solving inequalities students sometimes make an error manipulating the inequality. For example, a student solving the following inequality may multiply the 7 by 2 (forgetting to also multiply the 4 by 2) and then subtract 4. $$\frac{x}{2} + 4 \geq 7$$	Remind students of the BIDMAS order of operations and remind them that they should reverse the order when they are solving equations and inequalities. Remind students that all operations should be applied to every term in the inequality.

Developing conceptual understanding

9Ae11 Understand and use inequality signs (<, >, ≤, ≥); construct and solve linear inequalities in one variable; represent the solution set on a number line.

- FIX: begin writing inequalities about an unknown or variable by using word descriptions of the number.

  For example: 'a number is between 4 and 8' or 'Elena is no more than 5 years old' before replacing these with letters as a shorthand.

  For example: '$4 < n < 8$' or '$e \leq 5$'.
- FIX: liken solving inequalities to solving equations.

  For example, students should be happy to solve $2x + 3 = 7$. Explain to students that you use the same method for solving $2x + 3 < 7$, the difference being that the inequality symbol replaces the equals sign.

STRETCH: Students could explore solving simple two-sided inequalities.
For example, solve $4 < x + 1 \leq 7$ or $3 \leq 2x < 8$

- FIX: liken representing inequalities on a number line to showing a number on a number line. For example, if you were asked to show where -3 would be on a number line, you would put a dot on the number -3.

  Then ask students to show you which way you would draw an arrow to show greater than or equal to and less than or equal to.

  Finally, explain to students that to distinguish between less than/greater than and less than/ greater than or equal to, we show this in the same way but use an open dot/circle.

STRETCH: Use graphical software for students to explore regions by plotting linear inequalities on a graph.

End of chapter mental maths exercise

1. Write the correct inequality symbol between these two numbers: $$-7 \ldots -10$$	5. Write down the integers that satisfy this inequality: $$-3 < x \le -1$$
2. Write this inequality in words: $$-3 \le x < -1$$ Sam is x years old and Tyler is y years old.	6. Solve this inequality: $$4x + 1 \le 9$$
3. Tyler is more than three years older than Sam. Write this as an inequality.	7. Write down the smallest integer which satisfies this inequality: $$3(x + 2) > -6$$
4. Sam and Tyler's combined age is less than 12 years. Write this as an inequality.	8. Solve this inequality: $$-6x < 18$$

Technology recommendations

- There are a range of electronic versions of inequalities on number lines to support the approaches shown in this chapter. For example, you can quickly produce an inequality on a number line using this artificial apparatus and ask students to state the inequality they represent, or vice versa.

- You could use these electronic resources for your own modelling or enable the students to produce diagrams to support their responses more rapidly than they could by hand.

Investigation/research tasks

- **Construction**

  Construction workers are building a brick wall 12 bricks high. Each brick is 10 cm high to the nearest cm. What is the difference in the minimum and maximum height of the wall, ignoring any mortar between the bricks?

  How many bricks high is a wall where the minimum and maximum height is more than 20 cm?

  Investigate the difference in heights for bricks of any height.

- **Tennis**

  In a tennis match, a set is won by the first person to win six games, with a margin of at least two games over the other side (for example, a score of 6–4 or 7–5). There is a game called a tie-break to decide the winner if the score is 6–6, to decide the final game of the set. The score would then be 7–6.

  What are the minimum and maximum number of games that can be played in a set? Write this as an inequality.

  Matches are won by winning the best of five sets (winning three sets from the five) for men's singles matches and best of three sets (winning two sets from the three) for women's singles matches.

  What is the minimum and maximum number of games that can be played in both men's and women's singles matches? Write this as an inequality.

Investigate what the minimum and maximum number of games would be for any number of sets.

In some international tournaments, in the fifth set of a men's tennis match and in the third set of a women's tennis match there is no tie-break in the final game. Research the highest recorded number of games played in these situations.

Linear functions and graphs

Learning objectives

Learning objectives covered in this chapter: 9As3, 9As4, 9As5

- Find the inverse of a linear function.
- Construct tables of values and plot the graphs of linear functions, where y is given implicitly in terms of x, rearranging the equation into the form y = mx + c; know the significance of m and find the gradient of a straight-line graph.
- Find the approximate solutions of a simple pair of simultaneous linear equations by finding the point of intersection of their graphs.

Key terms

- function
- inverse
- gradient
- intercept
- simultaneous equations
- point of intersection

Prior knowledge assumptions

- Students know how to construct a table of values and plot the graph of a linear function.

Guidance on the hook

Purpose: This hook gives students practice using one- and two-step function machines in a game to introduce the concept of reversing a function machine to find an inverse function.

Use of the hook: Students need a copy of the function machines, and number and operation cards in the photocopiable resources. Start by explaining the rules as shown in the Student's Book. Students should then play this game in pairs.

Adaptation: You could adapt this game to include negative numbers.

TIP: You may want to get students to use a random number generator to generate negative numbers.

Extension: You could allow students working at a greater depth to include division as an operation.

BEWARE: Students may come into difficulty when using the division operation, depending on the number started with. You may wish to allow students to use calculators for the division, and you may need to prompt students to record their answers as a fraction to keep the accuracy.

Starter ideas

Mental maths starter

Expand $3(x - 4)$.	Expand $2(x + 5)$.	Expand $5(4x - 7)$.	Expand $4(1 - 3x)$.
Substitute $x = -5$ into $\dfrac{5 - x}{2}$.	Substitute $x = 9$ into $\dfrac{x}{3} - 5$.	Substitute $x = -4$ into $8 - \dfrac{x}{2}$..	Substitute $x = 8$ into $\dfrac{6}{x - 2}$.
Make y the subject of this equation: $y - 4x = 7$	Make y the subject of this equation: $6x = 1 - y$	Make y the subject of this equation: $2y + 8 = 6x$	Make y the subject of this equation: $2y - 3x = 4$
Substitute $x = -1$, $y = 2$ into $2x - 3y$.	Substitute $x = -3$, $y = -2$ into $3x + 2y$.	Substitute $x = 7$, $y = -3$ into $5x - y^2$.	Substitute $x = 3$, $y = -4$ into $4xy$.
Calculate y when $x = 0$: $2y - 3x = 6$	Calculate x when $y = 0$: $4 - 12x = 3y$	Calculate y when $x = 0$: $5x = y - 6$	Calculate x when $y = 0$: $2 = 3y - 4x$

Start point check

I am a number game

Give each student a copy of the grid from the photocopiable resources. Students should fill in their grid with any number from −10 to 10.

In a random order, read out the clues from the grid from the photocopiable resources. Students need to cross out the answer if they have it in their grid. The winner is the first person to cross out all of their answers.

This game could be adapted to a matching game, if you give students a copy of each of the clues and answers cut out.

Matching graphs

Give students a copy of the card sort from the photocopiable resources. Students then need to match a table of values with the corresponding graph.

STRETCH: You could ask students what the value of $x = 0$ in the table indicates and ask students what they notice about the pattern in the y-values.

Another format

Write down the equation $y = 2x - 3$ in 4 or more different formats.

You may want to start with a prompt like this:

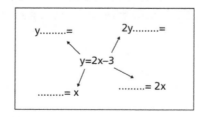

This could be played as a game where students could get a point for each unique and correct answer.

Discussion ideas

Probing questions	Teacher prompts
Will these two lines intersect? $2y - x = 8$ $9 - 0.5x = y$	You could ask students to plot the graph of both lines and then ask students what properties the lines have; i.e. the lines are parallel. Alternatively, you could prompt students to consider the circumstances when the lines would not intersect. Encourage students to rearrange the equations to the form $y = mx + c$ and then find the gradient of both lines; students may be able to spot that parallel lines have the same gradient. You could ask students if they can give you the equation of two more lines which will not intersect.
Will these two lines intersect? $y + 8 = 4x$ $4 - x = 4y$	You could ask students to plot the graph of both lines and then ask students what properties the lines have; i.e. the lines are perpendicular. Encourage students to rearrange the equations to the form $y = mx + c$ and then find the gradient of both lines; students may be able to spot that perpendicular lines have gradients where one is the reciprocal of the other.
Give me the equations of three lines which will form an isosceles triangle.	Encourage to students to plot three vertices of an isosceles triangle. Ask students to then draw lines through these points. Ask students what information they need for the equation of a line; i.e. the gradient and intercept. Students should be able to find the gradient and intercept from their graphs. You may need to show them how to use this to write the equation of the lines.
True or false? The inverse of this function will be the same as the function: $x \rightarrow 8 - x$	Encourage students to draw the function machine, to input different values for x and work out the output. Students should then think about what they have to do to return the output value back to the input value. Students should then be able to see that the inverse function will be the same as the function.

Common errors/misconceptions

Misconception	Strategies to address
The inverse of $x \rightarrow 4 - x$ is $x \rightarrow 4 + x$.	Ask students to input values of x into the function machine for $4 - x$, for example if $x = 3$ is input the output is 1. If $x \rightarrow 4 + x$ is the inverse then the input $x = 1$ and should return us to the original input which was 3, which it doesn't.

Misconception	Strategies to address
Students can often struggle to know where to start drawing the triangle underneath the line to calculate the gradient of a line. 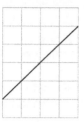	Encourage students to look for places where the line crosses the axis, if needed they can extend their lines to check the pattern continues. 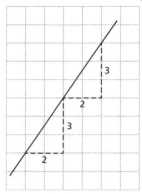
When the equation of a line is not given in the form $y = mx + c$ but is still explicitly in terms of y (for example, $y = 3 - 2x$) means that students often get the gradient and intercept mixed up.	When finding the gradient and intercept of a line encourage students to rearrange the equation so that it is in the form $y = mx + c$. For example, $y = 3 - 2x$ can be rearranged to $y = -2x + 3$. Students will then be able to read off the values of the gradient and intercept correctly.

Developing conceptual understanding

9As3 Find the inverse of a linear function.

- FIX: Begin using function machines; ask students to draw the function machine of the original function and then apply the order of operations (BIDMAS) in reverse to find the inverse function machine. Get students to check their inverse function by substituting values of x into the function machines. Students then need to put the output through the inverse function machine to check that they do return to the original value of x.

STRETCH: Use dynamic graphing software to plot a linear function and its inverse function. Ask students what they notice about the line of symmetry between the two functions.

9As4 Construct tables of values and plot the graphs of linear functions, where y is given implicitly in terms of x, rearranging the equation into the form $y = mx + c$; know the significance of m and find the gradient of a straight-line graph.

- FIX: Use dynamic graphing software to plot lines in the form $y = mx + c$ and use a slider to change the value of m and c so that students can see the effect on the graph.

  They should notice that the graph crosses the y-axis at the point $(0, c)$.

  They should also notice that the value of m determines the steepness of the graph.

STRETCH: Students may be able to determine the equation of a line from either a table of values or a graph by calculating the gradient and intercept.

STRETCH: Students working at a greater depth could begin to explore the properties of equations of parallel lines. Students may be able to find the equation of a line which is parallel to another line given the y-intercept.

9As5 Find the approximate solutions of a simple pair of simultaneous linear equations by finding the point of intersection of their graphs.

- FIX: Students can revisit tables of values and their corresponding graphs using the matching graph activity at the start of this chapter.

- FIX: Show students the graph of two lines which intersect and ask students which values of x and y would be in the table of values for both lines. Then help students to make the connection between this and the approximate solution.

STRETCH: Students working at a greater depth may be able to start to check the approximate solutions found on their graphs using algebraic methods.

End of chapter mental maths exercise

1. Write the inverse of this function $$x \rightarrow 4x - 5$$ 2. Write the inverse of this function $$x \rightarrow \frac{x}{3} + 2$$ 3. What are the gradient and intercept of this line? $$y = 3x - 1$$	4. What are the gradient and intercept of this line? $$4 - y = 2x$$ 5. What are the gradient and intercept of this line? $$5x = 2y - 4$$

Technology recommendations

- Use dynamic graphing software to plot lines in the form $y = mx + c$ and use a slider to change the value of m and c so that students can see the effect on the graph.

  They should notice that the graph crosses the y-axis at the point $(0, c)$.

  They should also that the value of m determines the steepness of the graph.

> TIP: Set the slider up to start with only whole number values of m and c from −10 to 10. You can then introduce decimals afterwards.

  Students could also use dynamic graphing software to investigate what graphs of non-linear equations look like, such as the graphs of $y = x^2$, $y = \frac{1}{x}$, etc.

Investigation/research tasks

- **Symbol puzzle**

  See the puzzle in photocopiable resources. Work out the value of each symbol and then the missing totals for each row.

  Solution:

  ✈ = 8   ✵ = 3   🏴 = 5   ❀ = 9

- **Equal expressions**

  Here are three expressions. Is it possible to find the values of a and b which make the expressions all equal?

  $4a - 3b + 25$ $7a + 4b + 59$ $3a - 9b - 1$

- **Parallel and perpendicular**

  Here are the equations of three lines. Two of these are parallel and the other is perpendicular to the other two.

  $$y + 9 = 4x \qquad 4y + x = 7 \qquad y = 4x - 1$$

  Use dynamic graphing software to investigate the equations of parallel and perpendicular lines.

Angles and geometrical reasoning

Learning objectives

Learning objectives covered in this chapter: 9Gs1, 9Gs2

- Calculate the interior or exterior angle of any regular polygon; prove and use the formula for the sum of the interior angles of any polygon; prove that the sum of the exterior angles of any polygon is 360°.
- Solve problems using properties of angles, of parallel and intersecting lines, and of triangles, other polygons and circles, justifying inferences and explaining reasoning with diagrams and text.

Key terms

- interior angle
- exterior angle

Prior knowledge assumptions

- Students should know how to solve problems involving angle properties of parallel lines, triangles and quadrilaterals.
- Students should be able to use the properties of the exterior angle of a triangle.

Guidance on the hook

Purpose: Through a practical activity, this task introduces the concept of the sum of the exterior angles of a polygon being equal to 360°. It does not mention the idea of an exterior angle.

Use of the hook: A think, pair, share approach could be used for the first part of the activity. (This is up to and including the first two questions.) When the students share, ask them to use full, complete mathematical sentences. A group-work approach could be used for the second part of the activity. Ask the students to discuss the total angle the pencil has turned through when the convex polygon is considered.

Adaptation: For lower-attaining pupils the task can be started using triangles and special quadrilaterals (for example, a square).

Extension: Students could draw diagrams of the shapes they use on paper, mark on the exterior angles, cut out them out and create angles at a point (therefore 360°). For example:

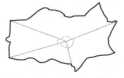

TIP: Students could estimate the angle the pencil is turning through as they do the task.

BEWARE: The convex polygon could create confusion for students with less confidence of angles.

Starter ideas

Mental maths starter

What is the sum of the interior angles of a triangle?	The sum of the interior angles of a quadrilateral is: a) 180° b) 320° or c) 360°?	What is the sum of the angles on a straight line?	Complete this sentence: Vertically opposite angles are ____.
A triangle has two interior angles of equal size. What is the name of the triangle?	Find the sizes of the missing interior angles: 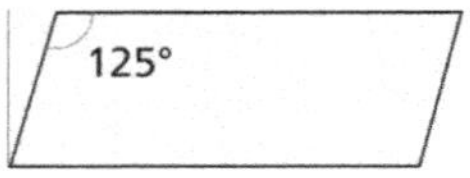 125°	Write down the value of y. 124° y 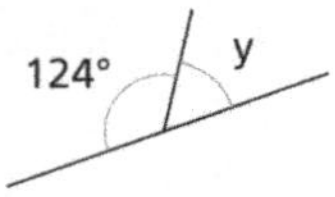	What is the value of x? 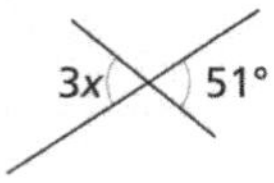 3x 51°
Find the sizes of all the interior angles. 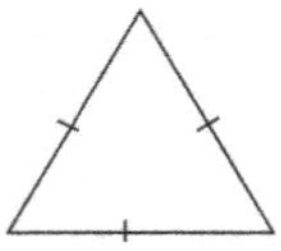	A quadrilateral has all four sides the same length and opposite interior angles the same size. What is the name of the quadrilateral?	The sum of three equal angles is 180°. What is the size of each angle?	The sum of four equal angles is 360° What is the size of each angle?
Complete this sentence: The exterior angle of a triangle is equal to the sum of the ____ interior opposite angles.	Three interior angles of a quadrilateral are 130°, 50° and 130°. What is the size of the fourth interior angle?	$5x = 180°$. What is the size of angle x?	$10y = 360°$. What is the size of angle y?
Write down the size of angle t: 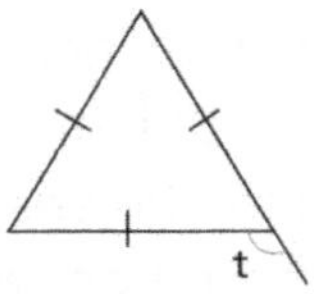 t	Write down the size of angle s: s 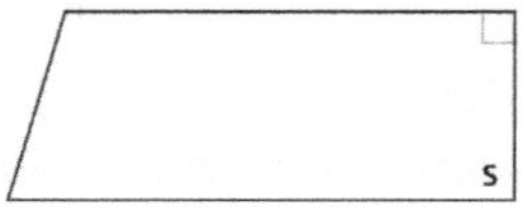	$10x + 90° = 270°$. What is the size of angle x?	$40z - 40° = 320°$. What is the size of angle z?

Vocabulary development

List a variety of polygons on the board. For example, include scalene triangle, parallelogram, regular pentagon, etc.

Ask the students to work in pairs and take turns to describe to each other the properties of the polygons. They should use full, complete mathematical sentences. Diagrams can be drawn to support the descriptions.

- FIX: For students who struggle with polygons such as a scalene triangle, restrict the list to, for example, square, rectangle, triangle, pentagon, hexagon.

Start point check

- **Alternate and corresponding angles**   *Problem solving*

  Ask students to create their own diagrams that explain what alternate and corresponding angles are. They then have to use full, complete mathematical sentences to explain to a partner what their diagram shows.

Discussion ideas

Probing questions	Teacher prompts
Pierre says this calculation finds the exterior angle of a regular decagon: $$\frac{180 - 10}{10}$$ How can you convince Pierre he is wrong?	Suggest to students that a drawing could be used when checking Pierre's method. *Problem solving* • FIX: Suggest that the method to find the exterior angle of a regular decagon could be compared with Pierre's method. TIP: A think, pair, share approach could be used for this question. TIP: Ask students to correct Pierre's method.
$$180 - \frac{360}{n}$$ n = number of sides of the polygon. Explain why the method shown finds the size of an interior angle of a regular polygon.	Encourage the students to break the method down into parts. Ask them to explain their answer to a partner using full, complete mathematical sentences. *Problem solving* • FIX: Support students who struggle with algebra by suggesting they try out examples to show that the method works.
Oli has measured all the interior angles of a polygon: 35°, 135°, 65°, 132°, 174° How can you determine if Oli's measurements are correct?	Any explanations could be written as full, complete mathematical sentences. *Problem solving* TIP: Ask students to work in pairs to answer this question. • FIX: Encourage the addition of the five angles as a first step.
  Five angle measurements are added to the diagram. What could they be?	Encourage the students think about what geometrical properties the diagram has. *Problem solving* • FIX: Suggest that a struggling student asks themselves the question, 'what is the diagram telling me?' TIP: Ask students to demonstrate their answers to the rest of the class.
  The diagram has not been finished. Andrea knows that: O is the centre of the circle. Line AC and line BD are diameters. ABCD is a quadrilateral. She says the quadrilateral is a rhombus. Give a reason why she is wrong.	Encourage the students to carefully complete the diagram. *Problem solving* TIP: Ask students to work in groups of three or four and provide A1 paper, or similar, to create a large version of the diagram TIP: Students might need reminding about the diagonals of quadrilaterals. • FIX: Provide hint/support cards/other forms of scaffolding that suggest steps that can be used to tackle the problem.

Common errors/misconceptions

Misconception	Strategies to address
Students can think that all polygons are regular.	Reinforce understanding by students drawing polygons with different numbers of sides. They can also be exposed to comparisons of regular and non-regular polygons.
Students make assumptions about diagrams and the properties of shapes within them.	Reinforce understanding by describing the properties of shapes in written form and verbally. Diagrams can also be divided up into their constituent parts.
Students assume that a calculation is enough evidence when asked to give a reason.	Reinforce understanding by describing polygons using reasons. For example: 'The shape is a regular pentagon because it has five sides of equal length, five interior angles of equal size and five exterior angles of equal size.' The reason has to be full and complete. Other mathematical topics can use the instruction, 'Give a reason why …'

Developing conceptual understanding

9Gs1 Calculate the interior or exterior angle of any regular polygon; prove and use the formula for the sum of the interior angles of any polygon; prove that the sum of the exterior angles of any polygon is 360°.

- FIX: To reinforce students' understanding that the sum of the exterior angles of any polygon is 360°, provide triangular tiles that students can manipulate. As they connect tiles, students can verbalise the addition of each 180° and write down the calculations. This activity can be done in pairs.

STRETCH: For those students confident with the learning objective, provide questions involving algebra. For example:

- o The diagram shows part of a regular polygon.
- o Write down the exterior angle in terms of y.
- o Find the number of sides the polygon has in terms of y.
- o Show that the sum of the interior angles of the polygon is $\dfrac{360y}{180 - y}$.

STRETCH: Ask students to work in pairs to create their own questions, based on those in Exercise 1. Solutions to the questions can be found by sharing with others. Students should be encouraged to explain and justify their solutions.

9Gs2 Solve problems using properties of angles, of parallel and intersecting lines, and of triangles, other polygons and circles, justifying inferences and explaining reasoning with diagrams and text.

- FIX: To support students' understanding of the properties of diagrams, provide the diagrams without any descriptions. Students have to write, or verbalise, the descriptions using full, complete mathematical sentences. Also, provide just the descriptions and students have to draw the diagrams.

Questions such as, 'What do you see? What do you know?' can be asked.

- FIX: To support students providing correct explanations, full, complete mathematical sentences can be provided verbally. This can be done in pairs.

- FIX: Problems can be scaffolded by the use of hint/support cards that students can refer to when solving them.

STRETCH: Ask students to work in pairs to create their own questions, based on those in Exercise 2. Solutions to the questions can be found by sharing with others. Students should be encouraged to explain and justify their solutions.

End of chapter mental maths exercise

1. Find the exterior angle of a regular pentagon.

2. The exterior angle of a regular polygon is 60°. What is the name of the polygon?

3. A polygon has five exterior angles. Four of the angles are: 30°, 56°, 78°, 124°.

   What is the value of the fifth angle?

4. Find the sum of the interior angles of an 11-sided polygon.

5. A polygon has six interior angles:

   150°, 72°, 102°, $y°$, $y°$, $y°$
   What is the value of $y°$?

6. The exterior angle of a regular polygon is 36°.

   What is the sum of the interior angles of the polygon?

7.

   Copy the diagram and find all possible angles using 25° and 125°, giving reasons to justify the choices.

8.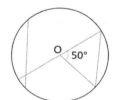

   Copy the diagram and find all possible angles using 50°, giving reasons to justify the choices.

Technology recommendations

- Use dynamic geometry software (such as GeoGebra) and spreadsheets to investigate the first learning objective (9Gs1 Calculate the interior or exterior angle of any regular polygon; prove and use the formula for the sum of the interior angles of any polygon; prove that the sum of the exterior angles of any polygon is 360°).

   For example:

Number of sides of the polygon	Sum of the interior angles	Interior angle (if regular)	Exterior angle (if regular)
3	180	60	120
4	360	90	90
5	540	108	72
7	900	128.57	51.43
10	1440	144	36

Formulae used:

Number of sides of the polygon	Sum of the interior angles	Interior angle (if regular)	Exterior angle (if regular)
3	=180*(D4−2)	=ROUND(E4/D4,2)	=180−F4
4	=180*(D5−2)	=ROUND(E5/D5,2)	=180−F5
5	=180*(D6−2)	=ROUND(E6/D6,2)	=180−F6
7	=180*(D7−2)	=ROUND(E7/D7,2)	=180−F7
10	=180*(D8−2)	=ROUND(E8/D8,2)	=180−F8

Investigation/research tasks

- **Present students with the following information.**   *Problem solving*

  A polygon has the following interior angles: 30°, 150°, 30°, 150°.

  Using a ruler and protractor, try to draw the polygon.

  Write down the lengths of the edges of the polygon in a) mm and b) cm.

STRETCH: Investigate drawing other polygons, using both interior and exterior angles.

- FIX: For students who struggle with using a protractor, provide a diagram with some of the sides of the polygon already drawn.

- **Present students with the following diagram.**   *Problem solving*

  Peter has drawn this diagram:

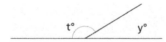

  Peter decides that $t° = 140°$ and that 140° is an interior angle of a regular polygon.

  Write down all the properties of Peter's polygon.

> TIP: Student's might need reminding what the properties could be.

STRETCH: Peter decides that $t° = 2y°$. Write down all the properties of Peter's polygon.

STRETCH: Peter decides that $t° = ky°$, where k is a multiple of 3. Peter says that his polygon is always a regular polygon. Is he correct? Justify your answer with calculations and reasons.

- **Create a poster that explains what the properties are of polygons up to 12 sides.**

Enlargements and transformations

Learning objectives

Learning objectives covered in this chapter: 9Gp4, 9Gp5

- Enlarge 2D shapes, given a centre and positive integer scale factor; identify the scale factor of an enlargement as the ratio of the lengths of any two corresponding line segments.
- Recognise that translations, rotations and reflections preserve length and angle, and map objects on to congruent images, and that enlargements preserve angle but not length.

Key terms

- scale factor
- centre of enlargement
- image
- object
- congruent

Prior knowledge assumptions

- Students should know how plot a set of coordinates.
- Students should be able to enlarge a shape.
- Students should be able to transform a shape by using a translation, reflection or rotation.
- Students should be able to recognise whether a transformation is a translation, reflection or rotation.

Guidance on the hook

Purpose: Through a practical activity, students reinforce their understanding of reflection.

Use of the hook: Students could work in pairs, with each partner creating one aspect of the pattern.

Adaptation: For students who struggle with reflections, partial diagrams can be created for them to then develop.

Extension: Students can develop their diagrams using lines at other angles.

TIP: Students could use A1/flip chart paper to create their patterns. These can then be displayed.

Starter ideas

Mental maths starter

Complete this sentence: The *x*-axis is per_____ to the *y*-axis.	Write down the coordinates of the points shown on this set of axes: 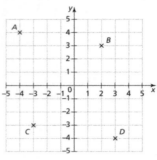 Plot E at (4, 1) and F at (−4, −2).	Draw a set of axes *x*: 0 to 4, *y*: 0 to 4. Draw a triangle with vertices at (1, 1), (2, 3) and (2, 1).	A rectangle has vertices at (−2, 1), (2, 1) and (−2, −2). What are the coordinates of the fourth vertex?
Complete this sentence: A translation, rotation, reflection and enlargement are all trans_____.	Enlarge the shape *L* with a scale factor of 5, centre (−5, 5). Label the image *M* and write down the coordinates of its vertices. 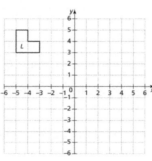	Draw a set of axes *x*: −2 to 6, *y*: −2 to 6. Draw a square with vertices at (1, 1), (1, 3), (3, 3) and (3, 1). Label it *N*. Enlarge it with a scale factor of 3, centre (2, 2). Label the image *P*.	*S* is an image after an enlargement with a scale factor of 2, centre (2, 0). 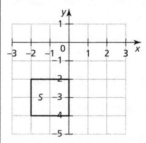 Two of the vertices of the object are at (0, −1) and (1, −1). What are the coordinates of the other two vertices?
Translate the shape *L* by six squares right. Label the image *N*. Write down the coordinates of the image. 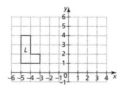	Reflect the shape *A* in the line *y* = 1. Label the image *B* and write down the coordinates of its vertices. 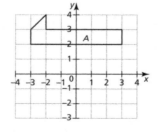	Draw a set of axes *x*: −1 to 5, *y*: −5 to 4. Draw a rectangle with vertices at (0, 0), (0, 4), (3, 4) and (4, 0). Label it *Y*. Rotate it by 90° clockwise, centre (0, 0). Label the image *Z*.	*T* is an image after a translation by three squares right and two squares down. What are the coordinates of the vertices of the original shape? 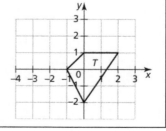

Which transformation could take shape *A* onto shape *B*?	Which transformation could take shape *B* onto shape *C*?	Which transformation could take shape *D* onto shape *E*?	Name all the transformations that could take shape *F* onto the other shapes.

Start point check

All the transformations

Ask the students to work in groups of three or four. Provide each group with A1, or similar, paper. Ask the students to draw their own set of axes and demonstrate all four transformations on the set of axes.

Drawing and describing transformations   *Problem solving*

Ask students to work in pairs. They create their own examples of all four transformations, writing a full, complete mathematical description of the transformation next to each one. Their set of transformations are then shared with another pair. Partners take turns describing one of the transformations verbally for the other partner to draw.

- FIX: Students who are struggling with any of the transformations can be given the diagrams and partial descriptions, which have to be completed.
- FIX: Students who are struggling with any of the transformations can be given the diagrams and they have to create the full, complete mathematical descriptions.

Discussion ideas

Probing questions	Teacher prompts
How could the diagram be changed so that a scale factor of 3 is used instead of 2? 	Suggest to students that they think about where a multiplication by 2 can be seen. *Problem solving* • FIX: Provide guidance on how to find the scale factor. TIP: A think, pair, share approach could be used for this question.

Probing questions	Teacher prompts
Oli states that his centre of enlargement is (1, 2). 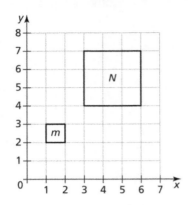 How would you prove that he is wrong?	Any explanations could be written as full, complete mathematical sentences. *Problem solving* • FIX: Suggest that lines are drawn from the image vertices back to the corresponding vertices in the original shape. TIP: Ask students to work in pairs to answer this question.
Abdul has measured and found his scale factor is both 2.9 and 3. Can you explain why he might have two values? 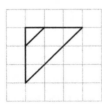	Any explanations could be written as full, complete mathematical sentences. *Problem solving* • FIX: Encourage lengths of corresponding sides to be measured. TIP: Ask students to work in pairs to answer this question.
Why is the scale factor of the enlargement 2? 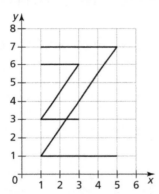	Encourage the students to completely justify their answer. (They need to be persuaded that all corresponding sides need to be measured, but without a direct instruction to do so.) *Problem solving* • FIX: Encourage lengths of corresponding sides to be measured. TIP: Ask students to demonstrate their answers to the rest of the class.

Probing questions	Teacher prompts
Samina says that the perimeter of the image S is three times the perimeter of the object R. Give a complete reason why she is wrong. 	Encourage the students to completely justify their answer. (They need to be persuaded that 'because the interior angles are wrong', or similar, is not a complete reason.) *Problem solving* TIP: A think, pair, share approach could be used for this question. TIP: Students might need reminding about the diagonals of quadrilaterals. • FIX: Suggest that the enlargement is redrawn to check Samina's errors. • FIX: Provide hint/support cards/other forms of scaffolding that support the reasoning that is needed.

Common errors/misconceptions

Misconception	Strategies to address
Students can misunderstand the multiplicative nature of the scale factor.	Reinforce understanding by students comparing images found using a scale factor of, for example 3, to those found by just, for example, adding 3 to each side of the object.
Students do not think the same scale factor is used for every side of an object.	Reinforce understanding by students using all the corresponding sides of the object and the image to find the scale factor; seeing that it is the same in each case. Use the same idea with shapes that are almost similar to show the scale factor is not the same.
Students do not understand the effect that the centre of enlargement has on the position of the image.	Reinforce understanding by students investigating what effect changing the position of the centre of enlargement has on the way an object and image relate to each other. Use verbal and written responses to consolidate understanding.

Developing conceptual understanding

9Gp4 Enlarge 2D shapes, given a centre and positive integer scale factor; identify the scale factor of an enlargement as the ratio of the lengths of any two corresponding line segments.

• FIX: To support students who struggle to visualise enlargement on paper, use alternative concrete approaches, for example, a pin board and elastic bands.

• FIX: To support students who struggle to enlarge a shape, suggest that one side of the image is found, then the rest of the image can be drawn using the scale factor.

STRETCH: For those students confident with the learning objective, provide questions such as:

An object has four sides. The diagram shows two of the sides and their images after an enlargement:

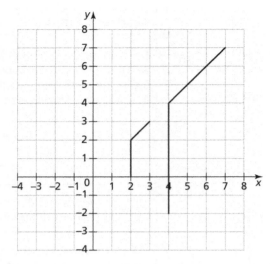

Complete the diagram by finding and using the scale factor of the enlargement.

> TIP: (Hints could be given to students, such as guiding them as they find the scale factor of enlargement, where it should be placed, the type of quadrilateral the object is.)

Write down the lengths of perimeters of the object/image. Divide the two lengths to check you obtain the same scale factor of the enlargement.

An example of what the student might produce:

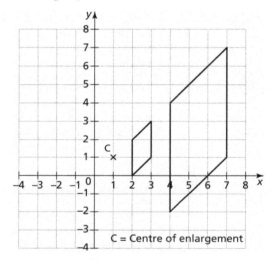

C = Centre of enlargement

STRETCH: Ask students to work in pairs to create their own questions, based on those in the example above. Solutions to the questions can be found by sharing with others. Students should be encouraged to explain and justify their solutions.   *Problem solving*

9Gp5 Recognise that translations, rotations and reflections preserve length and angle, and map objects on to congruent images, and that enlargements preserve angle but not length.

- FIX: To support student recognition of transformations, suggest that the corresponding angles/sides of the object and image are measured.

- FIX: To support student recognition of transformations, provide many examples at different orientations. For example, give students objects and images (see photocopiable resources).

- FIX: To support student provision of the correct explanations, full, complete mathematical sentences can be provided verbally. This can be done in pairs.

End of chapter mental maths exercise

1. Find the scale factor of the enlargement of object *A* to image *B*.

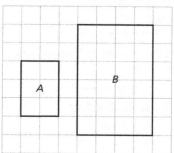

2. Find the scale factor of the enlargement of object *C* to image *D*.

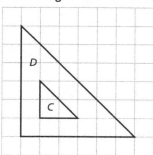

3. Copy the diagram and draw the enlargement of *P* with a scale factor of 2, centre (1, 0).

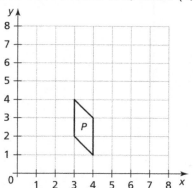

Label the image *T*.

4. Copy the diagram and draw the enlargement of *S* with a scale factor of 4, centre (2, 0). Label the image *T*.

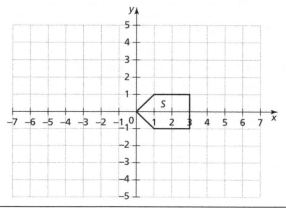

5. Find the scale factor of the enlargement of object *A* to image *B*.

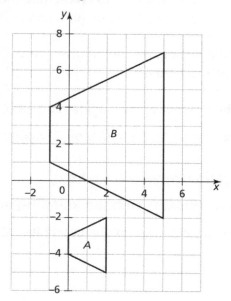

6. In the diagram, *B* is the object.

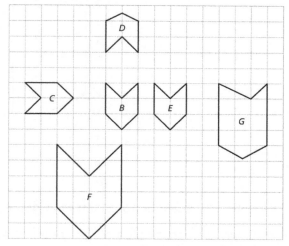

For each of the other shapes decide whether:

a) the shape is congruent, or not congruent, to *B*. If it is congruent, name the transformation of *B* which it could be.

b) the shape is an enlargement of *B*.

Technology recommendations

- Use dynamic geometry software (for example, GeoGebra) to investigate the enlarging shapes.

  You could ask students to investigate moving the centre of enlargement without changing the scale factor. Describe what happens to the object and image.

> TIP: The descriptions can be given verbally and in written form, using full, complete mathematical sentences.

- Use the internet to investigate the use of transformations by M.C. Escher.

  For example: http://www.mcescher.com/

Investigation/research tasks

- **Present students with the following information:**   *Problem solving*

  The diagram shows an object and its image.

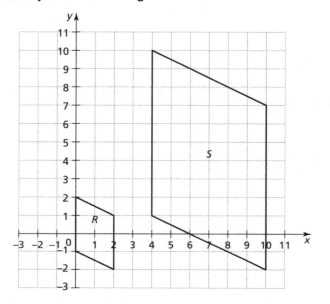

  Write down the scale factor of the enlargement.

  Write down the coordinates of the centre of enlargement.

  If the vertex at (0, −1) was translated to the position of its image it would move four squares right and two squares up.

  What happens to the other vertices of the object if they are translated?

  How do the translations change if the scale factor changes?

STRETCH: Students create their own enlargements and investigate the translations of the vertices of an object.

- FIX: For students who struggle with enlargement, provide the position of the centre of enlargement.

- FIX: For students who struggle with translation, provide one direction. For example, three squares up.

- Draw a set of axes x: −5 to 5, y: −5 to 5. Draw a triangle with vertices at (−1, 0), (1, 0) and (−1, −1).   *Problem solving*

    By enlarging the triangle, find the maximum size the scale factor can be as an integer. Justify your answer by drawing sets of axes that show the object, centres of enlargement and images that you use.

    STRETCH: Students can investigate other shapes and change the size of the axes.

- FIX: For students who struggle with enlargement, different positions of the centre of enlargement and one size for the scale factor could be investigated first.

    Dynamic geometry software could be used for this investigation.

- Investigate the use of enlargements in the production of, for example, photographs and prints of paintings. Use local sources, for example, photo printing shop.

Statistical graphs

<table>
<tr><td>

Learning objectives

Learning objectives covered in this chapter: 9Dp2
- Select, draw, and interpret diagrams and graphs, including:
  - frequency diagrams for discrete and continuous data
  - line graphs for time series
  - scatter graphs to develop understanding of correlation
  - back to back stem-and-leaf diagrams.

</td><td>

Key terms
- back to back stem-and-leaf diagram
- scatter diagram
- frequency diagram
- line graph

</td></tr>
</table>

Prior knowledge assumptions
- Students know how to draw and interpret simple frequency diagrams.
- Students can draw and interpret simple line graphs.
- Students know how to draw and interpret simple stem-and-leaf diagrams.

Guidance on the hook

Purpose: The purpose of this hook is to develop students' ability to interpret a line graph for time series.

Use of the hook: Start by presenting the students the men's winning times graph on its own. What information can they determine from it? Are they able to ask and answer sensible questions (such as, 'When was the fastest/slowest time?) Once the students have had an opportunity to analyse the data themselves, present the questions. Extend the questions by asking them to find out when the records were broken. After which year were the winning times consistently quicker than 10 seconds?

Adaptation: Students could draw both the men's and woman's time on the same graph. Do the students draw the same conclusions as before? Are they able to determine any more information/comparisons? Discuss other statistical representations that could be used to display this information. How useful are these other methods? Why was a line graph time series graph used to show this information?

Extension: Students research other statistics about the 100-metre race. Ask them to suggest their own investigations and to make a poster/presentation showing their findings. The students need to select the most appropriate graph to represent the data. Are the students able to suggest other appropriate graphs to show the same data? Why did they choose the one they chose?

Suggestions: How do the all race times in the 100-metre finals in 2016 compare with those in 1948?

Show the different nationalities that competed in the 100-metre finals for the past five summer Olympic games.

TIP: Encourage students to think about the data before selecting the graph.

BEWARE: Students tend to use bar charts or frequency graphs to display data. Encourage them to use other methods to display their data.

Starter ideas

Mental maths starter

What is 20% of 12?	What is 60% of 80?	What is 12% of 40?	What is 110% of 50?
The mean of three numbers is 10. Two of the numbers are 8. What is the missing number?	The mean of three numbers is 6. Numbers include 4 and 6. What is the missing number?	The mean of three numbers is 20. The numbers include 35 and 14. What is the missing number?	The mean of four numbers is 12. Two of the numbers are 10 and 14. The other two numbers are the same. What is the value of the missing numbers?
Write down three consecutive numbers that add up to 45.	Write down three consecutive numbers that add up to 21.	Write down five consecutive numbers that add up to 15.	Write down four consecutive numbers that add up to 22.
A train journey takes 45 minutes, it starts at 10 : 20. What time does the train arrive?	A car journey takes 1 hour and 5 minutes. It starts at 12 : 55. What time does it end?	A train journey starts at 15:56 and finishes at 17 : 10. How long was the train journey?	A car journey starts at 00:30 and finishes at 12 : 15. How long was the journey?

Start point check

Show the students different charts and diagrams that they are already familiar with (some are in the photocopiable resources). Remove the title and/or the axis labels/values and ask the student to write in some appropriate information of their own.

Ask each student in turn to think of a number between 1 and 100. Have the students, in turn, call out the number – everybody including the teacher records the number (this may need to be repeated if the class is small). Once all the numbers are recorded then ask each person to calculate the median and mode of the numbers. The teacher also completes the task, but by using a stem and leaf diagram (s)he will be much quicker than the students who probably kept their data in a list.

Discussion ideas

Probing questions	Teacher prompts
Here is an example of an incomplete stem-and-leaf diagram: 4 | 2 7 9 5 | 4 5 6 8 6 | 1 1 3 4 6 7 | 3 4 4 8 9 7 8 | 2 4 5 5 9 9 | 8 9 What information is this diagram showing? What other graph does it remind you of? What is the median? What is the mode? What is the mean?	Discuss what is missing from this diagram. What could this diagram be representing? Encourage the students to think what it could mean other than 4|2 = 42 (i.e. 420, 4.2, 0.42). Ask them to make a title and key for this diagram. Encourage the students to see it has a bar chart made up of numbers. Turning it on its side would demonstrate this clearly. Stem-and-leaf diagrams are a useful way to quickly find the median and mode of a set of numbers. Demonstrate this using games/races so the pupils see the benefit of a stem-and-leaf diagram.

Probing questions	Teacher prompts
Convert a stem-and-leaf diagram (above) to a frequency diagram. Use the frequency diagram to work out the median, mode and mean. What percentage of values were less than 5?	Encourage the students to use the title and key they suggested in previous question. Ask them to consider if it is continuous or discrete data. Discuss which diagram was easier to use to work out the averages and percentages.
Which graph would you use to show: • the number of goals each player scored in the Euro cup tournament or a season of football • the time taken for swimmers to swim 100 metres in the Olympics • the words per minute typed by university students • the colours of the cars in a car park • the number of siblings for each class member • population growth of a town over a decade • the length of the class students' legs and arms • the hours of revision and results in a test? Explain your reasoning.	Encourage the students to justify their answer. Different students may wish to portray different facts and therefore will choose different graphs.

Common errors/misconceptions

Misconception	Strategies to address
Stem and leaf: • Numbers are not written in sequential order or not evenly spaced. • Key and titles are forgotten. Back to back stem and leaf: • The numbers on the right-hand side are sequentially written left to right. • Two different stems are written.	Discuss the need for the leaves to be evenly spaced and sequential. When is this important? Discuss comparing results when the stems are different.
Students confuse when to put gaps between the bars.	Encourage them to understand that for discrete data (when something is counted) there will be gaps whether the data is grouped or not. The gap represents the space between two discrete values. Whereas continuous data has no breaks, so no gaps are represented in the diagram. Expose the students to lots of frequency diagram examples of similar data (e.g. yield of tomato plants and height of tomato plant data – discrete vs continuous within the same topic).
Students conclude only a strong correlation can be considered a correlation.	Show plenty of examples of weaker correlations and discuss at what point a weak correlation becomes no correlation.

Developing conceptual understanding

9Dp2 Select, draw, and interpret diagrams and graphs, including: frequency diagrams for discrete and continuous data, line graphs for time series, scatter graphs to develop understanding of correlation, back to back stem-and-leaf diagrams.

- Give the students sets of data and specify if they are to draw a stem-and-leaf or frequency diagram. There will be at least two copies of the data in the group – one for each type of graph. Once the students have drawn the instructed diagram, they must hide the raw data. One task is for another student to work out the median and mode from the data. The second task could be to find the diagram that was drawn from the same set of data. This can be adapted to include pie charts.

- FIX: Make some human scatter graphs or back to back stem-and-leaf diagrams with data collected from the class, such as birthdays, hair length, etc.

> TIP: Chalk and some outside space would work perfectly.

- Convert a local bus or train timetable into a stem-and-leaf diagram. Discuss if this is a beneficial way to display this kind of data.

End of chapter mental maths exercise

1. Is age continuous or discrete data?	6. What is the mean of 3, 5, 4, 7, 1, 6?
2. What is 80% of 400?	7. What is 42 + 15 + 63 + 45?
3. 520 − 42 = ...	8. What is 24 out of 40 as a percentage?
4. What is 5 680 462 to the nearest 100 000?	9. Is height continuous or discrete?
5. What is the median of 3, 5, 4, 7, 1, 6?	

Technology recommendations

- Draw and explore different graphs using spreadsheet packages.

- Use presentation packages to make posters or presentations to explain students' findings from a set of data.

- Use the internet to research uses of stem-and-leaf diagrams. For example, the Japanese underground system uses them to display their departure times, this website can be used to explore their timetables: http://www.tokyometro.jp/lang_en/station/honancho/timetable/

- Use data from online sources, such as those listed below, for students to conduct their own investigations. Support students in creating a question to ask, and with manipulating the large data sets:

  o https://www.olympic.org/olympic-results – official results from previous Olympic games

  o https://data.worldbank.org/ – World Bank Open Data (free and open access to global development data)

  o http://opendata.cern.ch/?ln=en – CERN – the European Organisation for Particle Physics (pen data on some of their experiments)

  o http://www.oecd.org/statistics/ – OECD statistics for each of the 30 OECD countries, arranged by topics (e.g. finance, agriculture, labour).

Investigation/research tasks

- Ask the students to find some real-life examples of frequency diagrams, line graphs and stem-and-leaf diagrams. They can look online, in newspapers or magazines, or in other curriculum textbooks (such as geography, history or science). What are these graphs showing? Can the students think of an alternative graph to use? Why would their choice have been better? Are they able to find a stem-and-leaf diagram (they are used infrequently, but can be found, for example in Japanese bus timetables)?

BEWARE: Publications are frequently mathematically incorrect or misleading. Use this opportunity to discuss what the publisher has done and why.

- John Tukey is quoted as saying 'There is no data that can be displayed in a pie chart, that cannot be displayed better in some other type of chart'. Discuss this comment. Show some pupils some simple pie charts and ask them to display the data using one of the three types of chart investigated in this chapter.

Interpreting and comparing data

Learning objectives

Learning objectives covered in this chapter: 9Di1, 9Di2, 9Di3

* Interpret tables, graphs and diagrams and make inferences to support or cast doubt on initial conjectures; have a basic understanding of correlation.

* Compare two or more distributions; make inferences, using the shape of the distributions and appropriate statistics.

* Relate results and conclusions to the original question.

Key terms

* correlated
* positive correlation
* negative correlation
* conjecture
* hypothesis

Prior knowledge assumptions

* Students know how to draw and read information from statistical graphs.
* Students know how to calculate the mean, median, mode and range for statistical data.
* Students know what the mean, median, mode and range tell you about a set of data.

Guidance on the hook

Purpose: The purpose of this hook is to promote discussion by considering a statistical graph of historical importance.

Use of the hook: Students could discuss the graph in pairs and come up with some conclusions from it. Then each pair could join up together with another pair to share the conclusions that they have made. This then could be followed by some whole-class discussion.

Some conclusions that could be made are:

* Much larger numbers of soldiers were dying in the period April 1854–March 1855 than in the second 12-month period.

* Deaths from preventable infectious diseases peaked in January 1855 and then fell steadily.

* Deaths from wounds peaked in November 1854. (They were high again in June 1855.)

Encourage students to notice that deaths from infectious diseases fell gradually from February 1855 onwards, coinciding with when new methods for preventing infection were introduced.

Adaption: Students could research historical statistical diagrams produced by other statisticians, such as those produced by Charles Joseph Minard – one of his diagrams has been voted the best statistical graph ever drawn. Hans Rosling also produced some influential graphs comparing data relating to countries (life expectancy, income, etc.).

Extension: Students could make up their own similar (rose) diagram to show a set of data and ask someone else to interpret what it shows.

Starter ideas

Mental maths starter

The range of a set of data is 31. Calculate the largest value if the smallest value is 89.	The range of a set of data is 0.45 metres. Calculate the largest value if the smallest value is 1.28 metres.	The range of a set of data is 13°C. Calculate the smallest value if the largest value is 5°C.	The range of a set of data is 1.8 cm. Calculate the smallest value if the largest value is 4.2 cm.
The means for two sets of data are: Set A: 6.5 Set B: 4.9 Calculate the difference between the two means.	The means for two sets of data are: Set A: 7.5°C Set B: −4.5°C Calculate the difference between the two means.	The means for two sets of data are: Set A: 1.84 m Set B: 1.39 m Calculate the difference between the two means.	The means for two sets of data are: Set A: 764 km Set B: 678 km Calculate the difference between the two means.
What measure of average would you use if you wanted to know the most common colour of people's shoes?	What statistic would you calculate if you wanted to know how spread out the exam marks in a class are?	What statistic would you calculate if you wanted to know the height that half the class jumped further than?	You know the total amount of rainfall for June. What measure of average daily rainfall could you calculate?
The total amount of money saved by eight people is $96. Calculate the mean amount saved by each person.	Here are the ages of six people: 11, 18, 19, 37, 45, 63. Calculate the median age.	The total cost of 12 items is $132. Calculate the mean cost of an item.	Here are prices of six books: $4.50, $4.70, $5.60, $6.20, $8.50, $8.50. Calculate the median price.
The mean mark scored by 11 people is 13. Calculate the total of the marks.	The mean length of 20 insects is 4.3 cm. Calculate the total length of all the insects.	The mean age of 15 people is 18 years. Find the total of the ages.	The mean time taken for 30 students to carry out a task is 16 minutes. Calculate the total of the times.

Start point check

Every graph tells a story!

Use the matching cards in the photocopiable resources.

With students working in pairs, ask them to match each card with its description.

STRETCH: Students could make up a graph and create a matching description.

The average is …?

Choose four of the cards below so that:

- The median is 18.
- The median is 21.5 and the range is 18.
- The mean is 10.

4	6	12	13	17	19	21	22	25	30

Discussion ideas

Probing questions	Teacher prompts
Sketch a scatter graph with five points plotted that shows: • weak negative correlation • strong positive correlation • no correlation.	Emphasise that the difference between positive and negative correlation is in whether the points show an upwards or downwards trend. Stress too that the adjectives 'weak' and 'strong' refer to how scattered the points are.
Think of a variable that is likely to be positively correlated with the time it takes someone to walk to school. Now think of a variable that is likely to be negatively correlated with it. Suggest a variable that is likely to have no correlation with the time it takes someone to walk to school.	Encourage students to give a reason why they think their variable will have the relationship that they claim.
This frequency diagram shows the heights of a group of people: 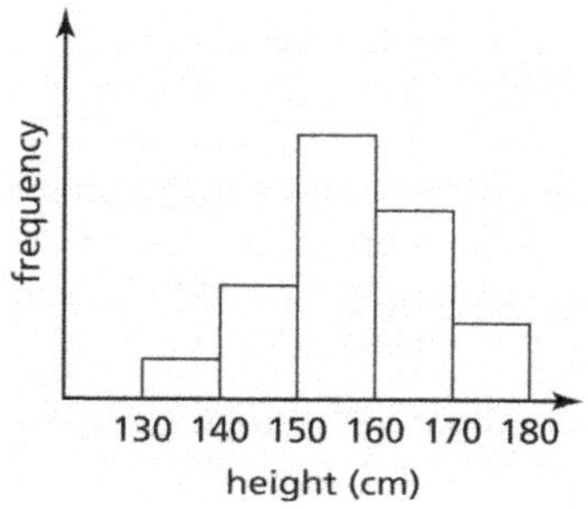 Show me a frequency diagram showing heights that, for example, has: • a lower mean value • a larger spread • the same modal class but a smaller spread.	Prompt students to see that to get a lower mean value, the frequency diagram could shift to the left. Discuss what would happen to the mean if every value became 10 cm smaller. Prompt students to appreciate that to get a larger spread, one or more additional bars will be needed (either below 130 or above 180).
Discuss the message this graph is trying to present: 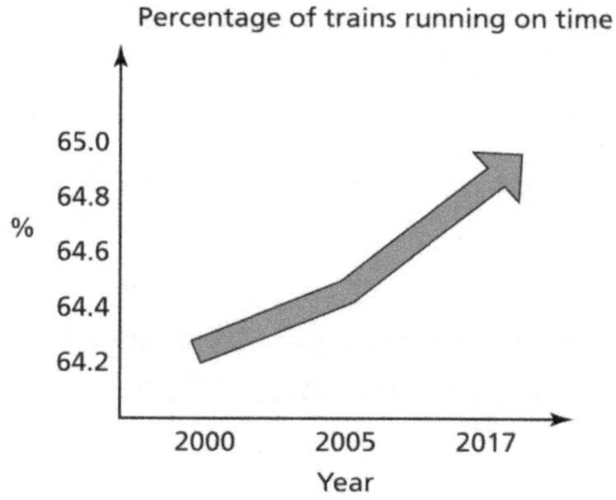 In what ways is the graph misleading?	Discuss issues such as: • The uneven scale on the horizontal axis making the rise look sharper than it is. • The fact that the rise is only from around 62.2% of trains running on time to about 64.8% of trains running on time. The rise is exaggerated by the scale on the vertical axis. • The thick line used to show the data – no points are actually plotted so it makes reading any specific data from the graph difficult.

Common errors/misconceptions

Misconception	Strategies to address
Students can think that a correlation between two variables means that increasing one variable causes the other to increase.	Discuss this scatter graph, which shows the life expectancy and the number of televisions per household in different areas.
	Discuss the correlation between the number of televisions per household and life expectancy.
	Stress that this does not mean that people will start to live longer if households are given more televisions. Life expectancy and number of televisions are instead both linked to another variable – wealth. (People in wealthier areas live longer and also tend to own more televisions.)
Students may use statistics as proof of a statement rather than as evidence in support of a statement.	Get every student to throw a coin ten times. Collect the results for the class showing how many heads each got. Highlight the different results that have naturally arisen from the same experiment.
	Discuss then how a single sample cannot on its own give definitive proof of a statement, rather just some evidence for or against it.
	Note the frequently quoted statement relating to different type of lies: 'lies, damned lies and statistics'. It highlights how careful you have to be when interpreting data.
Students sometimes do not give conclusions to hypotheses using the context of the question.	Discuss these two conclusions to an investigation:
	1. Boys have a higher mean than girls.
	2. The mean height for boys is greater than the mean height for girls, showing that boys are taller than girls on average.
	Discuss these two conclusions. Which one is more informative?

Developing conceptual understanding

9Di1 Interpret tables, graphs and diagrams and make inferences to support or cast doubt on initial conjectures; have a basic understanding of correlation.

- FIX: The scatter diagram shows two points.

Ask students to show how two points could be added to the scatter diagram so that the diagram shows:

- o no correlation
- o positive correlation
- o negative correlation.

- FIX: Ask students to find examples of statistical diagrams in the media. What messages are the diagrams being used to present? Discuss how effective the diagrams are at displaying the information.

> TIP: Make a display in the classroom showing a range of different types of diagrams from newspapers, magazines and the internet.

STRETCH: Students working at a greater depth could find examples of misleading graphs. Encourage students to explain why the graphs are misleading.

9Di2 Compare two or more distributions; make inferences, using the shape of the distributions and appropriate statistics.

- FIX: Students could represent values of an average and the range diagrammatically to help them to make comparisons. For example:

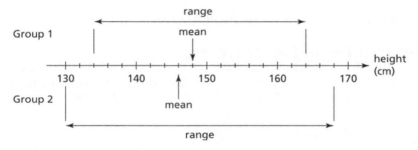

The diagram helps to reinforce the range as a measure of spread.

STRETCH: Students working at a greater depth could be introduced to the idea of skewness, to give another way to compare distributions: positive skew, symmetrical, and negative skew, as shown below.

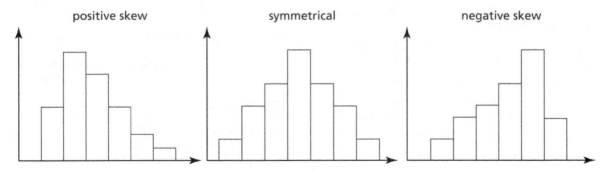

9Di3 Relate results and conclusions to the original question.

- FIX: Discuss with students the data handling cycle:

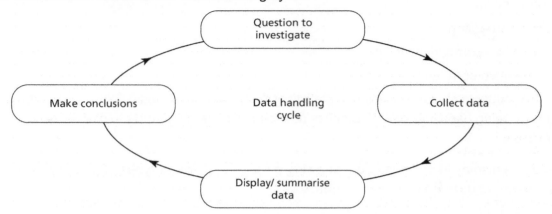

Emphasise that the final stage is to make conclusions from the data and link these to the original question being investigated.

- FIX: Give students the opportunity to work through the entire data handling cycle by:

    o deciding on a question to explore

    o collecting and analysing the data

    o making conclusions.

Some ideas for statistical investigations are given later in this chapter.

End of chapter mental maths exercise

1. The range of a set of data is 2.38 metres. Calculate the largest value if the smallest value is 4.26 metres.

2. The means for two sets of data are:

    Set A: 5.5°C

    Set B: −2.1°C

    Calculate the difference between the two means.

3. What statistic would you calculate if you wanted to know how spread out the heights of a group of people are?

4. Here are the temperatures (in °C) of eight cities: 16, 17, 18, 18, 21, 22, 23, 26.

    Calculate the median temperature.

5. The mean age of six students is 8.5 years. Calculate the total age of all the students.

6. Sandra thinks of five numbers.

    Four of her numbers are: 6, 2, 8, 11.

    The mean of her five numbers is 6.

    Find Sandra's fifth number.

7. Write down the type of correlation shown in this scatter diagram.

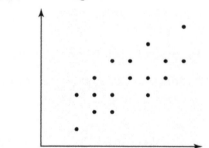

8. Two distributions have the same range.

	Smallest value	Largest value
Distribution 1	118	194
Distribution 2	143	?

Calculate the largest value in distribution 2.

Technology recommendations

- Use the internet to research average monthly temperatures in two different cities around the world (search using the keywords: average temperature city month).

- Use a spreadsheet package (or statistical software) to draw a graph to display these temperatures.

  Make some conclusions comparing the temperatures in the two cities throughout the year.

Investigation/research tasks

- **Exploring correlation**   *Problem solving*

  The Student's Book suggests that students could investigate the hypothesis:

  Students who have larger handwriting tend to write more slowly.

  Students could gather their own data related to this task. For example, they could time how long it takes people to write the sentence 'Scatter graphs are used to look for correlation.' The length (in centimetres) of the sentence would give a measure of handwriting size.

  Ask students to produce a scatter diagram of their results using a spreadsheet or statistics software.

  > TIP: Remind students of the importance of labelling axes.

  Encourage students to interpret their scatter diagram and to write a conclusion to the hypothesis.

  STRETCH: Students could compare differences in handwriting size and writing speed between males and females.

- **Used car prices**   *Problem solving*

  Ask students to investigate the price of used cars.

  Questions that could be explored include:

  - Do older used cars cost less than newer ones?
  - How do the prices of two different makes of cars compare?

  Students could collect data from the internet or from a local newspaper.

  STRETCH: Students working at greater depth should try to ensure that they keep other variables constant.

- **Height investigation**   *Problem solving*

  Students could collect data from other people in their class to investigate whether taller people have larger feet.

  Encourage students to:

  - form their own conjecture
  - collect suitable data
  - display the data in a suitable diagram
  - make conclusions.

TIP: Students could write up their investigations. The write-up should have sections containing their conjecture, descriptions of the data collection, a summary of the data, a diagram and conclusions.

STRETCH: Students could explore what other measurements might be correlated with height. For example, students could explore hand span, arm span, leg length or head circumference.

- **Sports investigation**   *Problem solving*

  Students could investigate a question of their choice linked to a sport. Examples could be:

    o Tennis: Do tennis games for male players last less time on average than those for female players?

    o Football: Do home teams score more goals on average than teams playing away?

    o Athletics: How do the points scored in different events by athletes in decathlon compare? For example, do athletes who score well in the 100 metres also do well in the high jump?

TIP: Work on this investigation would be very good for display.

Describing and combining transformations

Learning objectives

Learning objectives covered in this chapter: 9Gp6, 9Gp3
- Know what is needed to give a precise description of a reflection, rotation, translation or enlargement.
- Transform 2D shapes by combinations of rotations, reflections and translations; describe the transformation that maps an object onto its image.

Key terms
- reflection
- translation
- rotation
- enlargement
- combining transformations

Prior knowledge assumptions
- Students should know how carry out, recognise and describe translations, reflections, rotations and enlargements.
- Students should be able to write the equations of straight lines.

Guidance on the hook

Purpose: The activity deepens students' understanding of rotation. It provides one method students could use to find the centre of rotation.

Use of the hook: Begin the activity with a think, pair, share. Ask the students to think about how a rotation is described and what all the important properties are. Suggest that students use diagrams to explain their thinking.

Discuss with students the use of the centre of rotation. Ask students to demonstrate different amounts of turn and direction. Use a think, pair, share for students to consider how the centre of rotation could be found. Begin the activity with students in pairs, rather than as individuals. Suggest that students use diagrams to explain their thinking.

Ask students to work in pairs as they investigate how to find the centre of rotation. Ask pairs of students to demonstrate their findings to the rest of the class.

Adaptation: For students who struggle with rotation, partial diagrams can be created for them to then develop.

Extension: Students can develop their own diagrams with other amounts of turn; seeing whether the method works in all cases.

TIP: Dynamic geometry software could be used by students to demonstrate different amounts of turn and direction.

Starter ideas

Mental maths starter

In the diagram, decide which shape is an image of *A* after a translation: 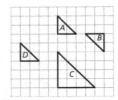	Describe the translation shown in the diagram. *A* is the object, *B* is the image. 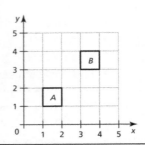	Draw a set of axes x: 0 to 5, y: 0 to 6. Draw a kite with vertices at (1, 1), (1, 2), (3, 3) and (2, 1). Label the kite *R*. Translate *R* two squares right and three squares up. Label the image *S*.	In the diagram *S* is an image after a translation by four squares left and two squares down. 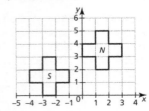 What are the coordinates of the vertices of the object *N*?
Write down the equation of each mirror line shown in the diagram. 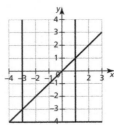	Describe the reflection shown in the diagram. 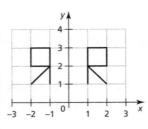	Draw a set of axes x: 0 to 5, y: −1 to 5. Draw a trapezium with vertices at (1, −1), (2, 1), (4, 1) and (5, −1). Label the trapezium *D*. Reflect *D* in the line y = 2. Label the image *E*.	In the diagram *S* is the object and *T* is the image. 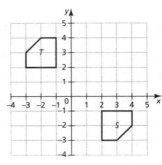 What is the equation of the line of reflection?
Complete this description: A rotation is described using …	Describe the rotation shown in the diagram. 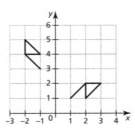	Draw a set of axes x: −3 to 3, y: −2 to 2. Draw a triangle with vertices at (−3, −2), (−2, −1), (−1, −2). Label the triangle *J*. Rotate *J* through 180° about the point (0, 0). Label the image *K*.	In the diagram *T* is an image after a rotation through 90° anticlockwise about the point (3,2). 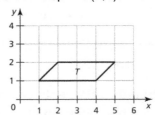 What are the coordinates of the vertices of the object?

| Complete the sentence:

The diagram shows an _____.

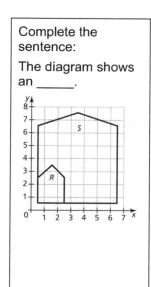 | Explain why the description for this enlargement cannot be completed.

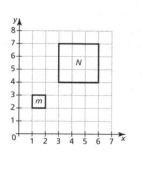 | Draw a set of axes x: −5 to 1, y: −2 to 4. Draw a triangle with vertices at (−3, 0), (−1, 2) and (−1, 0). Label the triangle B. Draw the enlargement of B with a scale factor of 3, centre (−2, 1). Label the image D. | In the diagram T is the object and Y is the image.

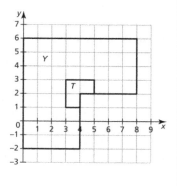

What are the coordinates of the centre of enlargement? |

Starter point check

Checking for errors in transformations   *Problem solving*

Ask students to work in pairs. They create their own examples of any of the transformations on a set of axes but with errors within any part of the diagram. For example, a translation can be drawn with the image slightly enlarged or an enlargement can be drawn with one edge of the image slightly short compared to the corresponding side on the object.

The transformations with errors are then shared with another pair who have to find and correct the errors.

Creating reflections

Ask students to work in pairs. They create their own examples of reflections on a set of axes, showing the object and the image each time. (The equations of the mirror lines need to be in the form y = k, x = k, y = x.) These reflections are then shared with another pair who have to find the mirror lines and write down their equations.

• FIX: For students who struggle with reflection, provide diagrams with, for example, the object shown; the image can then be drawn.

For an additional/alternative approach, student pairs choose their own mirror lines and other pairs have to create reflections using them.

Discussion ideas

Probing questions	Teacher prompts
What is wrong with this reflection? How can you correct it? 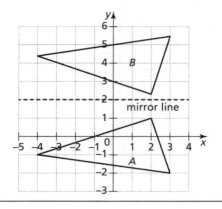	Any explanations could be written as full, complete mathematical descriptions. Suggest to students that they think about how many ways the diagram could be corrected. *Problem solving* • FIX: Suggest that the distance from the mirror line to both the object and image are checked first. TIP: A think, pair, share approach could be used for this question
Ahmed states that his centre of rotation is (8, 0). 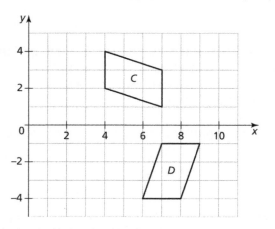 How would you prove that he is wrong?	Any explanations could be written as full, complete mathematical descriptions. *Problem solving* • FIX: Suggest that the diagram is drawn on paper so that it can be folded to find the correct centre of rotation. TIP: Ask students to work in pairs to answer this question.
How can we be sure that the image *F* has been found after two reflections? 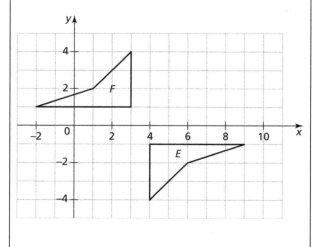	Any explanations could be written as full, complete mathematical descriptions. *Problem solving* • FIX: Encourage both reflections to be found and used. TIP: Ask students to work in pairs to answer this question.

Probing questions	Teacher prompts
Alice says that the image *K* can only be found using one transformation. 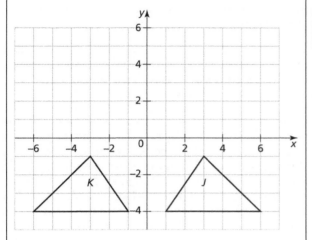 How can you convince her she is wrong?	Encourage the students to completely justify their answer. *Problem solving* • FIX: Encourage a rotation to be used first. TIP: Ask students to demonstrate their answers to the rest of the class.
Samina says that a single translation can also be a rotation and reflection. Give a complete reason why she is correct.	Encourage the students to completely justify their answer. *Problem solving* TIP: Ask students to work in pairs to answer this question. • FIX: Suggest that a shape such as a square is used in the explanation. • FIX: Provide hint/support cards/other forms of scaffolding that support the reasoning that is needed.

Common errors/misconceptions

Misconception	Strategies to address
Students misunderstand horizontal and vertical direction when describing/using translations.	Reinforce understanding by students through further practice of translations and examining how each vertex moves. Use verbal and written responses to consolidate understanding.
Students can confuse the terms clockwise and anticlockwise when describing/using rotations.	Reinforce understanding by students thinking about the direction of the hands on a clock.
Students misunderstand the concept of the image and object each being the same perpendicular distance from the mirror line when describing/using reflection.	Reinforce understanding by students measuring the perpendicular distance. Use equipment, such as small mirrors, for students to see how a reflection works.
Students can misunderstand the multiplicative nature of the scale factor.	Reinforce understanding by students comparing images found using a scale factor, for example 3, to those found by just, for example, adding 3 to each side of the object.

Misconception	Strategies to address
Students misunderstand horizontal and vertical direction when describing/using translations.	Reinforce understanding by students through further practice of translations and examining how each vertex moves. Use verbal and written responses to consolidate understanding.
Students can confuse the terms clockwise and anticlockwise when describing/using rotations.	Reinforce understanding by students thinking about the direction of the hands on a clock.
Students misunderstand the concept of the image and object each being the same perpendicular distance from the mirror line when describing/using reflection.	Reinforce understanding by students measuring the perpendicular distance. Use equipment, such as small mirrors, for students to see how a reflection works.
Students do not think the same scale factor is used for every side of an object.	Reinforce understanding by students using all the corresponding sides of the object and the image to find the scale factor, seeing that it is the same in each case. Use the same idea with shapes that are almost similar to show the scale factor is not the same.

Developing conceptual understanding

9Gp6 Know what is needed to give a precise description of a reflection, rotation, translation or enlargement.

- FIX: To support student recognition of transformations, use tasks that reinforce the concept of congruency. For example, give students objects and images (see photocopiable resources).

- FIX: To support student recognition of transformations, suggest that the corresponding angles/sides of the object and image are measured.

- FIX: To support student provision of correct descriptions of transformations, provide questions that use different sets of axes, different shapes/sizes of shapes, positive and negative coordinates for vertices, etc.

- FIX: To support student provision of the correct explanations, full, complete mathematical descriptions can be provided verbally. This can be done in pairs.

9Gp3 Transform 2D shapes by combinations of rotations, reflections and translations; describe the transformation that maps an object onto its image.

> TIP: Use dynamic geometry software, such as GeoGebra, to provide opportunities to combine transformations and manipulate their properties.

- FIX: To support student provision of the correct explanations, full, complete mathematical descriptions can be provided verbally. This can be done in pairs.

End of chapter mental maths exercise

1. Give a full, complete mathematical description of the transformation shown in the diagram. *A* is the object and *B* is the image.

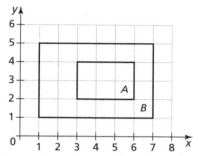

2. Find and describe the error in this sentence. Give an example of how the sentence can be corrected.

   Object *A* is rotated 90° anticlockwise about the point *y* = *x*.

3. Find and describe the error in this sentence. Give an example of how the sentence can be corrected.

   The image *R* was found after a translation by 180° squares left and *x* = 4 squares up.

4. Draw a set of axes *x*: −8 to 8, *y*: −6 to 8. Draw a trapezium with vertices at (2, −4), (4, 0), (6, 0) and (8, −4). Label the trapezium *P*.

   a. Reflect *P* in the line *y* = 2. Label the image *R*.

   b. Translate *R* five squares left and five squares down. Label the image *Q*.

   c. What single transformation takes *P* to *Q*?

5. Draw a set of axes *x*: −4 to 4, *y*: −1 to 4. Draw a parallelogram with vertices at (1, 2), (2, 3), (4, 3) and (3, 2). Label the parallelogram *B*.

   a. Rotate *B* through 180° about the point (0, 1). Label the image *C*.

   b. Reflect *C* in the line *y* = 1.5. Label the image *D*.

   c. Decide whether a single transformation can take *B* to *D*. Justify your answer.

Technology recommendations

- Use dynamic geometry software, such as Geogebra, to investigate both learning objectives.

  Enlargement

  An example of a task would be:

  Investigate moving the centre of enlargement without changing the scale factor. Describe what happens to the object and image.

  Translation

  An example of a task would be:

  Investigate moving the image, seeing how the translation changes. Describe what happens to the object and image.

  Rotation

  An example of a task would be:

  Investigate moving the object, seeing how the image changes its position. Describe what happens to the object and image.

  Reflection

  An example of a task would be:

  Investigate the relationship between the mirror line and the distance the object and image are from it. Describe what happens to the distance, object and image.

TIP: For all of the above, the descriptions can be given verbally and in written form; full, complete mathematical descriptions.

Investigation/research tasks

- Present students with the following information: *Problem solving*

  The diagram shows an object *J* and its image *W* (drawn and labelled on the board).

  Find four transformations (not including enlargement) that can be combined to take *J* to *W*. Provide full, complete mathematical descriptions of the transformations.

  STRETCH: Students create their own questions based on this investigation.

- FIX: For students who struggle with choosing and using transformations, provide hint/support cards/other forms of scaffolding that support the reasoning that is needed.

- Draw a set of axes *x*: −5 to 5, *y*: −5 to 5. *Problem solving*

  By drawing a polygon, investigate combining all four transformations, providing full, complete mathematical descriptions of the transformations.

  Find and describe any single transformations that represent the same combinations.

- FIX: For students who struggle with choosing and using transformations, provide hint/support cards/other forms of scaffolding that support the reasoning that is needed.

- Investigate the use of transformations in the local area through, for example, architecture and design.

Speed and land area

Learning objectives

Learning objectives covered in this chapter: 9Mt1, 9Ma2

- Solve problems involving average speed.
- Know that land area is measured in hectares (ha), and that 1 hectare = 10 000 m^2; convert between hectares and square metres.

Key terms

- average speed
- hectare

Prior knowledge assumptions

- Students should know how to find the difference between two times.
- Students should be able to divide two numbers to give integer or decimal answers.
- Students should be familiar with multiplying numbers by powers of ten.

Guidance on the hook

Purpose: This task uses the students' current concept of speed, placing it in a realistic context. It develops the skill of comparison.

Use of the hook: Begin by asking students to discuss in groups the speeds that different creatures can reach – mammals, reptiles, birds, insects, etc. Ask them to compare creatures, thinking about the fastest speed, slowest speed, etc.

Ask students to work in pairs to create a set of 12 cards (using the blank cards in the photocopiable resources), each with the name of a creature and its top speed. Ask students to play the game.

Adaptation: For lower-attaining pupils, cards can be created with speeds displayed just as integers.

Extension: Students could create new sets of cards with the speeds in different units. They could use the information on the cards as a source for the creation of their own questions, as part of their learning for 9Mt1.

TIP: Students could prepare the cards in advance of the start of Chapter 24, using the internet and other sources for all necessary information.

BEWARE: Sources of information for the cards could give speeds in different units.

Starter ideas

Mental maths starter

Calculate 8 × 70.	Calculate 0.5 × 90.	Calculate 90 ÷ 4.	Calculate 700 ÷ 14.
Find the value of 8 × 30 ÷ 60.	Find the value of 100 × 6 ÷ 8.	Find the value of 20 ÷ 16 × 2.	Find the value of 1000 ÷ 8 × 0.5.
Calculate 0.5 × 40	Calculate 0.4 × 60	Calculate 70 ÷ 0.5.	Calculate 60 ÷ 1.5.
How many hours are there between 4 a.m. and 10 a.m.?	How many minutes are there between 10:00 a.m. and 11:30 a.m.?	How many hours are there between 6:45 a.m. and 2:15 p.m.?	How many minutes are there between 11:45 p.m. and 3:15 a.m.?
Calculate 0.35 × 100.	Calculate 0.054 × 1000.	Calculate 7000 ÷ 10 000.	Calculate 680 ÷ 100 000.

Start point check

Card matching – multiplication and division *Problem solving*

Give students a set of cards (see photocopiable resources).

Ask students to work in pairs to match the cards, completing any blank cards. Explain that if a question needs to be written, it should be a multiplication or division. Students check each other's solutions, justifying to each other why new questions work.

* FIX: Limit the number of cards that need matching for any students who are struggling; do not include blanks.

STRETCH: Pairs of students can create their own set of cards, including blanks, for another pair to match (see photocopiable resources). Students check each other's solutions, justifying to each other why new questions work.

Conversion of time

Write the time 7.5 hours in the middle of the board. Gradually add combinations of times, as in the example below, using suggestions from the students:

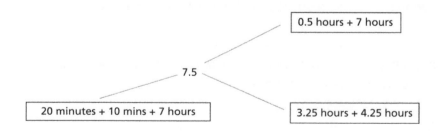

Ask the students to work in groups of three or four. Provide each group with A1, or similar, paper. Ask the students to write their own time (in hours as a decimal) in the centre of the paper and create different combinations of times that match it.

- FIX: Limit the number in the centre to an integer for any students who struggle with decimals and ask for combinations to only use hours or minutes, not both.

- FIX: Provide pre-prepared paper, with the combinations already provided with blanks to be filled in, as in the example below:

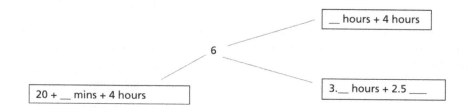

- FIX: Provide pre-prepared paper, with the combinations, with blanks to be filled in, written on cards that can be glued to the paper.

Discussion ideas

Probing questions	Teacher prompts
What is the same and what is different about 1.25 hours, 1 hour 25 minutes, 1 hour 15 minutes?	Suggest to the students that they think about how many minutes are in an hour.
Heinz cycles 18 km at 12 km/h. He rests for 15 minutes, then cycles 36 km at 16 km/h. Explain why his average speed is not 14 km/h.	Encourage the students to consider the overall time that Heinz takes for the journey and suggest they draw bar models/diagrams, etc. Ask them to answer using full, complete mathematical sentences. • FIX: Suggest that the individual times for each part of the journey are found first.
What is wrong with the statement: 'When you multiply by a power of 10 you just add zeros'? How can you correct it?	Ask the students to write out their explanation on paper and then explain it to a partner. Ask them to use full, complete mathematical sentences. TIP: Use think, pair, share as an approach when using this question.
A field has an area of 2.5 hectares. What could its length and width be in metres if one dimension is always a multiple of 10?	Encourage the students to draw bar models/diagrams to help them with the problem. *Problem solving* TIP: Ask students to demonstrate their answers to the rest of the class.

Common errors/misconceptions

Misconception	Strategies to address
Students consider there to be 100 minutes in an hour when adding hours expressed using decimals.	Provide extra exercises comparing hours and minutes. For example: 60 minutes = 1 hour 30 minutes = __ hours __ minutes = 0.25 hours Use appropriate bar models/diagrams, etc. to support any explanation.
When dividing by a number less than 1 the answer becomes smaller.	Provide a real-life example. For example: How many 0.5-litre bottles of water can be filled using a 1-litre bottle? Build up to other multiples of 1 and 0.5. For example: How many 0.5-litre bottles of water can be filled using a 2.5-litre bottle?
Students do not understand that division and multiplication are inverse operations and the effect this has on rearranging formulae.	Reinforce understanding using calculations, such as calculations using the multiplication tables. Reinforce understanding using the triangle for finding rearrangements of the average speed formula.

Developing conceptual understanding

9Mt1 Solve problems involving average speed.

- FIX: To support the understanding of the formula:

$$\text{average speed} = \frac{\text{total distance travelled}}{\text{total time taken to travel that distance}}$$

Use look and say. Students repeat a sentence. For example:

'The formula (for finding the average speed) is total distance travelled divided by total time taken to travel the distance.

Ask students to repeat the phrase to another student.

- FIX: The table used in Exercise 1 can be extended/modified to include a column involving minutes. This will reinforce the use of the correct units when finding the average speed.

For example:

	Total distance (km)	Total time (hours)	Total time (minutes)	Average speed (km/h)
a	100		240	
b	80	5		
c			300	40
d		7		60
e	200			50
f	75			25

- FIX: To support the use of the triangle representing formulae, suggest that students create a hint/support card that they can use to refer to when working on problems.

STRETCH: Ask students to work in pairs to create their own questions, based on those in Exercise 1, Questions 2 to 6. Information from cards used in the hook can provide data for the questions. Solutions to the questions can be found by sharing with others. Students should be encouraged to explain and justify their solutions.   *Problem solving*

9Ma2 Know that land area is measured in hectares (ha), and that 1 hectare = 10 000 m^2; convert between hectares and square metres.

STRETCH: Other units, for example km^2, could be used to extend the understanding for students who have mastered the objective. Converting between different units of area should also be considered.

STRETCH: Ask students to work in pairs to create their own questions, based on those in Exercise 2, Question 4. Solutions to the questions can be found by sharing with others. Students should be encouraged to explain and justify their solutions.   *Problem solving*

End of chapter mental maths exercise

1. Alfie travelled 80 km in 5 hours. What was his average speed in km/h?

2. Pierre rode for 3.5 hours at an average speed of 15 km/h. How far did he cycle?

3. Safira drove 1200 km at an average speed of 80 km/h. How many hours did she spend on her journey?

4. Andrea walks for 20 minutes, runs for 25 minutes and walks for 45 minutes.

   If she covered 6 kilometres, what was her average speed in km/h?

5. How many square metres is 2.4 hectares?

6. How many hectares is 350 000 hectares?

7. A rectangular field is 400 m long and 600 m wide. What is its area in hectares?

8. One field has an area of 0.25 hectares and another 24 500 square metres. What is the total area of the two fields in square metres?

Technology recommendations

- Use the internet to investigate land usage, biodiversity, etc. For example: https://data.worldbank.org/indicator

- Use spreadsheets to model the conversion between units for both learning objectives. For example, for solving problems involving average speed:

Finding average speed			
Distance (km)	Time (hours)	Time (minutes)	Average speed
12	4	240	3
13.5	3	180	4.5
18.6	4.2	252	4.43
27.8	5.9	354	4.71
43.56	7.56	453.6	5.76

The spreadsheet formulae could be as follows:

Finding average speed			
Distance	Time (hours)	Time (minutes)	Average speed
12	4	=C4*60	=ROUND(B4/C4,2)
13.5	3	=C5*60	=ROUND(B5/C5,2)
18.6	4.2	=C6*60	=ROUND(B6/C6,2)
27.8	5.9	=C7*60	=ROUND(B7/C7,2)
43.56	7.56	=C8*60	=ROUND(B8/C8,2)

Investigation/research tasks

- **Present students with the following information:**   *Problem solving*

Vehicle	Average speed for the journey (km/h^{-1})
A	40
B	50
C	60
D	70
E	80

Create the journey for each vehicle that shows the distances travelled, the average speeds and the times spent travelling. Use 30 minutes for lunch.

For example:

Vehicle A

	Time (hours and minutes)	Distance (km)	Average speed (km/h)
Before lunch	2 hours 15 minutes	90 km	40
Lunch	30 minutes		
After lunch	1 hour 15 minutes	70	56
Total	**4 hours**	**160 km**	
Average speed for the journey	40 km/h		

STRETCH: For students who are confident with using minutes and hours, suggest times could be, for example, multiples of 6 minutes.

STRETCH: For students who are confident with calculating using decimals, suggest that distances and average speeds could include decimals.

TIP: When tasks are completed ask students to check the solutions.

- **Present students with the following information:** *Problem solving*

  Fencing is in sections of 2 m.

  An L-shaped field has an area of 0.8 hectares.

  Investigate the amount of fencing that can be used for the field.

  For example (diagram not to scale):

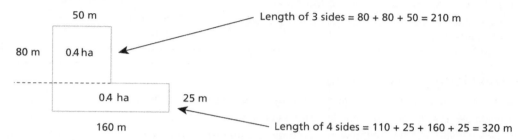

  Total perimeter of field = 210 + 320 = 530 m

  Number of fence sections = 530 ÷ 2 = 265

- FIX: For students who are struggling with calculating using decimals, use integer values for the area of the field.
- FIX: Provide hint/support cards/other forms of scaffolding that suggest steps that can be used to tackle the problem.

STRETCH: For students confident with calculating using decimals, suggest using values to two decimal places when dividing the field in to parts.

STRETCH: For students confident with calculating using decimals, the length of a section of fencing could be changed to, for example, 1.8 m.

STRETCH: Students can present solutions including the use of scale drawings.

> TIP: Encourage students to be accurate when they are creating their scale drawings.

> TIP: When tasks are completed allow students to check the solutions.

- Ask students to investigate the land area and usage for their local area, town, province or country.

STRETCH: Students can present their findings by including the use of scale drawings.

> TIP: Encourage students to be accurate when they are creating their scale drawings.

Trial and improvement

Prior knowledge assumptions

- Students know the meaning of the words **unknown**, **equation**, and **solve**.
- Students know how to solve an equation with an unknown on one side.
- Students know the meaning of the words **unknown**, **equation**, and **solve**.
- Students know how to expand a single bracket, for example $3(2x - 5)$.

Guidance on the hook

Purpose: This hook encourages students to check the answer to different calculations. Students use the information given to find the values that a, b and c stand for.

Use of the hook: Give each pair of students a copy of the puzzles shown in the photocopiable resources sheet. Students work together to solve them.

Adaptation: You could give students a list of the numbers that the letters can be. They need to use trial and improvement to check the value each letter can be.

Extension: Ask students to make up three new similar questions. Share the questions with the whole class and ask everyone to solve them.

BEWARE: Look out for students that guess numbers that work for one of the equations.

Once students have completed the task, gather the whole class together and discuss the numbers that they found.

Starter ideas

Mental maths starter

What is the value of $3(2x - 5)$ if $x = 2$?	What is the value of $2x^2 - 5$ if $x = -2$?	What is the value of $2x^2 + 7$ if $x = 0$?	True or false? $x^2 + 4 > 0$ for all x.
Solve $3(2x - 5) = 18$.	Expand $9(2x - 5)$.	Expand and simplify $3(2x - 5) - 2(x + 3)$.	Solve $2x - 5 = 11$.
Solve $26 = 2x - 5$	What is the value of $x^2 + 5$ if $x = 6$?	Expand $4(2x - 8)$.	True or false? If $3(2x - 4) = 33$, $x = 17$.
Simplify $3(8x - 2)$.	What is the value of $2(3x - 1)$ when $x = 4$?	Find an equivalent fraction to $\frac{5}{8}$ with a denominator of 24.	What is the value of $2x^2 + 7$ if $x = 0$?
Solve $5(2x - 5) = 20$.	Simplify $4(2x - 5)$.	What is the value of $x^2 - 8$ if $x = 2$?	Simplify $5(2x^2 + 7)$.

Start point check

Formula grid

Give students a copy of the formula grid from the photocopiable resources. Students work in pairs. They take it in turns to roll the dice. They write down the expression from the grid that corresponds to the number the dice landed. They roll the dice again and read the value of x that corresponds to this number. Students substitute the value of x in the expression they wrote. This is the number of points they receive. The winner is the one who collects the most points by the end of the game.

> TIP: This can be run as a game with students playing in teams with the first group choosing the expression and the second group choosing the value that x should be. Points are awarded for correct values.

You can make this easier or more challenging by changing the numbers that need to be substituted.

True or false? Show me.

Write a statement on the board that is wrong and ask students to check whether the statement is correct. For example, if $x = 4$, $2x^2 + 7 = 39$. Give each student a mini whiteboard and ask them to show you why this is not correct. Explain to the students that the aim of the task is not to just say 'true or false' but to show why this is the case. Rather than telling students they are right or wrong, encourage them to discuss and convince each other.

> TIP: If you don't have mini whiteboards, you can give students a sheet of paper to write their answers on.

> BEWARE: This question provides a good opportunity to notice whether there are students who need more support in substituting values into a formula and working out the answers. Look for misconceptions that students may have and clarify them before continuing with the rest of the lesson.

STRETCH: Adapt the questions so that the numbers used make the calculations more challenging.

What is the expression?

Write the following expressions on the board and ask students to find other expressions that can be simplified to give one of them:

a) $2x$

b) $3x + 5$

c) $5x - 4$

d) $3x^2 + x$

e) $3x$

> TIP: Provide students with an example. For instance, $3x^2 + 2x - x^2 - x$ can be simplified to $2x^2 + x$.

Allow students to work individually or in pairs. When students have finished, write different examples from their work on the board. To extend you could ask ten students to come and write their examples on the board for all to see. Students can group the examples according to the expression they represent.

> TIP: Ask students to explain each other's work rather than their own.

BEWARE: This question provides a good opportunity to notice whether there are students who have difficulties in simplifying expressions.

Discussion ideas

Probing questions	Teacher prompts
Convince me that $x = 2.3$ is not a solution to $3x^2 + x = 19$.	Ask students to substitute 2.3. Is the answer too big/too small?
A cube has a volume of 100 cm³. What is its length?	Encourage students to consider the factors of 6. You may prompt students by discussing what the factors of a number are.
The table shows the values of $2x^2 + x$. | x	$2x^2 + x$
2	10
2.1	10.92
2.2	11.88
2.3	12.88
2.4	13.92 | How can you use the table to find $2x^2 + x = 13$?	Ask: What does the table show? What value do you want the expression to be? Which of the values shown is the closest?

Common errors/misconceptions

Misconception	Strategies to address
Using the wrong starting value. For example, some students may start the table for $2x^2 + x = 13$ at $x = 2.4, 2.5$, and so on and notice that the values keep moving further from 13.	Start by asking students to substitute $x = 2$ and $x = 3$ and use a number line to estimate whether the answer to $2x^2 + x = 13$ will be closer to 2 or 3. $2x^2 + x = 10$ 13 $2x^2 + x = 21$ $x = 2$ $x = 3$
Not knowing how to use the table with the possible values that x can be. Some students get confused by the numbers in the table, what is included and what isn't.	Prior to students working independently, ensure that they are clear about the method that they are using.
Making mistakes when rounding. Some students give the wrong final answer as their rounding is incorrect. They think they need to round up or down rather than round to 1 or 2 decimal places (as the question requires).	Prior to starting the lesson ask students quick rounding questions. For example, round 2.348368 to one decimal place, or to two decimal places. Clarify any misconceptions students may have.

Developing conceptual understanding

9As6 Use systematic trial and improvement methods to find approximate solutions of equations such as $x^2 + 2x = 20$ (1, 2 and 7).

- FIX: Students need to be systematic in their approach. They need to be confident with substituting values for x and completing the calculations correctly. Ensure students can round correctly when giving their final answer.

STRETCH: Students working at a greater depth can find the answer to two or three decimal places.

End of chapter mental maths exercise

1. The product of two consecutive numbers is 420. What could the numbers be?	4. True or false? If $x^2 + x^3 = 82$, then $x = 5$ correct to the nearest whole number.
2. The area of a square is 80 cm^2. Will the length of the side (correct to the nearest whole number) be 8, 9 or 10?..	5. True or false? $x = 10$ is an answer to $\dfrac{55}{x+1} = x$
3. $x^2 = 21$, will $x = 4.6$ or 5.6 (correct to 1 decimal place)?	6. If $x^2 + 3x = 11$, is $x = 1$ or 2 correct to the nearest whole number?

Technology recommendations

- Use scientific calculators or a spreadsheet package to calculate the value of x using the trial and improvement method.

- Make a spreadsheet which starts with an expression. Substitute different values of x Use the table to predict what x can be when the expression equals different values.

Investigation/research tasks

- **Match the cards**   *Problem solving*

  Ask students to cut the equations and answers from the photocopiable resources and mix them. They need to rearrange the cards so that each equation and answer are together.

BEWARE: Prompt students to check the answers are correct rather than rush through them.

STRETCH: Ask students to choose one of the equations. Can they find the answer to two decimal places?

- FIX: Students could find the answer to the nearest whole number.

  Solution:

  $11x^2 + x = 115.8,$ $x = 3.2$

  $x^2 + 4x = 123.7,$ $x = 9.6$

  $x^2 + 2x = 67.9,$ $x = 7.3$

  $x^3 - x = 0.53,$ $x = 1.2$

  $x^2 + x = 35.8,$ $x = 5.5$

- **What is the question?** *Problem solving*

  Draw this table on the board.

x is between 0 and 1 (1 d. p.)	Between 1 and 2 (1 d. p)	Between 2 and 3 (1 d. p.)

  Ask students to work in pairs. They need to think of two equations that have an answer that is between 0 and 1, 1 and 2 and 2 and 3.

> TIP: Students can work in three groups. Write the equations that students make on the board and ask them to solve each other's questions.

  Every correct equation wins 2 points. Every correct answer to the equation wins 2 points.

- FIX: If students are stuck, ask them to start with the answer then build the equation from it. For example, if the answer is 0.6, then $0.6^2 = 0.36$, $0.6^2 + 2 = 2.36$. Students can write the equation $x^2 + 2 = 2.5$.

STRETCH: To make the task more challenging, ask students to use cubic equations and brackets.

- **What is the answer?** *Problem solving*

  Every correct equation wins 2 points. Every correct answer to the equation wins 2 points.

  Write an equation on the board. Underneath, place four decimal numbers. Only one of them is the solution to the equation. Students can use a calculator to check what the solution is.

  Allow students to discuss in pairs and decide which of the numbers is the solution. Share the results with the whole class. Ask students to explain their reasoning.

> TIP: This can be run as a game with students working in teams, with 1 point being awarded for each correctly reasoned answer.

> BEWARE: This question provides a good opportunity to notice whether there are students who may still need support with the trial and improvement method.

Ratio and proportion

Learning objectives	Key terms
Learning objectives covered in this chapter: 9Nf5, 9Nf6	• direct proportion
• Compare two ratios; interpret and use ratio in a range of contexts.	• ratio
• Recognise when two quantities are directly proportional; solve problems involving proportionality, e.g. converting between different currencies.	• proportion

Prior knowledge assumptions
- Students know how to change fractions to decimals.
- Students know how to solve simple problems, including direct proportion problems.

Guidance on the hook

Purpose: This task revisits the concept of ratios, fractions and proportion. The task also helps students to see that ratios and proportions can be used when making patterns.

Use of the hook: Using the information in the task, ask students to work in pairs to calculate the fraction of the triangles that are purple and the fraction of the triangles that are white.

Adaptation: You can get students to count all the triangles. They should notice that each colour follows a pattern (for example, the purple triangles are 1, 2, 3, 4, 5). Ask students to find the ratio between the purple and white triangles.

Extension: Ask students to discuss the difference between ratio and proportion.

Extension: Ask students to think of other real-life examples where proportion can be used.

TIP: You could ask students to make the pattern themselves. That way they can see for themselves the proportion of the triangles that are white and the proportion of the triangles that are purple.

BEWARE: Some students may be unsure as to what the difference between ratio and proportion is. Explain through examples the difference between ratio and proportion and encourage students to compare and discuss when ratio and proportion can be used.

Starter ideas

Mental maths starter

Divide $120 in the ratio 5 : 2 : 1.	Divide 49 kg in the ratio 2 : 4 : 1.	In a drink, the ratio of juice : water = 2 : 5. How much water is needed with 300 ml of juice?	There are 10 grey rabbits, 15 white rabbits and 20 spotty rabbits on a farm. What proportion of the rabbits are white?

Write $\frac{2}{25}$ as a decimal.	The ratio of red marbles : blue marbles : yellow marbles is 4 : 7 : 3. There are 21 yellow marbles. How many red marbles and blue marbles are there?	Five tickets cost $55. How much do 11 tickets cost?	Write $\frac{3}{16}$ as a decimal.
Simplify the ratio 12 : 10 : 16.	The ratio of flour : sugar : milk in a recipe is 3 : 4 : 2. There are 120 ml of milk. How much flour and sugar is needed?	If five apples cost 80 cents, how much do 12 apples cost?	A 2 m ribbon costs 90 cents. How much does a 1.5 m ribbon cost?
Simplify the ratio 36 : 54 : 18.	Change $\frac{5}{8}$ to a decimal.	The proportion of girls in a class is $\frac{5}{8}$. What is the ratio of boys : girls in the class?	The decorator mixes 300 ml of green paint with 700 ml of yellow paint to 100 ml of water. What fraction of the ingredients is water?
Mary decorates a frame with green ribbon : red ribbon : purple ribbon in the ratio 3 : 2 : 1. What fraction of the ribbon used is green?	Divide $320 in the ratio 3 : 7 : 10.	The ratio of mint cookies : chocolate cookies in a box is 3 : 5. There are 24 cookies in the box. How many chocolate cookies are there?	Tom plants 36 yellow flowers for every 30 pink flowers in the school garden. What proportion of the flowers are yellow?

Start point check

Equivalent ratios

Use the ratios grid from the photocopiable resources. There are green and orange marbles in each bag. Each fraction shows the fraction of orange marbles in each bag. Each ratio shows the ratio of orange : green marbles. (See photocopiable resources.)

Ask students to work in pairs and find sets of fractions and ratios that represent the same thing.

- How do you know they have the same value? What is the rule?
- Which of the fractions in your set is in the simplest form?
- How can you simplify a fraction?

> TIP: If students get stuck, prompt them to pick a ratio and write it as a fraction. Which of the fractions given is equivalent to this fraction?

Prompt students to multiply the numerator and denominator by the same number to get new fractions.

Representing ratios

Give students a piece of paper with 100 squares on it and ask them to colour some squares so that they can show the fraction of $\frac{1}{2}$.

Now ask students to shade a different number of squares in a different colour.

How many squares are left? Can they colour these squares in two different colours? What ratio is this showing?

STRETCH: Repeat for a different fraction, for example $\frac{1}{4}$, $\frac{1}{5}$, and so on.

> TIP: Encourage students to write each ratio in a simplified form.

> TIP: Students should have different coloured pencils that they can use to colour in.

STRETCH: Ask students to use five different colours. How many squares of each colour are shaded? What ratio do they make? What fraction of the whole shape does each ratio represent?

Ratio and proportion

Three students stand next to each other in front of the class. They each represent the number of ice creams sold. The first student represents chocolate ice cream, the second student represents strawberry ice cream, the last student represents vanilla ice cream. Each one writes a number on their whiteboard. They show the numbers to the whole class. Everyone else writes the proportion of the ice creams that are chocolate and the proportion of the ice creams that are strawberries.

STRETCH: Ask students to write the proportion in simplified form, and not simplified form. The first student to write it correctly wins 1 point

> TIP: Keep a list of the possible answers on a piece of paper and cross them off as you use them. Ask students not to use a number that has been used already.

> TIP: You can adapt the numbers used to less than 20 or less than 100 to make the question easier/harder.

Discussion ideas

Probing questions	Teacher prompts
The ratio of height : head circumference for the average person is said to be around 3 : 1. Investigate whether this is correct. Discuss your findings.	Students can use string to measure the circumference of their head, and a metre stick to measure their height. Ask students to write both values in cm and simplify the ratios.
Convince me that the ratio 500 mm : 75 cm : 1 m : 100 cm = 2 : 3 : 4 : 4.	Encourage students to pay attention to the units used. How many mm are there in 1 cm? How many mm are there in 1 m? How many cm are there in 1 m? You could try this practically by asking students to show each of the lengths in the playground.
Why do you think it is useful to represent ratios in the form 1 : n?	Discuss the importance of comparing ratios in the same way so that it is easier to compare. Encourage students to think of examples when this is useful. For example, when cooking rice, some chefs use the ratio 1 : 2 or 1 : 3 depending on the type of rice. That is 1 cup of rice for every 2 or 3 cups of water. The ratio 1 : n is easy to remember and follow. It also helps differentiate the types of rice that is being cooked.

Probing questions	Teacher prompts
How can you differentiate between variables that are in direct proportion and the ones that aren't?	Prompt students to refer to the examples used in the lesson. Can they explain why they are in direct proportion?

Common errors/ misconceptions

Misconception	Strategies to address
When changing ratio to proportion, some students get confused between ratio and proportion, between parts and ratio, and between proportion and the whole.	Use bar models to represent the parts. Label them appropriately. For example, the bar model below shows the ratio 3 : 5 : 1. As a proportion of the whole, each of the parts represents $\frac{3}{9}$, $\frac{5}{9}$ and $\frac{1}{9}$. 9 parts
Many students think that the ratio 1 : 5 is the same as 5 : 1.	Give an example where you share some sweets with your friend in the ratio 1 : 5. Your friend has five times more sweets than you, so if the ratio was reversed, the labelling will need to be reversed. Otherwise the ratio is not correct.
Not realising that the relationship between quantities in proportion are multiplicative, and so trying to use an additive relationship instead. For example, to make 12 biscuits, 200 g of flour is mixed with 1 egg and 100 ml of milk. To make 15 biscuits, the students add 3 g to the ingredients instead of multiplying by 1.3.	Explore the recipe example in more detail. If we only add 3 g of flour and 3 ml of milk will that be enough for an extra three biscuits? If we use one egg for 12 biscuits, do we need to add three eggs for three biscuits?
When comparing, some students may look at the actual numbers rather than the proportion that these numbers represent. For example, if there are 800 girls and 200 boys in a school, and 350 boys and 50 girls in a different school. Some students may think that the first school has a higher proportion of girls as 800 > 350.	Ask students to find the fraction of the students that are girls in each school. Encourage use of a bar model to visualise the findings better.

Developing conceptual understanding

9Nf5 Compare two ratios; interpret and use ratio in a range of contexts. Solve simple word problems including direct proportion problems.

- FIX: Encourage students to use bar models to visualise the ratio and proportion better. For example, a painter uses blue and yellow paint, as shown below, in the ratio of 4 : 5 and 2 : 3. The bar model shows that for every 1 part of blue, 1.25 parts of yellow are needed and for every 1 part of blue, 1.5 parts of yellow are needed. So, the second paint has a higher proportion of yellow paint in the mixture than the first paint.

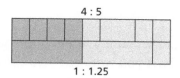

4 : 5

1 : 1.25

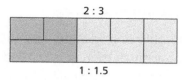

2 : 3

1 : 1.5

STRETCH: Students with a greater depth of understanding should work with ratios that also include decimals and fractions. They need to practise scaling up and down to simplify a ratio. For example, the ratio of sugar:calcium in a drink is 1.5 : 3, whilst in another drink it is 2 : 6. Which drink has the highest proportion of sugar?

9Nf6: Recognise when two quantities are directly proportional; solve problems involving proportionality, e.g. converting between different currencies.

- FIX: Encourage students to explore different methods when converting from one currency to another. Some students use one method only and are not keen on exploring new ones. For example, $80 cost 100 Euros. To calculate how many Euros you can have for $100, you could use the unitary method. Alternatively, you could find how many Euros you can get for $20, then multiply by 5.

  Encourage students to use bar models and diagrams to visualise the problem and also to check the answer at the end.

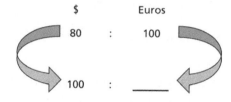

$ Euros

80   :   100

100   :   _____

STRETCH: Ask students to draw a conversion graph and use it to predict or convert from one currency to the other.

End of chapter mental maths exercise

1. Write the ratio of black:not black in the form 1 : *n*. Which of the rectangles has the highest proportion of black squares? 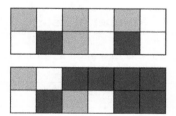 2. Simplify the ratio 120 : 80 : 60 : 50. 3. The ratio of oil:vinegar in two different salad dressings is 2 : 7 and 3 : 10. Which of the dressings has the highest proportion of vinegar?	4. 1 US $ = 6.65 Chinese Yuan. How many US dollars will you receive for 200 Chinese Yuan? 5. Ben has 84 red counters, 96 blue counters and 72 yellow counters. Write the ratio of counters in its simplest form. 6. Eight bread rolls cost $3.60. How much do 20 rolls cost? 7. Share 144 kg of apples in the ratio 3 : 6 : 2 : 1.

Technology recommendations

- Use the internet to research the currency of a different country to the one you live in. Investigate how much money you need to exchange if you were to live there for one week. Check whether the currency was the same five years ago. Would the amount you needed to exchange have been different then?

- Use a spreadsheet to calculate proportions for a recipe. Ask students to look at a cake recipe. Can they calculate the proportion of each ingredient? Ask students to record the results in a spreadsheet. How can they check their proportions are correct?

Investigation/research tasks

- **The highest proportion of squats**   *Problem solving*

  Ask students to measure how many squats they can do in 15 seconds.

  Write the ratio of squats: 15 seconds in the form 1 : *n*.

  Which of the students completed the highest proportion of squats?

BEWARE: Though it is good for students to collect the data themselves, ensure the focus of the task is in comparing different ratios.

TIP: Students need to have access to a stopwatch.

- FIX: Students can find the number of squats in 10 seconds, then divide by 10 to find the number of squats in 1 second.

  Ask students to draw a graph with the data they collected. Is the graph reliable to predict what the number of squats in 100 seconds can be? Encourage students to explain their reasoning.

- **What proportion of the day?**

  Ask students to write down a schedule of their day, for example, on a Monday. They need to include in their schedule the proportion of the day that they spend sleeping, eating, studying, reading.

  For example:

Activity	Time	Number of hours
sleeping		
eating		
studying		
reading	2pm – 3pm and 7pm – 8pm	2 hours

  o   Discuss the results with the whole class.
  o   Ask students to work in pairs and write the ratios in the form 1 : *n* to compare the results with each other.

TIP: Ask students to have a paper and pencil ready for their workings.

TIP: Record all the equivalent ratios you make.

- **Currencies**   *Problem solving*

  Exchange your currency to get $100.

  How much of your currency do you need? Make a list of five items that you could buy when food shopping. Now exchange all the prices to US $.

  If you had $100 when you started shopping, how many $ will you have left?

  > TIP: You could provide students with fake/paper US dollars that they can use for their transactions. Ask students to show their workings clearly. What did they spend? How much was left?

  STRETCH: Ask students to estimate the amounts that they will spend and the change they will receive.

Compound measures

Learning objectives

Learning objectives covered in this chapter: 9Mt2

- Use compound measures to make comparisons in real-life contexts, e.g. travel graphs and value for money.

Key terms

- compound measure
- speed
- population density

Prior knowledge assumptions

- Students know how to find the value of one unit.
- Students know how to solve a scaling problem.
- Students know how to find the speed of a car.

Guidance on the hook

Purpose: The purpose of this task is to revisit prior knowledge of direct proportion and begin to explore its application even further.

Use of the hook: Start by asking students to think about the questions posed in the hook. This could be done very effectively as a think, pair, share activity (individual students should think about their answers, then discuss as a pair with another student and then ideas can be shared as a class). Ask students to find two different ways of solving the question. When students give their answers, ensure that they can explain their methods clearly.

Adaptation: This can be made easier by breaking the question into smaller steps. For example, you could ask about the amount of money a footballer gets paid per day.

Extension: In addition to creating their own questions related to this context, students can also research other interesting facts from the football world. For example, the number of students playing football and the number of students becoming professional footballers. Share these facts with the whole class, encourage students' curiosity and emphasise the practical applications of mathematics now and in the future and the use of ratios and direct proportion in real life.

TIP: You can ask students to estimate rather than use a calculator. What calculations did they do? How does the real answer compare with the estimate?

BEWARE: Some students may be more interested in the facts rather than the mathematics in the hook. Allow students to be curious and ask questions. However focus their attention on the task ahead.

Starter ideas

Mental maths starter

500 g of pasta cost $0.90. How much do 100 g cost?	250 g of cheese cost $1.80. How much does 1 kg of cheese cost?	Three litres of juice cost $3.80. How much do 12 litres of juice cost?	Work out 2104 ÷ 8.
If eight loaves of bread cost $12, how many loaves of bread can you buy with $9?	Find the cost of one stamp if five stamps cost 120 cents.	125 g of almonds cost $3. How much do 500 g of almonds cost?	True or false? If 12 pens cost $15, four pens cost $3.
A car travels 120 km in 1.5 hours. How far does it travel in one hour?	Calculate 1254 ÷ 4.	Calculate 2168 ÷ 6.	Calculate 5.75 × 2.
A packet of 20 cookies costs $1.40. How much does one cookie cost?	A bus took 40 minutes to complete a journey 4 km long. How far does the bus travel in one hour?	Work out 1136 ÷ 4.	12 cupcakes cost $1.50. How much do 20 cupcakes cost?
If you walk 6 km in two hours, how long will it take you to walk 1 km?	Find how many ml of juice are there in three glasses, if four glasses have 900 ml of juice.	Nine lollies cost $6.30. How much do 12 lollies cost?	Five erasers cost 60 cents. How much do 22 erasers cost?

Start point check

Which car is the fastest?

Use the cards from the photocopiable resources. Ask students to cut out the cards, mix them and turn them upside down. Students work in pairs. They pick up a card and do not show it to their partner. They need to make a question that has an answer as shown on the card. For example, if the speed shown is 30 km/hour, the question could be; 'a car travels 45 km in 1.5 hours. What is its speed?'

Every correct question wins 1 point. Every correct answer wins 1 point. The winner is the one that collects the most points.

- FIX: Make simple questions, for example a car travels ... in one hour, a car travels ... in two hours.

STRETCH: Make the task more challenging by using decimal numbers. For example, a car travels 122.5 km in 2.5 hours.

How much?

Students work in pairs. Each pair has a sheet of the questions from the photocopiable resources. Each student has ten counters of different colours each. Students play rock-paper-scissors. The winner picks up a number from 1 to 10. The student reads and answers the question that corresponds to the chosen number.

If the answer is correct, a counter is placed in the box. If the answer is wrong, the other student can answer the question.

Students take turns to answer questions. Each student allocates a number to their partner. For example, once a student answers question 3, they allocate question 5 to their partner. Students continue until all the questions have been answered.

For questions 5 and 10, the student makes up their own question. The other student must solve the question.

The winner is the one who has the least number of counters left.

> TIP: Instead of using counters, students can cross out the boxes that they have answered correctly (using two different colour pens).

You can also ask students to represent these facts visually using a diagram (for example, a bar diagram).

Discussion ideas

Probing questions	Teacher prompts
Explain what population density means and how that can be calculated.	Encourage students to refer back to the examples used in the lesson and discuss how population density can be calculated.
Convince me that six pens for $7.50 is a better deal than eight pens for $10.	Encourage students to define what a better deal means. Encourage students to use a bar model to explain their answer.
There are 24 people on the bus. The journey takes 30 minutes and is 5 km long. How long will 2.5 km of the journey take if there are 48 people on the bus?	Encourage students to think of the variables that are in proportion. Will the journey change if there are more/fewer people on the bus? What does the speed of the bus depend on? Use this opportunity to encourage students to define proportion again and the relationship between the variables in direct proportion.

Common errors/ misconceptions

Misconception	Strategies to address
Students may not compare like for like. For example, some students think that a packet of ten biscuits, with a weight of 250 g costing $2 is a better deal than a packet of eight biscuits with a weight of 300 g costing $2. Students compare price per biscuit though the size of the biscuits is different.	Encourage students to discuss what they are comparing and the importance of comparing like for like. Ask students to calculate the price of biscuits per kg. If students use a bar model, discuss the size of each bar representing the biscuits if they are different sizes.
Not realising that the relationship between quantities in proportion are multiplicative and so trying to use an additive relationship instead. For example, thinking that if 12 kg of pears cost $16, then 5 kg of apples cost $9. Students subtract 7 from both sides rather than dividing by 2.4.	Students could calculate 1 kg of apples, then multiply the answer by 10. Alternatively ask students to draw a diagram or bar model to represent the problem. Pears (kg) Cost ($) ÷ 2.4 ⎰12 kg $16 ⎱ ÷ 2.4 ⎱5 kg ? ⎰

Misconception	Strategies to address
Using ratio and proportion without paying attention to the units. Students sometimes multiply or divide numbers that do not leave a remainder or give 'nice answers' rather than because they have to. For example, a roller coaster ride costs $5 for 3 minutes. To calculate the cost for 25 minutes some students multiply 3 by 5 and give the answer of $15. They focus on the numbers that are multiples of each other, rather than the actual ratio used in the question.	Encourage students to draw diagrams and bar models when solving proportion problems. The use of bar models will help students see the link between the variables and they will find it easier to determine what calculation they should use and why.

Developing conceptual understanding

9Mt2 Use compound measures to make comparisons in real-life contexts, e.g. travel graphs and value for money.

Encourage all students to use a bar model to represent a proportion problem. This will help them not only solve the problem, but also develop their conceptual understanding of what a proportional relationship is. For example, if a bus travels 450 km in eight hours, what is its average speed?

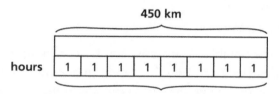

The use of the bar model makes it easy to see the relationship between the distance travelled and the time it took to complete this distance.

STRETCH: students working at a greater depth of understanding can look at proportional problems that use decimal numbers and a mixture of units. For example, a car travels 215.8 km in 3 hours and 20 minutes. What is its average speed?

End of chapter mental maths exercise

1. A train travels 600 km in 8 hours. Calculate the distance it will travel in 12 hours (assuming it travels at the same speed).

2. Seven identical cupcakes cost $4.20, or the same cupcakes cost 65 cents each if bought individually. Which is the better deal? Why?

3. Four pears cost 90 cents. How much do 12 pears cost?

4. A train has an average speed of 120 km/hour. A different train travels 420 km in 4 hours. Which of the trains is faster?

5. Tom runs 9 km in 1.5 hours. Amy runs 2 km in 30 minutes. Who is faster?

6. Six litres of lemonade costs $9. A bottle of 1.5 litres cost $3. Which of the bottles is the better deal?

7. The population of a town is 25 000 people. Its area is 70 km². A different town has a population of 8000 people and an area of 35 km². Which of the villages is the more densely populated?

Technology recommendations

- Use a spreadsheet to record the population of the village, town or city you live in and its area. Search on the internet how the population has changed over the last 100 years. Check how the change in the population has affected its population density. Draw a graph based on your results. Use your results to predict what the population will be ten years from now.

- Use the internet to investigate the time that it takes for different planes to travel around the world. What information do you need to know? How does a change in the speed affect the time that it takes to complete the journey?

Investigation/research tasks

- **Running**   *Problem solving*

  Run a distance of 100 m. Calculate your speed. Predict how long it will take you to travel 200 m. Run 200 m. Were your predictions correct? How long will it take you to run 500 m?

- FIX: Calculate the speed per second or minute.

STRETCH: Calculate the speed per hour.

> TIP: You could link this activity with a PE lesson. Students can use the data they collected to calculate and compare their speeds for different distances.

- **Deal or no deal**   *Problem solving*

  Use the cards in the photocopiable resources. Students pick up two cards of the same colour. They choose one of the cards. They have a choice to accept or not to accept. If they accept it and the second card is a better deal, they lose a point. If they accept and the second card is a worse deal, they win a point.

> TIP: Encourage students to estimate first. Then they can use a calculator to check their answers.

STRETCH: Students can make up their own questions and share them with each other to solve.

- **Input / output**

  Write this table on the board. Explain that the values of input and output are in direct proportion. Ask students to complete the missing values.

Input (number of km travelled)	40 km	160 km	200 km		320 km
Output (number of hours it took)		12 hours		18 hours	

STRETCH: Provide students with an empty input/output table and ask them to complete it.

STRETCH: Can students work out the formula that connects the variables that are in direct proportion?

> BEWARE: Students need to ensure that they look at both variables rather than focusing on the pattern that a single one follows.

Area and volume

Learning objectives

Learning objectives covered in this chapter: 9Ma3, 9Ma4

- Solve problems involving the circumference and area of circles, including by using the π key of a calculator.
- Calculate lengths, surface areas and volumes in right-angled prisms and cylinders.

Key terms

- circumference
- area

Prior knowledge assumptions:

- Students know how to calculate the meaning of area as a measure of the space inside a two-dimensional shape.
- Students know how to find the area of a rectangle from its length and width.
- Students know how to find the properties of triangles, parallelograms and trapezia.
- Students know what the net of a shape is.

Guidance on the hook

Purpose: The purpose of this task is to investigate how the area of a circle can be found. Students need to be clear about what area represents and use the area of the shapes they know to estimate the area of the circle.

Use of the hook: Start by asking students to think about the question posed in the hook. Discuss the different approaches that students use. Some students may count the squares. Other students may think about finding the areas of the squares or the triangles inside.

Discuss how the answer can change according to the approach used. When students give their answers, ensure that they can explain their methods clearly.

Adaptation: This can be made easier by breaking the question into smaller steps. For example, you could ask students to calculate the area of each of the triangles inside.

Extension: Ask students to draw circles of different radii and calculate their areas. Share these facts with the whole class. Encourage students' curiosity and generalising.

TIP: You can ask students to estimate the area. What calculations did they do? How does the real answer compare with the estimate?

BEWARE: Some students may focus on counting squares rather than thinking of different ways to calculate the area.

Starter ideas

Mental maths starter

Calculate the area of a square with length of sides of 6 cm.	Calculate the area of a rectangle with a width of 3 cm and length of 7 cm.	The area of a square is 81 cm². What is its side length?	The area of a rectangle is 35 cm². Its length is 2 cm longer than its width. What is the width?
The perimeter of a square is 18 cm. Calculate its area.	The perimeter of a rectangle is 20 cm. Its width is 4 cm. What is its area?	The perimeter of a rectangle is 20 cm. Its length is 2 cm longer than the width. What is its area?	The perimeter of a square is 30 cm. What is its area?
True or false? The area of triangle ABC = area of triangle ABD. C, D A, B	True or false? The perimeter of triangle ABC = perimeter of triangle ABD. C, D A, B	True, sometimes or never true? The area and perimeter of a rectangle can never be equal to each other.	True, sometimes or never true? The area and perimeter of a square can never be equal to each other.
True or false? The net of a cube is made of six identical squares.	True or false? The net of a cuboid is made of six rectangles.	Calculate the volume of a cube with a length of 5 cm.	Calculate the total area of a cube with length of 6 cm.
Calculate the volume of a cuboid with dimensions 3 cm by 5 cm by 6 cm.	The volume of a cube is 125 cm³. What is the length of its sides?	The volume of a cuboid is 100 cm³. The width = 4 cm, the length = 5 cm. What is its height?	The volume of a cuboid is 250 cm³. The base is a square with lengths of 5 cm. What is its height?

Start point check

The area is 20 cm²

Provide students with square grid paper. Ask them to draw five different shapes with an area of 20 cm². Encourage students to be creative and draw 'unusual' shapes and compound shapes.

Place the shapes on the board for all to see. Discuss the methods that students used to calculate the area of each shape.

STRETCH: Ask students to order the shapes according to their perimeter.

True or false?

Write on the board:

* If the length of the side of a square becomes two times bigger, its area becomes two times bigger.

- If the side lengths of a rectangle become three times bigger, its area becomes three times bigger.

Ask students to work in pairs and investigate whether these statements are true or false.

Share the results with the whole class.

- FIX: Encourage students to draw a square and check what happens when the length of its side becomes two times bigger.

STRETCH: Ask students to investigate what happens to the area of a square when the length of the side of the square becomes 2 cm longer.

Discussion ideas

Probing questions	Teacher prompts
True or false? The area of a circle can be equal to its circumference.	Encourage students to refer back to the examples used in the lesson and discuss how the area and the circumference of a circle can be calculated.
The perimeter of a semi-circle is greater than half of the circumference of a circle with the same radius. 10 cm 10 cm	Encourage students to describe what the perimeter of the semi-circle includes. Encourage students to use examples to support their answer.
Is it true? If the length of a cube becomes two times bigger, its volume becomes eight times bigger.	Encourage students to think of the variables that are in proportion. Encourage generalising.

Common errors/ misconceptions

Misconception	Strategies to address
When calculating the volume of a triangular prism, students multiply its length by its height. 12 cm 10 cm 8 cm 6 cm For example, students may calculate the volume of the prism = 6 cm × 8 cm × 10 cm × 12 cm.	Encourage students to write the formula for the volume of a prism. Ask: What shape is the cross section? What is its area?

Misconception	Strategies to address
When calculating the volume of a prism, some students are unable to identify the face that is the cross section. For example, some students may make the mistake of thinking that the orange rectangle is the cross section in this prism. 	Provide different 3D shapes for students to work with. Touching and seeing the shapes for themselves will help students see which of the faces is the cross-section face of the prism and why.
When calculating the perimeter of a semi-circle, some students forget to add the length of the diameter.	Ask: What does 'perimeter' mean? How can you calculate it?
When calculating the area of a circle, some students use the value of the diameter, rather than the radius. This can be because students are unsure what the diameter and radius represent or simply because they confuse the formulae of circumference and area of the circle.	Provide many opportunities for students to use the formulae for the area and circumference of a circle. Allow students to manipulate the formulae to find the radius or the diameter when the area is given.

Developing conceptual understanding

9Ma3 Solve problems involving the circumference and area of circles, including by using the π key of a calculator.

Encourage all students to draw the shapes for themselves and label the lengths that are given accordingly.

• FIX: Write the formulae for the area and the circumference of a circle somewhere in the classroom that is at all times visible by students. For example, this could be a poster or a formula card on the wall.

STRETCH: Students working at a greater depth of understanding can look at proportional problems that use the relationship between the changes in the area or circumference of a circle and the change in the length of the radius or the diameter.

9Ma4 Calculate lengths, surface areas and volumes in right-angled prisms and cylinders.

Ensure students are confident in what the formula for the volume of a prism represents.

• FIX: Provide students with different concrete prism shapes. Ask them to identify the face that represents the cross section of each of them.

STRETCH: Ask students to investigate what happens when the height of a prism becomes two or three times longer. How will the volume be affected?

End of chapter mental maths exercise

1. The circumference of a circle is 100 cm. Calculate its area.

2. Calculate the area of a semi-circle with radius of 1 cm.

3. Calculate the volume of this prism if the area of the cross section = 100 cm².

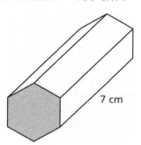

7 cm

4. Which has a greater volume − a cylinder with diameter and height of 10 cm or a cuboid of side length of 10 cm?

5. The volume of the cylinder = 340π m³. The area of the base is 17 m².

   Calculate its height.

6. Use $\pi = 3$ to calculate the area of the shaded part. Give your answer to the nearest whole number.

20 cm

Technology recommendations

• Use a spreadsheet to record the area of circles with circumferences of 1 cm, 2 cm, 4 cm, 8 cm, 16 cm. Investigate whether there is a pattern.

• Use a spreadsheet to record the volume of a cylinder with a base of a radius of 1 cm, 2 cm, 4 cm, 8 cm. Keep the height the same length and notice how the volume varies.

• Use the internet to search for buildings that are in the shape of 'unusual' prisms (not cuboids or cubes) or compound shapes. Make a presentation where you discuss how shapes are used in architecture. Estimate the surface area of each shape.

Investigation/research tasks

• **Boxes**   *Problem solving*

  Ask students to bring a cardboard box from home. This could be a cereal box or a different type of box in the shape of a cuboid.

  Ask students to calculate the volume of their prism.

  Ask students to change the box (cut it) to turn it into a triangular prism.

  Calculate the volume again and investigate how it has been affected by the change in the area of the cross section.

STRETCH: Encourage students to generalise where possible.

• **12 circles and semi-circles**

  Provide students with a square sheet of paper. Ask them to draw 12 circles and 12 semi-circles on it so that the circles cover as much of the page as possible, but do not overlap.

  Discuss with the whole class the strategies used to decide the radius that each circle and semi-circle should be.

  You could link this activity with an art lesson and ask students to colour or shade the circles they draw. Share the best results with the whole class. What is the perimeter of the artwork?

• FIX: Students should have access to the formulae for the area and circumference of circles.

STRETCH: Investigate the maximum value that the radius of one of the circles can have.

- **Cylinders**

  Provide students with a cylinder shape and ask them to calculate its volume. Ask students to estimate what the height of the water will be if you pour 100 ml of water into your cylinder.

  Investigate whether the height will be half of the value you found if you pour 50 ml of water.

  Repeat for a different cylinder which has a base with a diameter twice the length of the first cylinder.

  Investigate whether the height will be half of the value you found if you pour 50 ml of water.

  Investigate the relationship between volume and height.

  Generalise.

TIP: You could provide students with pictures of different cylinders or cardboard cylinders.

TIP: You could pour rice instead of water.

- FIX: Leave the answer in terms of π where possible.

Equations

Learning objectives

Learning objectives covered in this chapter: 9Ae8

* Construct and solve linear equations with integer coefficients (with and without brackets, negative signs anywhere in the equation, positive or negative solution); solve a number problem by constructing and solving a linear equation.

Key terms

* solve
* equation
* linear

Prior knowledge assumptions

* Students can solve linear equations with brackets.
* Students can solve linear equations with unknowns on both sides.
* Students can construct and solve linear equations from simple diagrams or word problems.

Guidance on the hook

Purpose: This task introduces students to the idea that an equation can have a solution that is negative or non-integer. Prior to this, students have worked with equations with positive integer solutions.

Use of the hook: Discuss the examples in the Student's Book showing how to build up an equation by starting from the solution. One example has a negative solution and one has a non-integer solution.

Students work on building their own equations, either individually or in pairs. If any students are finding this difficult, they could first try building several equations with positive integer solutions. Bring the whole class back together to share equations.

TIP: You could use some of the students' equations for demonstrating solving equations with negative and non-integer solutions.

Adaptation: The activity could be introduced by a teacher-led discussion in which the class contributes a range of different suggestions for building up an equation, which you (or a student volunteer) write on the board in the form of a spider diagram with the solution at its centre.

Extension: Students could try to build an equation with a solution that is both negative and non-integer. They could also make their equations more complicated than the ones shown, for example by having the unknown appear on both sides.

Starter ideas

Mental maths starter

What is 7 less than 6?	What is 5 less than 2?	What is 20 less than 19?	What is 18 less than 7?
What is $\frac{1}{3}$ less than 1?	What is $\frac{5}{6}$ more than $1\frac{1}{6}$?	What is $\frac{4}{3}$ more than $2\frac{1}{3}$?	What is $\frac{3}{5}$ less than $1\frac{1}{5}$?
Multiply $x + 3$ by 2.	Multiply $4 - x$ by 5.	Multiply $2x + 1$ by 6.	Multiply $4 - 10x$ by 3.
Solve the equation $x + 12 = 26$.	Solve the equation $3x - 2 = 13$.	Solve the equation $10 - 2x = 0$.	Solve the equation $3(8 - x) = 18$.
I think of a number. I double it, then add 6. I get 16. What number did I think of?	I think of a number. I treble it, then subtract 5. I get 4. What number did I think of?	I think of a number. I multiply it by 3, then subtract the result from 11. I get 8. What number did I think of?	I think of a number. I subtract 7 from it, then multiply the result by 4. I get 24. What number did I think of?
Naoki's age is twice Jan's age, plus 7. Jan is 6. How old is Naoki?	Moshe is 3 years younger than Nazim. The total of their ages is 17. How old is Nazim?	Hanna is 6 years older than Alia. The total of their ages is 30. How old is Hanna?	A father's age is 3 times his daughter's age, plus 4. The father is 40. How old is the daughter?

Start point check: Pairs equation solving

Give the class an equation to solve. Students work in pairs, one of whom starts by writing the equation on paper or a mini whiteboard and then writing the first step of a solution. The other student then checks the working so far, corrects it if necessary, and writes the next step. The two students continue to take it in turns to write a step until they have solved the equation.

TIP: The focus of this activity is on correct presentation of solutions, as well as on correct steps in solving. You could show an exemplar first, to remind students how to write their working.

TIP: After each equation, you could ask the class to hold up their working so that you can check whether they are writing their solutions correctly. Use mini whiteboards for this.

Below are some equations that you could use for this activity.

Equation	Solution
$2x + 5 = 17$	$x = 6$
$8 - 2x = 2$	$x = 3$
$3(p + 4) = 15$	$p = 1$
$2(3r + 3) = 30$	$r = 4$
$3s - 5 = s + 5$	$s = 5$
$2(t + 1) = t + 4$	$t = 2$
$6(3u - 1) = 3(10 + 2u)$	$u = 3$

Game/investigation

Simple equations bingo, with negative numbers and fractions.

This activity introduces students to solving equations with negative or non-integer solutions. Each equation can be solved in only one step.

Ask students to draw a 9 by 9 grid in their book. Write the solutions from the table on the board and ask students to fill in their grid using nine of those numbers (without using any number more than once).

Solution	−8	−7	−6	−5	−4
Equation	$x + 8 = 0$	$2x = -14$	$x - 3 = -9$	$x + 4 = -1$	$7 + x = 3$

Solution	−3	−2	−1	$\frac{1}{5}$	$\frac{1}{4}$
Equation	$x + 8 = 5$	$x - 3 = -5$	$5x = -5$	$5x = 1$	$2x = \frac{1}{2}$
Solution	$\frac{1}{3}$	$\frac{2}{5}$	$\frac{1}{2}$	$\frac{2}{3}$	$\frac{3}{2}$
Equation	$3x = 1$	$5x = 2$	$3x = \frac{3}{2}$	$3x = 2$	$2x = 3$

Write on the board, one at a time, equations from the table, in random order. Students should cross out the solution of each equation, if it is in their grid. Students look for a complete row or column, and after the first person gets this, students then look for the full grid completed.

> TIP: Before playing the game, show and discuss some examples of solving one-step equations where the answer is negative or non-integer, making sure that students understand how to do this.

> TIP: Keep a list of the numbers on a piece of paper and cross them off as you use them.

Extension: Include decimal solutions, and solutions that are both negative and non-integer. Examples are given in the table below.

Solution	$-\frac{1}{2}$	$-\frac{1}{4}$	−0.2	0.6	0.8
Equation	$2x = -1$	$12x = -3$	$x + 0.4 = 0.2$	$x - 1 = -0.4$	$5x = 4$

Discussion ideas

Probing questions	Teacher prompts
Here is a number line: $\leftarrow \!\!+\!\!-\!\!-\!\!-\!\!-\!\!+\!\!-\!\!-\!\!-\!\!-\!\!-\!\!+\!\!\to$ $\quad x \qquad\quad 0 \qquad\quad -x$ It has been drawn in the usual way, with positive numbers to the right of zero and negative numbers to the left. What values of x make this number line correct?	Students may find it difficult to accept that 'x' can be negative, or that '$-x$' can be positive. If they are familiar with 'think of a number' games, point out that we could start one of these games by thinking of a negative number, and we could still call it 'x'. Prompt students to try specific values of x. For example, they could try placing $x = -10$ on a number line, and then think about where to place $-(-10)$.
Are these statements always true, sometimes true or never true? If n is a positive number, then $n + 5$ is positive. If n is a positive number, then $n - 5$ is negative. If n is a negative number, then $n + 5$ is negative. If n is a negative number, then $n - 5$ is negative.	Students may start by suggesting particular values for n, but prompt them to try to generalise. For each question they could think about where n could be on a number line, and where to place $n + 5$, or $n - 5$, on that line.
If $3x = 1$ what is x? If $2x = 5$ what is x?	If students are unsure how to solve equations like these (where the solution is a fraction), discuss approaches that can help. For example, for the first equation: • a bar model: | x	x	x | |---|---|---|
1	 • think about what we get if we divide both sides of the equation by 3. Compare the equation with a similar numerical example, such as $4 \times \dfrac{1}{4} = 1$.
What would be your first step when solving this equation? $$7(1 - 2n) = 7(34 - n)$$ What first steps could you use when solving this equation? $$24(4m - 2) = 36(m - 2)$$ What first step would you use when solving this equation? Could you start by dividing by a number? $$6(k + 12) = 11(k + 7)$$	Students may assume that if there are brackets in an equation, the first step should always be to expand them. This may also lead to the incorrect assumption that in mathematics the expanded form of an expression is considered to be 'better', or simpler, than the factorised form. Ask the class for possible first steps. Students can discuss which first step they prefer, and why. You could demonstrate that it is possible to start solving the third equation by dividing by 6 (or by 11), and then discuss why division is not the most helpful first step in this case.
Wei is 3 years older than Kingston. Write an equation relating their ages. Tapani's age is 3 times Vicente's age. Write an equation relating their ages.	If students give the answer $k = w + 3$ or $v = 3t$, ask who is older in each pair, and which of the two unknowns should be the larger number. Show students that the incorrect answer $k = w + 3$ would make k larger than w, and so Kingston would be older than Wei (or that $v = 3t$ would make v larger than t, and so Vicente would be older than Tapani).

Common errors/misconceptions

Misconception	Strategies to address
Thinking that you can literally 'move' any part of an equation from one side to the other and switch its sign. For example: $$-2x = 8$$ $$x = 8 + 2$$ (student moves '−2' to the other side and changes its sign) or: $$5(x + 3) = 20$$ $$5x = 20 - 3$$ (student moves '+3' to the other side and changes its sign). Thinking that you can add like terms no matter which side they are on. For example: $$3x + 5 = 2x + 10$$ $$5x = 15$$ (student adds $3x$ and $2x$, and adds 5 and 10)	These errors usually come from the misapplication of rules that students have learnt but do not understand. A visual model can be used to remind students why some manipulations are valid and others are not. This could be a bar model, but with equations where it is not known whether the solution is positive or negative, a balance model can be easier to work with. See the section on Developing conceptual understanding (below) for more about using a balance model. It can also help to give students an equation of similar form to the one they have incorrectly manipulated, but with the unknowns replaced by known numbers. For example, for the three equations on the left you could give: $$-2 \times 3 = -6$$ $$5(2 + 4) = 30$$ $$3 \times 2 + 4 = 4 \times 2 + 2$$ Ask students to manipulate the equation without carrying out any arithmetic. They can then use arithmetic to check that their steps are valid.
Performing an operation twice on one side of an equation: $$3x - 4 = 11$$ $$3x + 4 = 11 + 4$$ (student adds 4 to the left side twice)	The student may be attempting to perform the operation 'add 4' to both sides, but thinks that the left side should then read '+4' to show that the step has been taken. Using a bar model or balance model can help the student to see why this is not correct.
Given an equation such as $5x = 7$, writing $x = \dfrac{5}{7}$ instead of $x = \dfrac{7}{5}$.	This can happen if the student lacks understanding and is simply guessing how to rearrange the numbers. (Students are less likely to make this type of mistake when working only with integers. For example, given $2x = 10$, the student can more easily reason that if 2 times a number is 10, the number must be 5. In fact, working with fractions or decimals can help to reveal where the student's understanding of how to manipulate equations is not yet secure.) The bar model or the balance model can help students here, or they can simply consider dividing both sides by 5 to get $\dfrac{5x}{5} = \dfrac{7}{5}$.

Misconception	Strategies to address
Not applying the order of operations correctly. For example, given the equation: $$8 - 3(x + 2) = 11$$ the student then writes: $$5(x + 2) = 11$$	Ask the student for, or remind them of, the correct order of operations, and ask them to check whether their working follows it. Show a similar expression without an unknown. For this example you could use $15 - 4(5 - 2)$. Discuss how to perform this calculation correctly, and why it is not equivalent to $11(5 - 2)$. In some cases it may help to show the student an expression that does simplify to the incorrect expression they have found. For this example, you could show: $$8(x + 2) - 3(x + 2) = 5(x + 2)$$ Discuss why this simplification *is* correct.
When expanding a bracket, multiplying only the first term, for example: $$3(x + 4) = 3x + 4$$	It may be that the student has forgotten to multiply the second term and simply needs to be reminded. Drawing an area model (featured in Chapter 31, Expanding brackets) can remind the student to multiply both terms: $\begin{array}{c c c} & x & 4 \\ 3 & \boxed{3x} & \boxed{12} \end{array}$ However, this error may instead be due to a misunderstanding of the order of operations, where the student does not see the significance of the brackets and proceeds as if they were not there. In this case, discuss what difference the brackets make to the expression, and remind students of the correct order of operations.
Writing two related unknowns using different symbols and then being unable to progress. For example, a student tries to solve the problem 'A number is 4 more than another number. The sum of twice the smaller number and five times the larger number is −1.' They write $2a + 5b = -1$ and then cannot proceed further.	Ask the student if any piece of information from the question has not been used. Point out that their equation is not incorrect, but it treats the two numbers as two separate unknowns. Prompt them to write one number in terms of the other. If students have particular difficulties getting started on questions that do not suggest symbols for the unknowns, have them practise creating equations from statements like the one on the left.

Developing conceptual understanding

9Ae8 Construct and solve linear equations with integer coefficients (with and without brackets, negative signs anywhere in the equation, positive or negative solution).

- FIX: The bar model is difficult to use if it is not known at the start whether the solution will be positive or negative. If students are ready at this stage to work with equations without referring to a visual aid, they should do so.

  Students who are not yet confident without a visual aid can be shown a 'balance' model of equation solving, in which the two sides of an equation are represented by the two sides of a seesaw or a pan balance. Negative numbers can be represented by helium balloons or simply by imagining 'negative mass'.

For example, the equation $2(x - 3) = 3(3x + 5)$ could be represented like this:

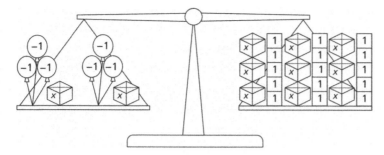

As the diagram suggests, the model becomes more time-consuming to sketch the more complex the equation. The model should only be used until the student feels able to work without it.

BEWARE: To use this model, the student needs to be clear that a '−1' balloon does not equal a '1' block. Removing a balloon makes a side heavier. So if a balloon is removed from the left side of the balance above, that side gets heavier by 1, and a '1' block needs to be added to the right side.

- Even when a visual model is not being used, there are still multiple ways to approach an equation. Show students different ways of thinking that lead to the same result, and let them select which work best for them. For example, when considering the first move in solving $7(2x - 3) = -14$, you could start by:
    - expanding the bracket to create an equivalent equation, $14x - 21 = -14$;
    - viewing the equation as 7 × something = −14 to see that $2x - 3 = -2$;
    - performing the same operation, ÷7, on both sides, which also leads to $2x - 3 = -2$;
    - or seeing the equation as a description of a 'think of a number' trick where the last operation was to multiply by 7 (giving the result −14), and carry out the inverse operation, ÷7, which again produces the equation $2x - 3 = -2$.

    Point out that it is acceptable to use different approaches for different equations, or even at different stages in solving one equation.

- FIX: Write an equation on the board. At each stage in solving the equation, ask the class to suggest the next step. Demonstrate each step on the board. A student may suggest a step that is not helpful (for example, for the first step in solving $2(x - 2) = 3(x - 1)$ they may say 'add 2 to both sides' or 'multiply both sides by 3', perhaps through misunderstanding the effect that step will have). Instead of telling the student that it is the wrong step to take, show what happens when the step is taken correctly. Allow the class to ask you to undo a step if they realise it is unhelpful. During this activity, take the opportunity to distinguish between three types of step in equation solving: steps that are incorrect (for example, performing an operation on one side only); steps that are correct and helpful (that is, steps that move you closer to finding the solution); and steps that are correct but unhelpful.

STRETCH: Students can try solving equations involving decimals, or equations involving both decimals and fractions.

STRETCH: Students can try solving equations in which the unknown is in the denominator of a fraction, such as $2 - \frac{8}{x} = 6$.

9Ae8 Solve a number problem by constructing and solving a linear equation.

- This is a topic where it can be helpful for students to see several worked examples which show how to approach, for example, questions involving one unknown or two related unknowns; questions in which no symbols are suggested for the unknown(s); questions involving angles or the geometry of polygons; questions consisting of multiple statements.

- FIX: Equation construction problems require two skills – constructing the equation, and solving the equation – and a student may be proficient in one skill but need more practice with the other. If a student is proficient at equation solving but needs practice in constructing equations, let them just do this first step for a set of questions. If the student is proficient at setting up equations but has difficulties solving them, you could give more practice in questions that simply give an equation to solve.

End of chapter mental maths exercise

1. If $-x = -4$, what is x?
2. If $2x = -6$, what is x?
3. If $7x = 2$, what is x?
4. Solve the equation $3x = 5 - x$
5. Solve the equation $4 - 2x = x + 2$
6. Bella is 4 years older than Srijita. Their two ages add to make 18. How old is Srijita?

7. A regular pentagon has a side length of $x - 1$. The perimeter of the pentagon is 55 cm. Find x.
8. I think of a number, x. I add 3 to my number and then multiply the result by 5. I get -20. What is x?
9. The angles in a triangle are $2x°$, $50°$ and $2(2x + 5)°$. Find x.
10. Three consecutive even numbers add to 36. What are the three numbers?

Technology recommendations

- Work with an interactive version of the balance model of equation solving. To find some websites that provide this, search for the following: equations balance model interactive. Some allow negative amounts to be placed on the balance, while others only allow positive amounts.

- Use a spreadsheet program to test an identity (an equation for which any real number is a solution) by checking that both sides give the same answer for a selection of values of the unknown. The consolidation exercise in the Student's Book includes a question about testing possible solutions of the equation $3(2 - q) = q - 2(2q - 3)$.

Students could create a table like this, including a list of possible values of the unknown (which could include negative numbers and decimals):

	A	B	C
1	q	3(2-q)	q-2(2q-3)
2	-3		
3	-2		
4	-1		
5	0		
6	1		
7	2		

and enter suitable formulae for calculating the two sides of the equation:

	A	B
1	q	3(2-q)
2	-3	=3*3(2-A2)
3	-2	

	A	B	C
1	q	3(2-q)	q-2(2q-3)
2	-3	15	=A2-2*(2*A2-3)
3	-2		

Then copy these formulae down the columns to calculate the value of each side of the equation for different values of the unknown.

	A	B	C
	q	3(2-q)	q-2(2q-3)
1			
2	-3	15	15
3	-2	12	12
4	-1	9	9
5	0	6	6
6	1	3	3

BEWARE: Spreadsheet programs usually do not allow the multiplication symbol (*) to be omitted. For example, to multiply the bracket (2−A2) by 2, students need to enter 2*(2−A2) instead of 2(2−A2).

TIP: Instead of typing a column of consecutive values for the unknown, students can use the 'fill down' function in the spreadsheet: fill in two or three consecutive numbers, then select them all and pull down on the drag handle to continue the sequence

• Use graphing software to plot the graphs of each side of an equation, and find the solution by reading the x-coordinate of the intersection point.

For example, to solve the equation $10(x + 6) = 5 − x$, plot $y = 10(x + 6)$ and $y = 5 − x$ as shown.

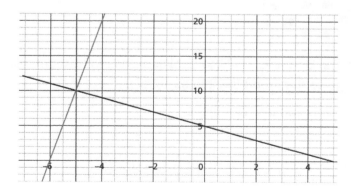

TIP: It may not be obvious to students why this method works. Remind them that each *x*-coordinate on a graph represents an input to the function, and the corresponding *y*-coordinate represents the output. So the intersection of the two graphs is where one input (*x*-coordinate) gives the same output (*y*-coordinate) to both functions

Ask students to try this method with an equation that has no solution, such as $2x + 4 = 2x + 5$. The two graphs do not cross. Discuss the significance of this.

Investigation/research tasks

* **Solving and creating a word puzzle**

  There are three bags of marbles.

  The second bag has six times as many marbles as the first bag.

  The third bag has 15 more marbles than the first bag.

  The third bag has 20 marbles fewer than the second bag.

  Construct and solve an equation to find the number of marbles in each bag.

  Now create your own puzzle about three bags of marbles, with different statements and a different answer from the one above. Give it to another student to solve.

  Solution:

  There are *x* marbles in the first bag.

  There are 6*x* marbles in the second bag.

  There are *x* + 15 marbles in the third bag, which equals 6*x* − 20.

  $$x + 15 = 6x - 20$$

  $$5x = 35$$

  $$x = 7$$

  The first, second and third bags contain 7, 42 and 22 marbles respectively.

* **Domino trick**

  Each domino shows two numbers from 0 to 6, represented by dots. The two numbers on a domino can be the same or different. For example:

  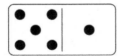 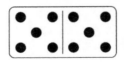

  Miremba knows a trick using dominoes. She asks a friend to pick a domino, without telling her what she has chosen, and then gives the friend these instructions:

  o   Choose one of the numbers on the domino. Double it.

  o   Add 3.

  o   Multiply the answer by 5.

  o   Add the other number on the domino.

  o   Tell me the answer you now have.

  Miremba subtracts 15 from the answer, and gets a two-digit number. Each digit shows one of the numbers on the domino. Miremba can impress her friend by saying what numbers were on the chosen domino.

Try this trick with a partner.

Express the steps using algebra, and show how the trick works.

Create a different set of instructions that can be used for this trick.

'Double-twelve dominoes' are a variation of the standard set of dominoes. The number of dots on each half of the domino ranges from 0 to 12. Investigate whether the trick works with all double-twelve dominoes.

Now imagine a set of dominoes showing the numbers −6 to +6. A domino can show two positive numbers, two negative numbers, or one negative and one positive. Investigate whether the trick works with these dominoes, and try to explain why.

Solution:

If a is the first number chosen, and b is the other number on the domino, the steps can be represented algebraically as:

$$5(2a + 3) + b = 10a + b + 15$$

After Miremba subtracts 15, she has $10a + b$.

With double-twelve dominoes, the trick only works when the second number, b, is 9 or below.

If the domino shows two negative numbers, or one positive and one negative number, the trick does not work.

> TIP: If there are no dominoes available, students can simply choose two numbers from 0 to 6 and make a note of them – or print and use the set of dominoes in the photocopiable resources.

- **Creating geometry equation problems**

  $x = 25°$. Create a problem in which a triangle's angles are labelled and x has to be found.

  $x = 17°$. Create a problem involving angles on straight lines, where x has to be found.

  $x = 3$ cm. Create a problem involving sides of a polygon, where x has to be found.

  Basic: x appears once, and no more than one pair of brackets is used.

  Challenging: x appears more than once, and at least two pairs of brackets are used.

  Write a solution for each problem that you create.

> TIP: Students can create simpler or more complex problems, depending on their level of proficiency. An example of a simpler problem is:
>
> The three angles of a triangle are $2x°$, 30° and 100°. Find x.
>
> An example of a more challenging problem is:
>
> The three angles of a triangle are $3(x − 5)°$, $2(32 − x)°$ and 106°. Find x.

- **Finish the equation**

  The equation $x + 5 = 2x − 4$ is true for one value of x.

  The equation $x + 6 = x + 8$ is not true for any value of x. It is an equation with no solution.

  The equation $2(x + 3) = 2x + 6$ is true for any value of x. This type of equation is called an 'identity', and it has an infinite number of solutions.

Below are some half-finished equations. Complete each equation in three different ways:

1. Create an equation that has one solution.

2. Create an equation that has no solution.

3. Create an equation that has an infinite number of solutions.

$$x + 2 =$$
$$5(x + 3) =$$
$$4(1 - x) =$$
$$2(3x - 5) =$$
$$5x - 3(x + 2) =$$

TIP: Students may need to see an example before they start the activity. You could show the following ways of completing $2(4 - x) =$, for example:

$2(4 - x) = 3(x + 6)$ has one solution ($x = -2$)

$2(4 - x) = 2(2 - x)$ has no solution

$2(4 - x) = 3(3 - x) -1 + x$ has an infinite number of solutions

Simultaneous equations

Learning objectives	Key terms
Learning objectives covered in this chapter: 9Ae9	• simultaneous equations
• Solve a simple pair of simultaneous linear equations by eliminating one variable.	• equation
	• simultaneous
	• solve
	• coefficient
	• unknown
	• variable
	• eliminating/elimination

Prior knowledge assumptions
- Students can solve a linear equation, including where the solution is a negative number or decimal.
- Students are fluent in negative number arithmetic.
- Students can substitute into a (linear) formula (for example, $3x + 2y = 18$) and hence find a missing value.

Guidance on the hook

Purpose: This task introduces the idea of an equation containing two unknowns and the range of possible solutions to this. It then shows students how a second equation can pin down the precise solution that is true for both.

Use of the hook: A guessing game is described in the Student's Book: encourage students to play this game in pairs initially to help them get used to rolling the dice and then using the total, predicting the possible scores on each of the two dice.

Ask the students to think about which scores have fewer possibilities (i.e. $\frac{2}{12}$, then $\frac{3}{11}$ and so on) and which have more (that is, 7, then $\frac{6}{8}$ and so on) and so which scores are easier to get three points.

They should be able to deduce the numbers directly when told the difference also – but they only get 1 point for doing this.

Bring the group back together and tell them that you have rolled two dice and have a total of 7.

Record this as an equation by letting x = score on dice 1 and y = score on dice 2, hence $x + y = 7$.

Ask them what the possible values of x and y could be.

Then ask students how they could record a difference of 3 using an equation, that is $x - y = 3$.

BEWARE: Students may try to use different letters here. Ensure they use x and y again as the unknowns are the same unknowns as in the first equation (that is, they are still the scores on each of the two dice).

Ask the students to try their different combinations for x and y in the second equation to find which one is the solution to both equations (5 and 2). This is the solution to the pair of simultaneous equations.

Adaptation: You could give students larger dice that go beyond 6 to produce more possibilities to help them realise why the first equation is not enough on its own to find a single solution.

Extension: Students could write their own equations to support their totals and differences when playing the game alone.

Starter ideas

Mental maths starter

Multiply $5x$ by 5.	Multiply $6y$ by 4.	Multiply $-8y$ by 2.	Multiply $-3x$ by -6.
Multiply $6y$ by -2.	Halve $-8x$.	Double $-16x + 4$.	Multiply $4 - x$ by 3.
Add together -2, 4 and 17.	Add together -16 and -3.	Find the sum of 5 and -9.	Find the sum of -3 and -4.
Find the difference between 14 and -6.	Find the difference between -20 and -13.	Subtract -6 from 18.	Subtract 21 from -12.
Divide -30 by 10.	Divide -15 by 3.	Divide -40 by 4.	Divide $21x$ by -7.

Start point check

Same and different

$13y = 26$ $8y = 56$ $3y = -42$ $2x - 5 = 57$ $3 + 4y = 11$

Write the five equations on a board for the students to look at.

Ask them:

- Which equation is the hardest to solve? Why?
- Which equations are the easiest to solve? Why?
- Are there any equations that you can solve in your head?
- Tell me something that is the same in each equation, tell me something that is different about each equation.

Game: Last man standing

This game will help students to understand that an equation with two variables has many different values of x and y that will work. It will encourage them to think creatively about their solutions, especially using negative and fractional values.

Write an equation with two variables on the board. For example, $3x + y = 17$.

Ask the students to write down one set of possible values for x and y. For example, $x = 5$, $y = 2$.

Tell all students to stand up. They take it in turns to say their values to the class. If someone else has the same values then they both sit down.

Anyone left standing up when all values have been read out will have found a unique solution and wins a point.

Play the game again with a new equation. This time, discuss the different strategies that students can use to help them win. You could use the prompt sheet in the online photocopiable resources for this chapter to select suitable equations.

Game: In a minute

Write a simple equation on the board, such as $3x = 9$.

Give students one minute to write down as many equivalent equations as they can (for example, $6x = 18$).

Encourage students to consider adding and subtracting terms too (for example, $6x + 1 = 19$).

Discussion ideas

Probing questions	Teacher prompts
Convince me that if I add $10x + y = 23$ and $3x - y = 3$, I will get the equation $13x = 26$.	Prompt students to use a visual representation, such as a bar model, to demonstrate what happens when we add these. That is: can be added to give: This rearranges as: which simplifies to: They could also show this more abstractly by listing all of the terms and then simplifying. That is: $10x + y + 3x - y = 23 + 3$ so $10x + y + 3x - y = 26$. Rearranging: $10x + 3x + y - y = 26$. Simplifying: $13x + 0y = 26$ $13x = 26$.
Convince me that $4x + 10y = 48$ is equivalent to $2x + 5y = 24$.	Prompt students to use a visual representation here rather than simply stating that everything has been halved. They could show this using a bar model, for example, to show that rearranging $4x + 10y = 48$ into two pieces gives two equations of $2x + 5y = 24$.
Write a pair of simultaneous equations that can be solved by adding the equations. Now write a different pair of simultaneous equations that can be solved by subtracting the equations.	Encourage students to start by writing one equation, using a value for x and y in their mind. For example, $x = 5$ and $y = 3$. This will help them to calculate the RHS of the equation. Then ask students what the second equation needs to look like if adding the equations will eliminate one of the unknowns. Students will need to use the values of x and y that they assigned in the first equation to produce a correct second equation. Prompt students to check whether their pair of equations really is solved by adding the equations. You could ask students to swap over to solve another person's equations to check their answers. You can encourage students to generalise their answers. For example: If the first equation is of the form $ax + by = c$, then a second equation of the form $-ax + dy = e$ or $fx - by = g$ will work (where a, b, c, d, e, f and g are real numbers). Repeat for subtraction.

Probing questions	Teacher prompts
Does it matter whether you eliminate x or y in your equations?	Ask students which is the best to eliminate in these examples: $$6x + y = 25; \quad 3x - y = 11$$ $$2x + 5y = 24; \quad 2x + 3y = 20$$ $$10x + 3y = 46; \quad 7x + y = 30$$ $$x - y = 2; \quad 2y - x = 2$$ to help them see that there is usually one easier variable to eliminate. TIP: Give students angles in increasing size to begin with to help them use their previous answer to help them estimate the next angle. Look out for students who always prefer to eliminate the x unknown here, who may do a lot of additional work in order to approach a problem in this way. Then ask students to solve: $$2x + y = 15; \quad 2x - y = 13$$ to show that you could eliminate either unknown here and still solve the pair efficiently. You could use the prompt sheet in the photocopiable resources for this chapter to select two equations that are best to solve by subtracting the equations, and then two that are best to solve by adding the equations.
How can you check your solutions to make sure they are correct?	Try giving students these equations: $$3x + 4y = 57$$ $$5x - 4y = 31$$ and the solution: $x = 7$, $y = 9$. Ask the students to check whether this solution is correct by substituting these values into each equation. You may need to prompt them to check both equations (as this solution works for the first equation but not the second) to realise that the solution is not correct. You could link this back to the hook task where there were a number of possible solutions to the first equation, but not all of these worked for the second equation. You could then ask students to use elimination to find the real answer and then convince you of their solution using substitution. Note that the correct solution is $x = 11$, $y = 6$.

Common errors/misconceptions

Misconception	Strategies to address
Struggling to calculate the difference between two equations when approaching equations involving a negative. For example, students may reverse the order of the subtraction in order to achieve a positive answer on each side. Alternatively, students may make an error with their negative number calculation saying, for example, with $2y - 6y$ that the answer is $-4y$.	Allow students to follow through an error in a negative calculation as this will usually result in an unexpected solution or value for an unknown. This should trigger them to go back and check their work to see whether there is an error. Sound out the calculation verbally (for instance '$2y$ subtract negative $3y$') to help emphasise the operations required. It is advised that you involve some negative number arithmetic starters and activities in this chapter to ensure students are confident and fluent in this prerequisite skill.

Misconception	Strategies to address
Finding it hard to see that in just one equation, x and y are variables and can hold multiple values whereas once a second equation is introduced, this pinpoints the specific values that they must be.	Give students a single equation and ask them what the solution is. For example, $3x + y = 17$. Show that different students in the group have found different values for x and y and test these out to show that they all work. You can then give a second equation where only one of these solutions works to demonstrate that only when we have two equations do we know for sure what the answer is.

Believing that you cannot add two equations to get a further valid equation.	You could show students some numerical equations first to help convince them of this approach.
	
	For example,
	  if 2 + 3 = 5
	  and 7 + 9 = 16,
	  then 2 + 3 + 7 + 9 = 5 + 16
	
	You could also look at equations with one unknown before those with two unknowns.
	
	For example,
	  if $3x + 1 = 19$
	  and $2x + 5 = 17$,
	  then $3x + 1 + 2x + 5 = 19 + 17$
	
	Students can then simply this to see why we collect the terms in the 'vertical' way so often modelled.

Developing conceptual understanding

9Ae9 Solve a simple pair of simultaneous linear equations by eliminating one variable.

- FIX: Make use of the bar model representation shown in the worked example in the Student's Book. Some students may benefit from trying to solve some of the 'Doing' questions using this visual approach first, before translating this to the abstract algebraic method.

- FIX: You might want to use an even more visual method to help those who find the bar model too abstract.

  For example: you could represent 'let x be the cost of a pen and y be the cost of a pencil'.

  To solve $x + 5y = 9$ and $x + 2y = 6$, try using these images:

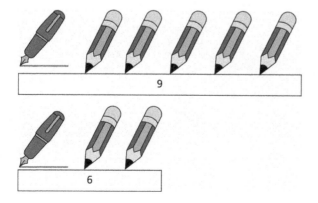

Students should be able to see quickly that the extra three pencils in the top equation account for an extra value of 3 and so deduce that each pencil has a cost of 1.

- FIX: As in the Student's Book, commence with examples involving subtracting the equations, as this can be seen as simply 'finding the difference' between the equations. You might want to use a numerical example to show why this approach is valid: for example:

    if 7 + 3 = 10

    and 2 + 4 = 6

    then (7 + 3) − (2 + 4) = 10 − 6

Ask pupils for applications of this – for example, tiled floors. Get them to find examples on the internet.

You can then explore what happens when we add two equations for situations with equal and opposite coefficients of one unknown.

STRETCH: Students who grasp the concept quickly could be challenged to try to represent their solutions to the more complex problems involving multiplying a variable using the bar model (from the second exercise).

For example, students might represent $2x + y = 11$ and $3x - 2y = 6$ as:

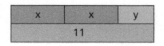

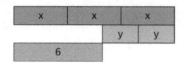

They can then multiply the first equation by 2 to obtain:

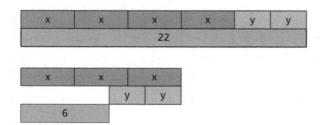

before adding the equations to get:

This simplifies to give:

So:

Students can then find the value of y by substituting $x = 4$:

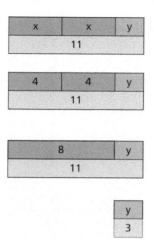

STRETCH: for those finding this approach straightforward, you could introduce them to examples where both variables must be multiplied to eliminate an unknown.

Here is a further example using the bar model for a pair of equations involving such a scaling up.

$$2x + y = 11;\ 3x - 2y = 6$$

We can represent the two equations like this:

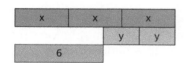

To eliminate x, we need to multiply the equations so they are comparable (that is, have the same number of xs). So, we multiply the first equation by 3 and the second by 2 to get:

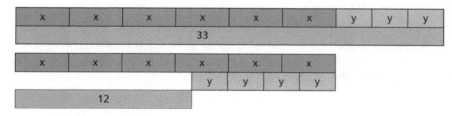

We now need to look at the difference between the two equations.

The xs are the same but there is a difference in the numbers and the ys.

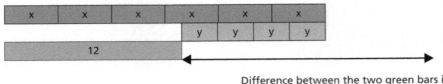

Difference between the two green bars is:
a) 33 − 12 = 21
b) 3y + 4y = 7y

Therefore 7y = 21
y = 3

Now we know that $y = 3$, we can substitute and so find that $x = 4$.

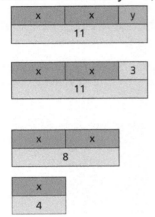

Encourage students to clearly communicate their work, showing each step of their solution on a new line. You could give students some examples of incorrect solutions to a simultaneous equation. Ask them to mark the solutions and identify the error that has been made. Discuss with students how easy it was to identify each error and ask them to suggest how the solution could have been presented more clearly.

Encourage students to check their work by substituting their values back into the original equation.

STRETCH: Students working at greater depth could explore simultaneous equations with no solution (e.g. $x + y = 12$, $2x + 2y = 9$) or an infinite number of solutions (for example, $2x + y = 7$, $6x + 3y = 21$). This relates to the 'Always, sometimes, never?' question in the consolidation exercise.

End of chapter mental maths exercise

1. Multiply $7x$ by 3.	8. Solve $7y = 84$.
2. Divide $24x$ by 8.	9. Solve $-2x = -8$.
3. Multiply $7x + 2y$ by 4.	10. Solve $3y = -21$.
4. Find the sum of $9x$ and $-3x$.	11. Three pens and two pencils cost 72 cents. Write an equation to represent this.
5. Find the sum of $-2y$ and $-3y$.	12. I think of two numbers, x and y. They sum to 13 and they have a difference of 9.
6. Find the difference between $2y$ and $-7y$.	
7. Find the difference between $-3x$ and $-8x$.	Write two simultaneous equations to represent this problem.

- Use a spreadsheet to generate pairs of numbers to satisfy each of the equations and then compare the lists of values to find a common solution to both.
- For example, for the equations:

$$3x + y = 19 \text{ and } 2x - y = 6$$

you could ask students to produce a table like this to find solutions:

	A	B	C	D	E
1	3x+y=19			2x-y=6	
2					
3	x	y		x	y
4	0	19		0	-6
5	1	16		1	-4
6	2	13		2	-2
7	3	10		3	0
8	4	7		4	2
9	5	4		5	4
10	6	1		6	6
11	7	-2		7	8
12	8	-5		8	10
13	9	-8		9	12
14	10	-11		10	14
15					

TIP: Encourage students to use a formula to find the value of y if possible. For instance, in the first equation students would use =19−3*A4 for the first value of y in the table on the left and so on.

- Use graphing software to plot the graphs of both equations to find the solution as the intersection of the graph. You can then encourage students to explore why some equations have no solutions or infinite solutions (based on their graphs).

Investigation/research tasks

- **Word problem**

  Erika bought 20 sweets for $2.42.

  Erika bought lemon sweets and strawberry sweets only.

  Erika bought two more strawberry sweets than lemon sweets.

  How many of each of kind of sweet did Erika buy?

  Encourage students to solve this problem formally by setting out their unknowns first and then writing the equations.

  For example:
  - Let x be the number of lemon sweets bought.
  - Let y be the number of strawberry sweets bought.
  - Then $x + y = 20$ and $y = x + 2$.

Students can rearrange the second equation to give $-x + y = 2$ and then solve.

STRETCH: Alternatively, students can consider substituting into the first equation to explore an alternative method of solving these equations.

Solution: 9 lemon sweets and 11 strawberry sweets.

TIP: If students finish, encourage them to write a similar problem of their own and then swap with a partner to see if they can solve each other's.

- **Solution or no solution?**   *Problem solving*

Investigate the solutions to these three sets of equations:

Set 1	Set 2	Set 3
$6x + 2y = 26$	$6x + 2y = 26$	$6x + 2y = 23$
$3x - y = 5$	$3x + y = 13$	$3x + y = 5$

What do you notice about the solutions to the second and third sets of equations?

Why is this happening?

Try drawing these using graphing software to see what happens visually? Does this help you see why your solutions above happened?

Students should find a standard solution to Set 1 ($x = 3$, $y = 4$).

They should then discover that there is more than one solution to the second set of equations. In fact any solution to one of them solves the second one too, making an infinite set.

Finally, they should find that there is no solution to the final equation.

TIP: Use graphing software to show why, when the equations are fundamentally equivalent, the lines overlap and so all points on the line are a solution. Additionally, show that when the lines are parallel, there are no intersection points and hence no solutions.

- **Fibonacci simultaneous equations**   *Problem solving*

The Fibonacci sequence is the number sequence in which each term is the sum of the previous two terms.

It starts 1, 1, 2, 3, 5, 8, ...

Continue this sequence to find the first 15 terms of the Fibonacci sequence.

Investigate solutions of simultaneous equations where the coefficients are consecutive numbers in the Fibonacci sequence.

For example:

$$x + y = 2 \text{ or } 2x + 3y = 5$$

$$3x \times 5y = 8 \text{ or } 8x + 13y = 21$$

Students should discover that the solution to these equations is always $x = 1$ and $y = 1$.

BEWARE: Some of these combinations will require only one multiplication of an equation, which is the level of the chapter (as in the two examples given above). However, other combinations will require both equations to be multiplied, which may be too challenging for some students. For example, $3x + 5y = 8$ and $13x + 21y = 34$.

TIP: Students can also investigate simultaneous equations where the coefficients are members of a Fibonacci sequence starting with values other than 1, 1, ... For example, they could use the sequence 1, 3, 4, 5, 9, 14, 23, ... instead if further exploration is needed with more straightforward equations. The solution will now change too.

Students could also explore other types of sequences, such as equations where the coefficients are arithmetic progressions. For instance, $x + 4y = 7$ and $10x + 13y = 16$ (coming from 1, 4, 7, 10, 13, 16, ...).

STRETCH: For significant challenge, students could show this algebraically by considering the equations:

$$ax + by = a + b$$

$$(a + 2b)x + (2a + 3b)y = 3a + 5b$$

Expanding brackets

Prior knowledge assumptions
- Students can expand a bracket.
- Students can simplify expressions by writing powers.
- Students can simplify expressions by collecting like terms.

Guidance on the hook

Multiplication using the grid method

Purpose: this hook introduces students to a method for multiplying two numbers, each of which is split into two parts. They will use a similar method when multiplying two brackets.

Use of the hook: Start by asking students if they know the grid method of multiplication. Work through the example from the Student's Book, 59 × 38, on the board. One way to help students understand the method is to use an area model, where 59 and 38 represent the lengths of a rectangle's sides. The area of the rectangle can be calculated by splitting it into four smaller rectangles, like this:

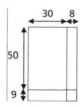

and calculating the four areas, then adding them up.

The Student's Book shows a second way of doing this multiplication, $(60 - 1) \times (40 - 2)$, which can be understood in terms of the area model shown:

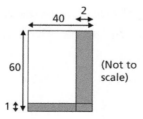

The required area, 59 × 38, equals the area of the 60 × 40 rectangle minus the areas of the three shaded rectangles.

Adaptation: Students can sketch their rectangles approximately to scale, to help them see the connection between the grid method and the area model. They will need to take particular care when representing the calculation $21 \times 79 = (20 + 1)(80 - 1)$.

Since the focus is on conceptual understanding, consider allowing students to use calculators for the final step (addition and/or subtraction), if this step is likely to take up a lot of the available time.

Extension: Ask students if they can think of any other way, instead of drawing a grid, to ensure that they remember to multiply each term in the first bracket by each term in the second bracket.

TIP: Remind students that when two brackets are written next to each other, such as $(50 + 9)(30 + 8)$, this means that the value of one bracket is to be multiplied by the value of the other.

TIP: Encourage students to see the bigger picture: the two brackets simply show the product of two numbers (where each number is made up of two parts). Before they do each multiplication, ask students to write out the multiplication using two brackets.

Starter ideas

Mental maths starter

Calculate 21×3.	Calculate 42×3.	Calculate 32×4.	Calculate 31×8.
Calculate 11×31.	Calculate 51×21.	Calculate 19×41.	Calculate 29×21.
Expand $2(x + 3)$.	Expand $4(3 - x)$.	Expand $6(x - 2)$.	Expand $3(12 - x)$.
Expand $5(2x + 1)$.	Expand $3(3x - 4)$.	Expand $-2(6 - x)$.	Expand $4(2x + 5)$.
Simplify $x \times x$.	Simplify $x(x + 1)$.	Simplify $x(3 - x)$.	Simplify $-x(2 - x)$.

Start point check

Give students the set of expanding brackets loop cards (in the photocopiable resources). Each card contains an expression in factorised form and a different expression in expanded form.

Ask students to find pairs of equivalent expressions (for example, $x(3 + 4x) = 3x + 4x^2$) and place them next to each other. If they do this for all of the cards they can make a complete loop.

Game/investigation

Give students the Worksheet from the photocopiable resources, which guides them to discover that two brackets of the form $(x + a)(x + b)$ can be rewritten as $x(x + b) + a(x + b)$ or $x(x + a) + b(x + a)$.

Discussion ideas

Probing questions	Teacher prompts
State which of the following expressions is/are equivalent to $2(4 + 5)$: $(2 \times 4) + (2 \times 5)$ $2 \times 4 + 5$ $(2 \times 4) \times (2 \times 5)$ State which of the following expressions is/are equivalent to $2(4 \times 5)$: $(2 \times 4) \times (2 \times 5)$ $2 \times 4 \times 5$ $(2 \times 4) + (2 \times 5)$	These questions prompt students to think about when they can use the distributive law. It applies to $2(4 + 5)$ – each of the terms in the brackets is multiplied by 2 – but does not apply to $2(4 \times 5)$. If students are unsure, they can try evaluating the expressions to see which are equivalent. After this, ask students how to expand $2(x + 3)$ and $2(3x)$, and check that they are not writing the second expression as $2 \times 3 \times 2 \times x$.
Is $(x + 3)(x - 4)$ the same as $(x - 4)(x + 3)$?	This question tests whether students see the big picture: the expression $(x + 3)(x - 4)$ can be viewed as the product of two numbers, so the order of the two brackets does not affect the answer. If students are unsure, they can use an area model to show each expression as a rectangle, and think about whether their two rectangles have the same area.
Expand $(x + 4)(x - 4)$ and simplify. What is unusual about the answer?	Ask students to explain why the answer has fewer terms than other simplified products of two-term brackets. Ask them to create other pairs of brackets that expand and simplify to give two terms.
Expand $(x + 3)^2$.	If students think the expanded form is $x^2 + 9$, ask them to use the area model to do the expansion, and show that they have omitted the areas of two of the rectangles. Students can try a similar calculation with known numbers, for example: $(3 + 2)^2 = 5^2 = 25$ or $(3 + 2)^2 = 3^2 + 6 + 2^2 = 25$, whereas $3^2 + 2^2 = 9 + 4 = 13$.

Common errors/misconceptions

Misconception	Strategies to address
Omitting one or more terms in the expansion of two brackets.	One way for students to make sure they include all terms is to use the area model. A quicker method is to use lines to connect terms that need to be multiplied, for example: $(x + 4)\,(x - 5)$ Another way is to use the word 'FOIL' as a reminder to multiply 'firsts' (the first term in each bracket), 'outers', 'inners' and 'lasts': O F $(x + 4)\,(x - 5)$ I L

Misconception	Strategies to address
Confusing x^2 with $2x$.	If the student does remember that x^2 is read as 'x squared', then remind them that the term 'squaring' comes from the method for calculating the area of a square. Ask them to think about how we do this. You could also point out that we already have '2x' as the way to express 'the product of 2 and x', so 'x^2' has a different meaning.
Part way through expanding, switching to adding instead of multiplying, for example: $(x + 2)(x + 3) = x^2 + 2x + 3x + 5$ (student calculates final term as $2 + 3$ instead of 2×3).	Students can lose track of which operation they should be doing, especially if they do not have a good understanding of the big picture (that we are multiplying two numbers, each of which is the sum of two numbers). Students can use the area model to see that we need to *multiply* pairs of terms to find four areas, and then *add* the results to find the total area.
Trying to continue simplifying an expression that cannot be simplified, for example: $x^2 + 5x + 6 = 6x + 6$	Students may think that an answer that contains one or more operators is 'unfinished', since they may interpret an operator as an instruction to do something. Remind students to think about like terms and unlike terms when considering whether to simplify. If students write, for example, $x^2 + 5x = 6x$, ask what are the two x values that make this true. Show that it is not true for any other value of x, and so $x^2 + 5x = 6x$ cannot be written since it is not true for all x (and it is untrue for most x).

Developing conceptual understanding

9Ae10 Expand the product of two linear expressions of the form $x \pm n$ and simplify the corresponding quadratic equation.

* FIX: The area model introduced earlier for multiplying two brackets can help students to understand what they should multiply, and why.

* FIX: Algebra tiles can be used by students to model the expansion of two brackets. This is similar to the area model, but it can be practised using manipulatives. A set of algebra tiles is included in the photocopiable resources. Below is an example showing how to use algebra tiles to show the expansion $(x + 1)(x + 2) = x^2 + 3x + 2$.

The set of tiles includes negative tiles ($-x^2$, $-x$ and -1). Below is an example showing the expansion of $(2 - x)(x - 1)$.

TIP: Print negative tiles on paper of a different colour to make them easy to distinguish from the positive tiles.

STRETCH: Students can try multiplying brackets where the coefficients of x are not 1, such as $(2x + 3)(4x - 1)$.

STRETCH: Students can try multiplying brackets containing more than two terms each, such as $(x + y + 3)(x + y - 2)$. It may help to use an area model at first.

STRETCH: Students can try solving equations of the form $(x + 3)(x - 2) = 0$.

TIP: Ask students to think how the product of two numbers can be zero.

End of chapter mental maths exercise

1. Calculate 31×61	7. Expand $(x + 2)(2 - x)$
2. Calculate 29×19	8. Expand $(3 - x)(x + 4)$
3. Calculate 16×32	9. A rectangle has side lengths of $x + 6$ and $x - 1$. Find the area of the rectangle in expanded form.
4. Calculate 73×59	
5. Expand $(x - 1)(x + 3)$	
6. Expand $(x - 4)(x - 5)$	10. A rectangle has side lengths of $10 - x$ and $x + 5$. Find the area of the rectangle in expanded form.

Technology recommendations

- There are interactive websites where students can explore expansion of brackets using algebra tiles. To find some of these websites, search for the words: algebra tiles interactive.

- Students can use a spreadsheet program to check that the expanded and factorised forms of a quadratic expression are equivalent, by substituting values for the variable into the two forms. For example, to check that $(x - 5)(x + 6) = x^2 + x - 30$, students could create a table like this, including a list of possible values of x:

	A	B	C
1	x	(x-5)(x+6)	x^2+x-30
2	-3		
3	-2		
4	-1		
5	0		
6	1		
7	2		

and enter suitable formulae for calculating the values of the two expressions:

	A	B
1	x	(x-5) (x+6)
2	-3	=(A2-5)*(A2+6)

	A	B	C
1	x	(x-5) (x+6)	x^2+x-30
2	-3	-24	=A2^2+A2-30

Then copy these formulae down the columns to calculate the value of each side of each expression for different values of the variable:

	A	B	C
1	x	(x-5) (x+6)	x^2+x-30
2	-3	-24	-24
3	-2	-28	-28
4	-1	-30	-30
5	0	-30	-30
6	1	28	28

BEWARE: Spreadsheet programs usually do not allow the multiplication symbol (*) to be omitted. For example, to multiply (A2 − 5) by (A2 + 6), students need to enter (A2 − 5) * (A2 + 6) instead of (A2 − 5)(A2 + 6)

TIP: Instead of typing a column of consecutive values for the variable, students can use the 'fill down' function in the spreadsheet: fill in two or three consecutive numbers, then select them all and pull down on the drag handle to continue the sequence.

STRETCH: Students can use graphing software to plot graphs of quadratic functions and explore the relationship between the function and its graph.

Investigation/research tasks

* **Deducing rules** *Problem solving*

  When you expand $(x + 6)(x + 8)$, you get $x^2 + 14x + 48$.

  1. Try to find rules showing how the numbers 14 and 48 are related to the two constant terms in the brackets, 6 and 8.

  2. Check your rules by expanding other pairs of brackets, including brackets containing negative terms.

  3. Use your rules to predict the expanded form of $(x + q)(x + s)$. Now expand the brackets and check whether your answer agrees with your prediction.

STRETCH: When you expand $(2x + 3)(4x + 5)$, you get $8x^2 + 22x + 15$.

4. Try to find rules showing how the 8, 22 and 15 are related to the numbers 2, 3, 4 and 5 in the brackets.

5. Check your rules by expanding other pairs of brackets where the coefficients of x are not 1.

6. Use your rules to predict the expanded form of $(px + q)(rx + s)$. Now expand the brackets and check whether your answer agrees with your prediction.

- **Difference of products**

  Take a 100 square, one is provided in the photocopiable resources, and lay a 2 by 2 square over the top.

  Find the product of the numbers in the opposite corners of your 2 by 2 square. And then find the difference between these products

  For example, on this 100 square the product of the opposite corners is

  $11 \times 21 = 231$

  $20 \times 12 = 240$

  The difference between these two products is 9.

  Move the 2 by 2 square and repeat. What do you notice?

  Can you use algebra to write a formula which shows this will always happen?

  Students should be able to use algebra to generalise a 2 by 2 square on a 10 × 10 grid and show why the difference in the products of the opposite corners is always 9.

  For instance, they may produce a general 2 by 2 square like this:

x	$x + 1$
$x + 9$	$x + 10$

  and show that

  $x \times (x + 10) = x^2 + 10x$

  $(x + 1) \times (x + 9) = x^2 + 10x + 9$

  The difference between the two expressions is 9.

  BEWARE: Students may have met a similar task in Stage 7 where they explored the sum of the numbers in opposite corners.

  TIP: You could encourage students to use different size squares to see how this affects the difference in the products of the opposite corners. Students should be able to use algebra to generalise an n by n square on a 10 × 10 grid.

  STRETCH: Students working at greater depth could consider rectangles or explore grid sizes to see how this affects the difference in the products of the opposite corners. Students should be able to use algebra to generalise an n by m rectangle on a $p \times p$ grid.

- **Multiplication using the line method**   *Problem solving*

   Use the worksheet in the photocopiable resources. This investigation explores the line method of multiplication, and gives students another way to approach the expansion of two brackets. The distributive law is illustrated visually by the crossing of lines.

   > TIP: After students have seen the example and tried the method, you may wish to have a class discussion about how the method works. Students will learn more from this activity if they can understand the line method, rather than seeing it as a mysterious 'trick'.

- **Proofs using algebra**   *Problem solving*

   Prove each statement.

   - For any value of x, $(x + 5)(x + 2)$ is 4 greater than $(x + 6)(x + 1)$.
   - For any value of x, $(x + 2)(x - 1)$ is 1 less than $x(x + 1) - 1$.
   - For any value of x, $(x + 4)(x - 4) - x2$ equals -16.
   - For any value of x, $(x + 2)(x - 2) + 4$ is a square number.
   - For any value of x, $(x + 2)(x - 1) + 2$ is divisible by x.

STRETCH: For any value of x, $(2x + 1)^2 - 1$ is divisible by 4.

   Now try writing your own statements, and show how to prove them.

   BEWARE: Students may think that if they substitute one or more values of x and find that the statement is true for these values, they have proved the statement. Before starting the activity, make sure students understand that a proof must show that the statement is true for all x values, and should be carried out algebraically rather than by calculating specific examples.

Real-life graphs and direct proportion

Learning objectives

Learning objectives covered in this chapter: 9As7, 9As8

- Construct functions arising from real-life problems; draw and interpret their graphs.
- Use algebraic methods to solve problems involving direct proportion, relating solutions to graphs of the equations.

Key terms

- linear function
- *y*-intercept
- gradient
- direct proportion

Prior knowledge assumptions

- Students can draw and interpret graphs in real-life contexts.
- Students can plot and interpret a graph of a linear function.
- Students understand and can work with ratios.

Guidance on the hook

Purpose: This activity introduces students to the idea that a directly proportional relationship between two variables can be expressed in the form of a graph.

Use of the hook: Students use spreadsheet software to produce a table of values of the masses of two spices that are used in the ratio 2 : 3 for a recipe. They then plot a graph to show the relationship between the two quantities, find the gradient and *y*-intercept, and write the

formula for the graph. The correct formula is $g = \frac{3}{2}n$ or 2g = 3n). By doing this, they see that

a real-life graph showing direct proportion can have its formula expressed in terms of the two variables.

Students can find the gradient of the graph by plotting a trendline and then displaying its equation, which will be $y = 1.5x$ or equivalent.

Students can find the *y*-intercept of the graph either by realising that when $n = 0$, $g = 0$, or by extrapolating (or 'forecasting') the trendline backward.

Adaptation: Students could create the table and graph by hand instead of using the spreadsheet software.

Extension: Students could use the ratio to deduce a formula for calculating values of *g*:

	A	B
1	n	g
2	2	=A2*3/2
3	4	

Students can explore the effect on the graph of changing the ratio of masses of the two spices.

Starter ideas

Mental maths starter

If $y = 3x$, what is y when $x = 4$?	If $y = 12x$, what is y when $x = 3$?	If $y = -4x$, what is y when $x = 20$?	If $y = -8x$, what is y when $x = -3$?
If $y = 3x + 2$, what is y when $x = 6$?	If $y = 4x + 1$, what is x when $y = 29$?	If $y = 2x - 6$, what is y when $x = 1$?	If $y = 10 - 4x$, what is x when $y = -10$?
What is the y-intercept of the graph $y = 3x + 2$?	What is the gradient of the graph $y = 4x + 1$?	What is the y-intercept of the graph $y = 2x - 6$?	What is the gradient of the graph $y = 10 - 4x$?
y is directly proportional to x. If $y = 6$ when $x = 3$, what is y when $x = 4$?	y is directly proportional to x. If $y = 24$ when $x = 8$, what is y when $x = 10$?	y is directly proportional to x. If $y = 5$ when $x = 1$, what is y when $x = 3$?	y is directly proportional to x. If $y = 1$ when $x = 2$, what is y when $x = 4$?
The cost of hiring a car is \$15 per hour. Write a formula for the cost, \$$c$, of hiring the car for time t hours.	The cost of taking a taxi ride is \$3 plus \$1 per kilometre. Write a formula for the cost, \$$c$, of travelling distance d km by taxi.	A plant is 5 cm high, and it then grows by 1 cm each day. Write a formula for the height, h cm, of the plant after time t days.	An empty container is filled with water. The depth of water increases by 2 cm every second. Write a formula for the depth, d cm, of water in the cylinder after time t s.

Start point check: Directly proportional or not?

This activity reminds students what it means for two variables to be directly proportional. Later in this chapter they will work with graphs of real-life variables that are directly proportional.

Ask students to create tables of values for pairs of variables, some of which are proportional and some are not. Examples of pairs of variables to give students are:

- length, L, and perimeter, p, of a square
- length, L, and area, A, of a square
- total mass of a box of marbles, M, and number of marbles, n, of mass 5 g each, where the mass of the box is 100 g
- total mass of marbles, m, and number of marbles, n, of mass 5 g each
- length in metres, L, and length in centimetres, L.

STRETCH: area in metres, A, and area in centimetres, a.

Students then state whether each pair of variables is directly proportional, and write a formula relating the two variables in each pair.

Ask what the formulae for the directly proportional variables have in common. (All have the form $y = mx$.)

STRETCH: Ask students to describe or sketch the graph, or to draw it using online graph plotting software, for each of the pairs of variables above.

TIP: If students do not remember the meaning of 'directly proportional', start by showing a table of values of two variables that are directly proportional (e.g. y = 3, 6, 9, … when x = 1, 2, 3, …, so the relationship is $y = 3x$) and a table of values of two variables that are not (e.g. y = 2, 3, 4, … when x = 1, 2, 3, …, so the relationship is $y = x + 1$).

For each pair of variables they investigate, students could write the ratio of the two values in each row of their table, simplify the ratios, and check whether the ratios are all the same.

Game: Treasure hunt

This game gives students practice in relating straight line graphs to their formulae. They will use this skill later in this chapter.

Students work in pairs, with each pair sharing a pair of axes with a number of crosses marked (see photocopiable resources).The two students take turns, where a turn involves writing the formula for a straight-line graph and then (with the help of the other player, if needed) drawing that graph onto the axes. The player scores a point for each cross their graph passes through. (You could tell students that each cross marks a spot where treasure is hidden.)

The students play until they have drawn three graphs each. The player with more points at the end is the winner.

There are two different graphs in the photocopiable resources for this game, so students can play the game twice.

BEWARE: Students may choose to write formulae for horizontal and vertical graphs only (for example, x = 2, or y = 12), because these are particularly easy to write and draw. You may wish to make a rule that these are not allowed.

Discussion ideas

Probing questions	Teacher prompts
On each of the following graphs, state what the y-intercept represents: • heart rate (on y-axis) against number of sit-ups done (when the person was previously resting) • height of a person (on y-axis) against the person's age in years • mass of a block of ice (on y-axis) against time, after the block is taken out of a freezer and left in a warm place.	You could give students mini whiteboards and ask them to hold up their answers. Students may find that sketching the graph helps them to think about what the y-intercepts represent. (The answers are: resting/normal heart rate; height at birth; initial mass of ice/mass of ice immediately after it is taken out of the freezer.)
'The more people work on a task, the sooner the task will be finished.' Sketch a graph for this situation, with the number of people on the y-axis and the time taken to complete the task on the x-axis.	Some students may incorrectly draw a straight line through the origin, with a positive gradient. If so, ask them to describe what happens, according to their graph, to the time taken as the number of people increases. Ask if this is consistent with the information given.

Probing questions	Teacher prompts
What does it mean when we say that 'y increases with x at a constant rate'? Sketch a graph showing this relationship. Sketch graphs showing y increasing with x at a rate that is not constant.	Students may have difficulty understanding the meaning of the word 'rate'. Rate often means 'per unit time'. Discuss examples of this, such as: • speed is rate of change of distance with time, in units such as m/s • if a plant grows 0.5 cm per day then its growth rate is 0.5 cm/day; if it grows 5 cm every 2 days then its growth rate is 2.5 cm/day. Sometimes rate means 'per unit (variable other than time)'. Examples include: • rate of change of cost with distance travelled (in a taxi), in dollars per kilometre • rate of change of length of a spring with amount of mass hung from it, in centimetres per gram (as shown in Worked Example 2 in the Student's Book). Point out that if we divide a change in one variable, y, by the corresponding change in another variable, x, we get the rate of change of the first variable with the second (which equals the gradient of a graph of y against x).
Consider the graph of $y = 3x = 4$. When $x = 0$, what is the value of y? What name do we give to the point on a graph where $x = 0$? If x increases by 1, by how much does the value of y increase? How does this relate to the gradient?	Although students may know that a straight-line graph has a formula of the form $y = mx + c$, where m is the gradient and c is the y-intercept, they may not understand why. This understanding can be helpful when they are relating real-life formulae to the corresponding graphs. Students are likely to find it harder to see why 3 is the gradient than to see why 4 is the y-intercept. Demonstrate that the '3' in the formula makes y increase by 3 each time x increases by 1. Gradient $= \dfrac{\text{change in y - coordinates}}{\text{change in x - coordinates}}$, which is $\dfrac{3}{1}$, or 3.
Why is the graph showing the relationship between two directly proportional variables a straight line through the origin?	Students can consider the two aspects (straight line; passes through origin) separately. Ask students to think about why if one variable has the value zero, the other variable must also be zero. One way to show why a direct proportion graph is a straight line is to draw steps under the graph. Demonstrate that every time x increases by 1, y increases by a constant amount, m, as expressed by the relationship $y = mx$.

© HarperCollins*Publishers* 2018

Probing questions	Teacher prompts
If 3 Moroccan dirhams are worth 4 South African rand, write a formula relating a number of dirhams, d, to the number of rand, r, that have equal value.	If students give the incorrect answer $3d = 4r$, it may be because they read this formula incorrectly as '3 dirhams equal 4 rand', instead of the correct interpretation '3 times a number of dirhams has the same value as 4 times a number of rand'.
	Ask which needs to be larger, the number of dirhams d, or the number of rand r, for the two sides to be equal in value according to the incorrect formula $3d = 4r$, and according to the correct formula $4d = 3r$. If needed, demonstrate using numerical values for d and r.
	Alternatively, show that the formula $4d = 3r$ correctly shows that if the number of dirhams $d = 3$ and the number of rand $r = 4$, then the two sides are equal. This is consistent with the information given. This does not work with the incorrect formula $3d = 4r$.
If the ratio of two quantities p and q is $1 : 3$, state the gradient of: • a graph with p on the y-axis and q on the x-axis • a graph with q on the y-axis and p on the x-axis. What are your two answers if the ratio of $p : q$ is changed to $2 : 3$?	Ask students how much q increases when p increases by 1. (This is easier than working out how much p increases when q increases by 1.) It may help for students to try sketching the graphs, showing this relationship between p and q.
	For the second ratio, it is less obvious what happens to either of the variables when the other increases by 1. If needed, remind students how to convert the ratio to a unitary ratio ($1 : \frac{3}{2}$ or $\frac{2}{3} : 1$). (You may wish to point out that the previous ratio, $1 : 3$, can also be written as $\frac{1}{3} : 1$, which makes it easier to see how much p increases when q increases by 1.)

Common errors/misconceptions

Misconception	Strategies to address
Thinking that the formula for a graph must have x and y as the variable names.	Use plenty of examples and questions (such as those in the Student's Book) where the variable names are not y and x. Point out that students have previously seen graphs of distance against time, for example, and that the axes are still called the x- and y-axis, but the variable names can be changed to reflect the quantities they represent.
When interpreting a graph, counting squares on the graph paper instead of using the scale, for example when finding a gradient.	Make sure students encounter plenty of examples of graphs where the scales do not use 1 square to represent a change of 1 in the value of the variable.
	Sometimes students simply forget to check the scale and need a reminder. However, if students are confused about how to use graph scales which do not use 1 square for 1 unit, choose an example where the real-life significance of the gradient is easy to understand, such as a distance–time graph with constant gradient. Plot the graph so that it *does* have 1 square representing a value of 1. (Online graph plotting software could be used for this.)
	Ask students to find the gradient, and ask what it tells us about the moving object (its speed). Then replot

Chapter 32: Real-life graphs and direct proportion

Misconception	Strategies to address
	the graph with a different scale on one or both of the axes, taking care to show that the plotted values are the same as before, so the graph is still describing the same journey. Ask students if the speed should be the same or different when found from this graph.
	Show what happens when you work out the gradient (speed) incorrectly using one square to mean one unit, and then show the correct method, using the axis scales.
Thinking that if one variable increases as another variable increases, then the two variables must be directly proportional.	Demonstrate that if a graph is not a straight line, then you cannot draw equal steps going up the graph. This is because when x increases by 1, y increases by different values in different parts of the graph. This means the two variables are not proportional as they are not in a constant ratio.
Thinking that two variables are directly proportional if when one increases by an amount, the other increases by the same amount.	When teaching direct proportion, emphasise the idea that when two variables are directly proportional, their values are always in the same ratio.
	The table shows an example of the type of relationship that students may mistakenly think is directly proportional.

x	y
1	2
2	3
100	101

Remind students that direct proportion implies a constant ratio, and ask them to compare the ratios 1 : 2 and 100 : 101 – which are quite different, since 100 : 101 is very close to 1 : 1.

Developing conceptual understanding

9As7 Construct functions arising from real-life problems; draw and interpret their graphs.

- Sketch several different straight-line graphs on the board (with both positive and negative gradients, and with zero and non-zero y-intercepts). Ask students to suggest an example of a pair of variables that matches a particular graph, and then ask the class what the y-intercept and the gradient each represent in that example. Students could show their responses using mini whiteboards.

- FIX: Students may need a reminder about how to choose a suitable scale when drawing a graph. They should make the graph as large as possible on the paper while at the same time choosing a scale that is easy to use. Ask the class to suggest scales that are easy to use, such as one large square (10 small squares) to represent 1, 2, 5, 10, 20, 50, etc. Discuss using one large square to represent 4 (or 40) – this is more difficult, and best avoided if possible. Discuss or show why it is difficult to accurately use a scale where one large square represents 3 or 7, for example.

- If they have mobile phones, students can find out about their own contract, and construct a formula to show the relationship between cost and time (for an all-inclusive contract) or cost against call time or data usage. Then they can plot a graph of the relationship.

9As8 Use algebraic methods to solve problems involving direct proportion, relating solutions to graphs of the equations.

- FIX: Ask students to investigate direct proportion graphs, drawing steps under each graph to show how much y increases each time x increases by 1. Students can use graphs they have drawn, or they can use the graphs on the photocopiable resources 'Step by step'. Start with graphs that have whole-number gradients. For each graph, students make a table of pairs of x and y values taken from the graph. They can then check that all of the pairs are in the same ratio, to confirm that the two variables are directly proportional. Students then write a formula for the relationship represented by the graph.

STRETCH: Ask students to sketch a graph of $y = -2x$, and then discuss whether the two variables x and y are directly proportional. (They are, since the ratio $x : y$ is always the same. However, students may not have seen a negative number in a ratio before.) Ask students to suggest why these graphs are not often seen for real-life relationships. (Most real-life variables are positive numbers. Even where a variable can have negative values, such as bank balance or temperature, it is rare to find that it is directly proportional to a variable that has positive values.)

BEWARE: Make sure students do not use the phrase 'inversely proportional' to describe this type of relationship, since this has a different meaning. Sometimes the phrase 'negatively proportional' is used.

End of chapter mental maths exercise

1. The distance travelled by a toy car is directly proportional to the time it spends travelling.
   a. Sketch a graph of distance against time for the toy car.
   b. Describe the motion of the car.

2. A bag is full of sand. Sand pours out of the bag at a constant rate, until there is no sand left. Sketch a graph of volume of sand, V, in the bag against time, t.

3. The cost of hiring a bicycle is a fixed fee of $10 plus $5 per day. A student draws a graph of cost (in dollars) on the y-axis against time (in days). State:
   a. the gradient
   b. the y-intercept.

4. A bamboo shoot is 10 cm high. It then grows 8 cm every 2 days. A student draws a graph of height, h cm, against time, t days. State:
   a. the y-intercept
   b. the gradient.

5. 1 Euro has the same value as 5 Turkish lira. A conversion graph shows the number of lira on the y-axis and the number of Euros on the x-axis.
   a. Find the gradient of the graph.
   b. State whether the graph passes through the origin.

6. The cost of 3 lemons is $1. Find the gradient of a graph of cost in dollars (on the y-axis) against number of lemons bought.

Technology recommendations

- Use either a graphing calculator or online graph drawing software to draw graphs of real-life relationships. This can allow you to explore the appearance of graphs of many different functions without spending a lot of time drawing axes and plotting points. Some online graph plotters, such as https://www.desmos.com/calculator, allow the gradient and y-intercept to be changed dynamically using sliders.

- Do the online activity 'Water Line', in which students sketch graphs showing height of water against time for glasses of different shapes being filled at a constant rate. Then students draw their own glasses and try to sketch graphs for each other's designs. The activity can be found at https://teacher.desmos.com/waterline.

Investigation / research tasks

- **Taxi comparison**

  Use the internet to research one of the following:
  - costs of using a taxi for different taxi companies in your area (check whether the companies charge per unit of distance or per unit of time)
  - costs of hiring a car for different car hire companies in your area (check whether the companies charge per unit of distance or per unit of time)
  - costs of using mobile phones on 'pay as you go' rates (where you pay per minute of call instead of having a contract) with different companies.

  For each company, construct a formula to express the relationship between cost and one other variable (for example, time, distance).

  On one set of axes, plot a graph of cost (on the y-axis) against the other variable (on the x-axis) for each company.

  Create a guide to which company has the lowest cost for different ranges of the other variable. This could include a table showing when to use which company.

- **Currency conversion**

  Choose your home currency and one currency that is not normally used in your country. Use the internet to find out the relationship between amounts of money in the two currencies.

  Draw a conversion graph that can be used to find the costs of small everyday items in the overseas currency.

  Find the gradient of your graph. (It may not be a whole number.)

  Write an equation for your graph.

  Use your equation to find the costs of buying larger items (such as a laptop or a car) in the overseas currency.

  TIP: Students could use spreadsheet software for this activity.

- **Bicycle hire puzzles**   *Problem solving*

  Solve the two puzzles below.

Bicycle hire puzzle 1

  Company A and company B are bicycle hire companies.

  Each company charges a fixed fee plus an added fee per day.

  The graphs of cost, $C, against time, t days, for the two companies do not intersect.

  Company A charges a fixed fee of $10 plus $12 per day.

  Company B charges a total of $70 for 5 days.

  Find the formula relating cost C and time t for each company.

Bicycle hire puzzle 2

Company P and company Q are bicycle hire companies.

Companies P and Q charge the same amount for hiring a bicycle for 4 days.

Company P charges a fixed fee of $20 plus $5 per day.

The graph of cost, $C, against time, t days, for company Q has a y-intercept of 8.

Find the formula relating cost C and time t for each company.

> TIP: If students are finding it difficult to get started on these puzzles, any of the hints below could be given.

Puzzle 1:

- Start by writing a formula for company A.
- If two graphs do not intersect, they must be parallel.
- If two graphs are parallel, what can you say about their gradients?
- Construct a formula for company B, writing the y-intercept as c.

Puzzle 2:

- Start by writing a formula for company P.
- If the y-intercept of the graph for company Q is 8, what does that tell you about the formula for company Q?
- Construct a formula for company Q, writing the gradient as m.

Solutions:

Bicycle hire puzzle 1

The two companies charge a fixed fee plus an added fee per day, and their graphs do not intersect, so their graphs must look like this:

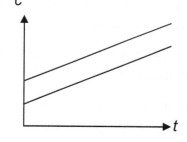

The formula for company A is $C = 12t + 10$.

The graph for company B has the same gradient, so its formula is $C = 12t + c$, where c is the y-intercept.

Company B charges a total of $70 for 5 days, so it must pass through the point (5, 70). Substituting into the formula gives $70 = 12 \times 5 + c$, and solving this gives $c = 10$.

So the formula for company B is $C = 12t + 10$.

Bicycle hire puzzle 2

The formula for company P is $C = 5t + 20$.

The formula for company Q is $C = mt + 8$, where m is the gradient.

Both companies charge the same amount for 4 days, so when $t = 4$, C is the same for both P and Q: $5 \times 4 + 20 = 4m + 8$. Solving this equation gives $m = 8$.

So the formula for company Q is $C = 8m + 8$.

Constructions

Prior knowledge assumptions
- Students can make constructions (for example, perpendicular bisector) using a straight edge and compass.

Guidance on the hook

Purpose: This task introduces students to the construction of regular polygons using only a straight edge and compasses. It involves following a simple method for constructing a regular octagon.

Use of the hook: Students follow the instructions to construct a regular octagon, following a method used by architects and builders for designing and constructing octagonal structures, and published in 1488.

The method is fairly straightforward, but encourage students to take care to draw their construction as accurately as possible. Students can check the accuracy of their octagon by measuring and comparing the side lengths, or by measuring and comparing the lengths of lines joining opposite vertices.

Students can then use the internet to research methods of creating regular polygons using origami (paper folding).

Extension: As a challenge, students could try to do the construction by looking at the diagrams only, without reading the text.

Ask students to calculate the interior angle of a regular octagon, and then use a protractor to check the interior angles of the octagon they have constructed.

TIP: Give students squared or graph paper to help them quickly and accurately draw a square in which to construct their octagon.

Starter ideas

Mental maths starter

Sketch a regular hexagon.	Sketch an irregular hexagon.	Sketch a regular octagon.	Sketch an irregular octagon.
Sketch a circle and label the diameter and the radius.	Sketch the construction lines for constructing an equilateral triangle.	Sketch the construction lines for constructing the bisector of an angle.	Sketch the construction lines for constructing the perpendicular bisector of a line.
A line of length 54 cm is bisected. Find the length of one of the two halves.	A line of length 13 cm is bisected. Find the length of one of the two halves.	A line of length 9.8 cm is bisected. Find the length of one of the two halves.	A line of length 6.42 cm is bisected. Find the length of one of the two halves.
An angle of 36° is bisected. Find the value of one of the two angles created.	An angle of 63° is bisected. Find the value of one of the two angles created.	An angle of 132° is bisected. Find the value of one of the two angles created.	An angle of 77° is bisected. Find the value of one of the two angles created.
Add the number of sides in a hexagon to the number of sides in an octagon.	Calculate the exterior angle of a regular octagon.	Calculate the exterior angle of a regular hexagon.	Add the sum of the interior angles of a triangle to the sum of the interior angles of a square.

Start point check

Bisectors group memory game

In Stage 8, students learned how to construct perpendicular bisectors and angle bisectors. These constructions will be needed again for some of the activities in this chapter. If students do not recall the methods, they can play this group memory game.

Students work in groups of two to four. The aim is for every student in the group to construct a perpendicular bisector and an angle bisector correctly and accurately. The instructions for these two constructions are fixed somewhere in the class (for example, on the teacher's desk, or on the wall at the back of the room).

A group can only send one student at a time to look at the instructions. That student then returns to the group and describes the next step in the construction, and all of the group members follow it. This continues until everyone in the group has completed the two constructions.

Adaptation: Using a timer, allow 'observation periods' of 10 to 20 seconds, during which one student from each group is allowed to look at the instructions. Between observation periods, allow one to two minutes for the groups to discuss and draw.

Investigation: Proving that the angle bisector method works

This guided investigation leads students through the steps in proving the angle bisector construction method, which they learned to use in Stage 8. Thinking about how a construction method works can help students to remember the steps in the method, and to see it as a logic problem rather than simply a series of instructions.

The diagram shows an angle ABC that has been bisected using the standard method.

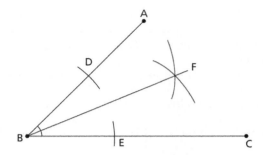

Draw an angle of around 60° and construct the angle bisector. (Your construction does not have to be exactly the same size as the one shown here.)

1. Label points A–F on your construction as shown in the diagram.

2. Explain why line BD must be the same length as line BE. Add markings on your diagram to show that the lengths are equal.

3. Draw a straight line joining D and F.

4. Draw a straight line joining E and F.

5. Explain why line DF must be the same length as line EF. Add markings on your diagram to show that the lengths are equal.

6. Explain why triangles BDF and BEF must be congruent.

7. Explain why angles ABF and CBF must be equal (and so the original angle, ABC, must have been successfully bisected).

Extension: Give students only the diagram and the instruction to draw lines DF and EF (and also, if needed, the hint that the proof involves congruent triangles), and ask them to write a proof.

Students can then research how to prove that the perpendicular bisector method works. This is more challenging than the proof above. Proofs using congruent triangles can be found on the internet.

Discussion ideas

Probing questions	Teacher prompts
Explain how the method for inscribing a square in a circle ensures that the resulting quadrilateral is a square.	Ask this question just after students have practised this construction. How does the construction method ensure that the side lengths are all equal? Alternatively, what are the properties of the diagonals of a square, and how does the construction method ensure that the diagonals have these properties?

Probing questions	Teacher prompts
A student tries to inscribe a square in a circle. He draws a diameter and then bisects it with a line that is not perpendicular. Without doing the construction, predict the shape he makes when he joins the four points on the circumference. Justify your prediction. He tries again, but this time he draws a perpendicular to the diameter that does not bisect the diameter. Without doing the construction, predict the shape he makes when he joins the four points on the circumference. Justify your prediction.	For both questions, think about the properties of the diagonals of the constructed shape. (The diagonals of the first shape have equal length – both equal the diameter – and bisect each other, but not at right angles. The shape is a rectangle.) (The diagonals of the second shape have different lengths and intersect at right angles. One diagonal is bisected and the other is not. The shape is a kite.) Students can check their answers by trying the constructions.
Explain how the method for inscribing a regular hexagon in a circle ensures that the hexagon is regular.	Ask this question just after students have practised this construction. If students are unsure, ask what they know about the sides of a regular hexagon. How does the construction make the sides equal – or equivalently, how does it ensure that the vertices are equal distances apart?
Describe what happens to the size of the interior angles of polygons as the number of sides increases.	Students may say that the angles get smaller, by assuming that there is some angle (perhaps 360°) that is divided between the interior angles. Prompt students to think about the interior angles in equilateral triangles and in squares, or to sketch polygons with increasing numbers of sides.

Common errors/misconceptions

Misconception	Strategies to address
Confusing the three methods for constructing a perpendicular to a line (perpendicular bisector, perpendicular from point to line, perpendicular through point on line).	Students could play a group memory game (similar to the one in the 'Start point check') to help them remember the three methods. Alternatively, they could play charades in small groups, where one student acts out one of the methods (using a prompt sheet if needed) without actually using any drawing tools, and the others try to say which method it is.
Allowing the compass opening to change between drawing the two final arcs when constructing the perpendicular from a point to a line or the perpendicular to a point on a line.	Demonstrate, or ask students to try, doing the construction but changing the compass opening significantly between drawing the final two arcs. It should be obvious that the resulting 'perpendicular' is not, in fact, perpendicular. Students are less likely to make this type of mistake if they are able to understand how the method works. In one of the investigations in this chapter, 'Proving that the perpendicular construction methods work', students work through a proof that the construction method for a perpendicular from a point to a line does, in fact, produce a perpendicular. Students can think about which part of the proof is undermined if they change the compass opening between drawing the final two arcs. The method used to construct a perpendicular through a point on a line is the same as the method used to bisect an angle when the angle is 180° (and

Misconception	Strategies to address
	students are asked to show this in the investigation 'Proving that the perpendicular construction methods work'). The starter investigation 'Proving that the angle bisector method works' leads students through a proof that the construction method for an angle bisector does, in fact, bisect the angle. Students can think about which part of the proof is undermined if they change the compass opening between drawing the final two arcs.
Thinking that in any construction, the compass opening must always stay the same throughout	After students have practised the construction of a perpendicular to a point on a line, which involves drawing three arcs in total, have a class discussion on whether the compass opening needs to stay the same throughout. If needed, demonstrate (or ask a student to demonstrate) that the compass opening can be changed after drawing the first arc, without affecting the accuracy of the construction.
	The same applies to the construction of a perpendicular from a point to a line.
	Emphasise that when the compass opening does need to stay the same, there is always a reason for this.
	One of the investigations for this chapter, 'Proving that the perpendicular construction methods work', involves proving why the method for constructing a perpendicular from a point to a line works. This will help students to think about which distances in this construction need to be equal, and which do not.

Developing conceptual understanding

9Gs6 Use a straight edge and compasses to:

- **construct the perpendicular from a point to a line and the perpendicular from a point on a line**
- **inscribe squares, equilateral triangles, and regular hexagons and octagons by constructing equal divisions of a circle.**

- Ask students to check that their compasses do not have a loose hinge, which can cause the compasses to change their opening at times when this is not wanted, leading to inaccurate constructions. Remind students that the pencil lead of the compasses needs to be sharp.

- FIX: You can model construction methods for students on the board using large-scale geometry equipment, or by using online construction software in which the movements of the ruler, pencil and compasses are shown, such as https://www.mathspad.co.uk/i/construct.php. Students can use this software to explore and invent a wide range of different constructions (and investigate what happens when different mistakes are made in the construction methods they have learned), since it allows constructions to be performed more quickly than by drawing.

- Ask students to carry out the construction methods they have learned, but to introduce one mistake (such as incorrectly positioning the compass point, or changing the compass opening at an inappropriate time) into each method and find out what effect this has on the result. Students could write their findings as an investigation, describing each mistake and demonstrating and describing (and if they can, explaining) its effect. Alternatively, they could share the work in small groups, with each member trying one incorrect method and presenting their findings to the rest of the group.

- Ask students to try following a method for inscribing a regular 12-sided polygon (dodecagon) in a circle:
  - First draw the six arcs as for inscribing a hexagon, making six points on the circumference of the circle.
  - Join two neighbouring points to the centre of the circle.
  - Bisect the acute angle this makes, extending the bisector so that it intersects the circumference.
  - Starting with the compass point at this intersection point and with the opening the same as for the before, go round the circle making equally spaced arcs.
  - Join the 12 points on the circumference to make a regular 12-sided polygon, or dodecagon.

  (This method can be used to construct a dodecagon for the inscribed polygon investigation later in this chapter.)

  Ask students what other shapes could be made by opening the compasses to smaller divisions of the radius of the circle.

STRETCH: Ask students to try to work out how to inscribe a dodecagon in a circle, but without giving the set of instructions above. For this, students could use the online construction software at https://www.mathspad.co.uk/i/construct.php, so that they can undo incorrect steps rather than having to erase individual pencil lines or start again.

STRETCH: The web page http://www.cutoutfoldup.com/108-fold-a-regular-octagon-method-i-.php shows a method for folding a regular octagon from a square piece of paper. After students have tried this, ask them to write instructions for following this method by constructing the lines (using a straight edge and compasses) instead of creating them by folding.

End of chapter mental maths exercise

1. Sketch the construction lines for a perpendicular from a point to a line.	4. Sketch the construction lines for inscribing a square in a circle.
2. Sketch the construction lines for a perpendicular through a point on a line.	5. Sketch the construction lines for inscribing a regular hexagon in a circle.
3. Sketch the construction lines for inscribing an equilateral triangle in a circle.	6. Sketch the construction lines for inscribing a regular octagon in a circle.

Technology recommendations

- Use web-based games to create constructions.

  The web-based game https://www.euclidea.xyz/en/game/packs presents players with a series of construction challenges, beginning with very simple constructions that students will already know, and becoming increasingly difficult. Completing challenges unlocks new construction shortcuts and new challenges. The game can be installed on mobile phones.

The website https://sciencevsmagic.net/geo/ is similar, but there are fewer challenges (shown on the right-hand side of the screen) and students can try them in any order. Students can also use this website for creating their own constructions.

STRETCH: The website http://www.robocompass.com/app lets the user write a step-by-step program to carry out a particular construction. Programs consist of a series of simple commands. The drop-down menu 'Examples' shows a series of example programs which can be selected and then run by clicking on the play button (green arrow) near the top left. Click 'How to' at the top right to see the list of possible commands. This activity is likely to be of particular interest to students who enjoy computer programming.

Investigation/research tasks

• **Proving that the perpendicular construction methods work**

1. Perpendicular from a point to a line:

   a) Construct a perpendicular from a point to a line, and label points on your construction as shown in the diagram.

   b) On your construction, draw lines PA, PB, CA and CB.

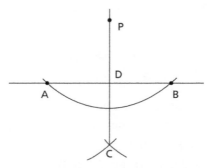

   c) Explain why line PA must be the same length as line PB. Add markings on your diagram to show that they are the same length.

   d) Explain why line AC must be the same length as line BC. Add markings on your diagram to show that they are the same length.

   e) Explain why triangle PAC must be congruent to triangle PBC.

   f) Explain why angle APC must equal angle BPC. Add markings on your diagram to show that these angles are equal.

   g) Explain why triangle APD must be congruent to triangle BPD.

   h) Explain why angle PDA must be congruent to angle PDB.

   i) Explain why angles PDA and PDB must sum to 180°.

   j) Explain why angles PDA and PDB must both be right angles (and so the constructed line must be perpendicular to the original line).

2. Show that the method for constructing a perpendicular through a point on a line is equivalent to the method for bisecting an angle of 180°.

Extension: Students could be given the proof for the construction of the perpendicular from a point to a line with some steps missing and asked to work out the intermediate steps. Alternatively, ask students to construct the perpendicular and add the lines PA, PB, CA and CB to their construction, and then try to work out a proof. (You could give the hint that the proof involves congruent triangles.)

- **Inscribed polygon investigation**   *Problem solving*

    In this investigation, you will draw inscribed regular polygons with increasing numbers of sides (equilateral triangle, square, hexagon and octagon), and investigate their perimeters.

    Inscribe each polygon in a separate circle, and make the **radius** of every circle 5.0 cm.

    Keep an organised record of: the type of polygon, the length of one of its sides (measured with a ruler), and its perimeter (calculated from the measured length). When you have finished, answer the questions below.

    1. Calculate the circumference of the circle.
    2. Describe the pattern followed by the perimeters of polygons with increasing numbers of sides.
    3. Make a prediction about the perimeter of a regular pentagon inscribed in a circle.
    4. For a regular inscribed polygon with a very large number of sides (say, over 10 000):
        a) State the other shape that it closely resembles.
        b) Predict its perimeter and explain your prediction.

Extension: Ask students to inscribe a regular dodecagon (12-sided shape) in addition to the other polygons. (A method for this construction is described in the 'Developing conceptual understanding' section.)

You may wish to tell students that a similar method was used by the Chinese mathematician Liu Hui in the 3rd century to find an approximate value of pi (π). However, he used a regular 96-gon (96-sided polygon) and he found its perimeter by calculation instead of by measurement.

Solution:

Inscribed regular shape	Side length (cm)	Perimeter (cm)
triangle	8.7	26.0
square	7.1	28.3
hexagon	5.0	30.0
octagon	3.8	30.6
dodecagon	2.6	31.1

1. $\pi d \approx 3.14 \times 10 = 31.4$ cm.
2. The perimeters increase.
3. It lies between 28.3 cm and 30.0 cm.
4. a)   Circle
   b)   31.4(15...) – the circumference of the circle

- **Dividing hexagons and octagons**

For each part of the questions below, first sketch your ideas. When you think you have found a method that works, construct it.

1. Find methods, using only a straight edge and compasses, to accurately divide a regular hexagon into:
   a) two congruent shapes (two methods, each making a different shape)
   b) three congruent shapes
   c) four congruent shapes
   d) six congruent shapes (two methods, each making a different shape).
   Name the shapes made by each method.

2. Find methods, using only a straight edge and compasses, to accurately divide a regular octagon into:
   a) two congruent shapes (two methods, each making a different shape)
   b) four congruent shapes (two methods, each making a different shape)
   c) eight congruent shapes (two methods, each making a different shape).
   Name the shapes made by each method.

Solution:

Some possible methods are described below.

1. Dividing a hexagon:
   a) Method 1: Draw a line joining two opposite vertices to make two congruent trapezia (which are isosceles). Method 2: Construct the perpendicular bisector of one side and extend it so that it meets the opposite side, to make two congruent irregular pentagons.
   b) From the centre of the hexagon (which is the centre of the circle in which it is inscribed), draw lines to alternate vertices. This makes three congruent rhombuses. Draw a line joining two opposite vertices. Construct the perpendicular bisector of this line. This makes four congruent trapezia.
   c) Method 1: Draw lines joining each pair of opposite vertices, to make six equilateral triangles. Method 2: Construct the perpendicular bisector of a side and extend it to the opposite side, and repeat for the other two pairs of opposite sides. This makes six congruent kites.

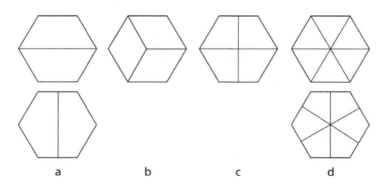

a   b   c   d

2. Dividing an octagon:
   a) Method 1: Draw a line joining two opposite vertices to make two congruent irregular pentagons. Method 2: Construct the perpendicular bisector of one side and extend it to the opposite side, to make two congruent irregular hexagons.

b) Method 1: Draw a line joining two opposite vertices, and draw the line perpendicular to this that joins two opposite vertices, to make four congruent kites. Method 2: Construct the perpendicular bisector of a side and extend it to the opposite side, and then construct the perpendicular bisector of this bisector. This makes four congruent irregular pentagons.

c) Method 1: Draw lines joining pairs of opposite vertices, to make eight congruent isosceles triangles. Method 2: Construct the perpendicular bisector of a side and extend it to the opposite side, and repeat for the other three pairs of opposite sides, to make eight congruent kites.

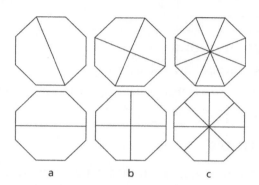

a   b   c

TIP: It could take students a long time to construct all of the hexagons and octagons needed for this activity. If they have already had enough practice at inscribing these polygons in circles, you could give them copies of the photocopiable resources 'Hexagons' and 'Octagons' which contain ready-drawn hexagons and octagons to dissect.

Pythagoras' theorem

Learning objectives

Learning objectives covered in this chapter: 9Gs7
- Know and use Pythagoras' theorem to solve two-dimensional problems involving right-angled triangles.

Key terms
- hypotenuse
- theorem
- pythagoras' theorem

Prior knowledge assumptions
- Students know the types of triangle and their names.
- Students can find the square of a number, and the square root of a number.

Guidance on the hook

Purpose: This activity gives students a hands-on way to discover Pythagoras' theorem.

Use of the hook: Make copies of the photocopiable resources 'Pythagoras dissection 1', 'Pythagoras dissection 2' and 'Pythagoras dissection 3', and give one diagram of each of the three types to each student. (Each resource sheet has two copies of the same diagram on a single page.)

Each diagram shows a way of cutting up the two smaller squares on a right-angled triangle. For each one, students should try to rearrange the shapes to exactly cover the largest square.

Solutions:

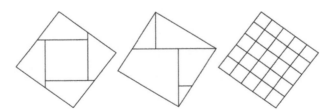

Adaptation: There are websites where students can do this type of activity using virtual manipulatives, for example: http://www.etudes.ru/en/etudes/pythagorean-theorem/.

Extension: Students could try to create their own dissection puzzle based on the squares on a right-angled triangle's sides.

BEWARE: For the third diagram, tell students they do not have to cut out all of the very small squares individually. It is possible to cut them into larger groups and rearrange those to fill the largest square.

Starter ideas

Mental maths starter

What is 3^2?	What is 5^2?	What is 11^2?	What is 20^2?
What is $\sqrt{16}$?	What is $\sqrt{49}$?	What is $\sqrt{64}$?	What is $\sqrt{144}$?
Find the area of a square with side length 6 cm.	Find the side length of a square with area $100\,\text{m}^2$.	Find the area of a square with side length 30 m.	Find the side length of a square with area $81\,\text{cm}^2$.
What is $\sqrt{3^2 + 4^2}$?	What is $\sqrt{6^2 + 8^2}$?	What is $\sqrt{30^2 + 40^2}$?	What is $\sqrt{5^2 + 12^2}$?
Which two integers does $\sqrt{2}$ lie between?	Which two integers does $\sqrt{11}$ lie between?	Which two integers does $\sqrt{50}$ lie between?	Which two integers does $\sqrt{95}$ lie between?

Start point check

Squares and square roots loop cards

This activity can be used to check whether students remember the meaning of squaring and square rooting, and can calculate squares correctly and remember some of the perfect squares up to 100.

Give students the set of squares and square roots loop cards (in the photocopiable resources). Each card contains a number on the left side and an instruction to find the square or the square root of a number on the right side.

Ask students to find pairs of equal numbers (for example, $\sqrt{49}$ = 7) and place them next to each other. If they do this for all of the cards they can make a complete loop.

Adaptation: Instead of handing out sets of dominoes to students, give students mini-whiteboards and ask them to write squares or square roots of particular numbers and hold up their answers.

Activity: Make a right-angled triangle using knotted string

Divide students into groups of three and give each group a length of string. Ask the groups to make a loop which is divided by knots (or by marks on the string) into 12 equal sections. (It is possible to do this without a ruler, by creating one section and then folding the string back on itself and marking it to make the next equal section.)

Then ask the groups to pull their string into triangles, finding the triangles they can make if each side length must be a whole number of sections. Students try to find a triangle which has a right angle. (This is the triangle that has side lengths of 3, 4 and 5 parts.)

Tell students that there is evidence that this method was used in ancient Egypt to make right angles when laying out new buildings.

> TIP: It is not essential to tie the ends of the string to make a loop. Instead, one student can hold the two string ends together to make one of the vertices of a triangle.

Adaptation: To save time, give students strings with the knots already tied.

Adaptation: Do this as a whole-class activity: prepare a very long knotted rope and, in a large space such as a gym or playground, ask the class to pull the rope into a triangle with side lengths of 3, 4 and 5 parts each. Ask what they notice about one of the angles.

Discussion ideas

Probing questions	Teacher prompts
What is the square of $\sqrt{9}$? What is the value of the square root of 4^2?	These questions test whether students really understand the meaning of 'square root'. If they are unsure of the answers, have a class discussion, with examples, about what square rooting means (finding the number that squares to make another number).
What kinds of triangle can be right-angled? How do you know?	Ask students to try to draw a right-angled triangle that is equilateral, or isosceles, or scalene. Students may not realise that an isosceles triangle can be right-angled; ask for the sum of the two smaller angles in a right-angled triangle, and then ask if it is possible for these two angles to be equal.
If you are given the lengths of a triangle's sides, how can you work out whether the triangle is right-angled, without making an accurate construction of the triangle?	What does Pythagoras' theorem say about the sides of a right-angled triangle? What can you say about the two sides of the equation for a particular triangle, if it is right-angled?
If you are given two of the angles of a triangle (and neither of them is a right angle), can you work out whether it is right-angled? If you are given only one of the angles of a triangle, can you work out whether it is right-angled? Can you ever work out from one angle that a triangle is *not* right-angled?	How can you find the third angle of the triangle? If you are told that a triangle has one angle of 30°, is it possible for the triangle to be: right-angled; not right-angled? If a triangle is right-angled, what do the other two angles add up to? What is the largest value either of these two angles can have?
A triangle with side lengths 3 cm, 4 cm and 5 cm is right-angled. If you enlarge this triangle, you get a similar triangle. Think about what type of triangle the enlarged triangle is. Suggest possible side lengths for this triangle. (This is a 'Think about' question in the Student's Book chapter.)	What is the relationship between the side lengths of two similar triangles? For example, what would be the side lengths of the image of a 3-4-5 triangle under an enlargement of scale factor 2? What would be the side lengths of images of a 3-4-5 triangle enlarged by different scale factors?

Common errors/misconceptions

Misconception	Strategies to address
Thinking that x^2 gives the same result as $2x$.	Remind students that $x^2 = x \times x$ and $2x = 2 \times x$. Point out that there are only two values of x for which $x^2 = 2x$, and ask students if they can find the two values (0 and 2). Demonstrate, or ask students to show, that for other values of x, the expressions x^2 and $2x$ have different values.

Misconception	Strategies to address
Thinking that the unknown side length is always found by squaring and *adding* the other two side lengths, and then square rooting.	When teaching this topic, emphasise that c in the formula $c^2 = a^2 + b^2$ always represents the length of the hypotenuse. Ask students to rearrange this formula to make a^2 or b^2 the subject. (Alternatively, express the formula as $h^2 = a^2 + b^2$ to remind students that h is the hypotenuse length.) Show examples of how to calculate a side length when that side is not the hypotenuse (in which case a subtraction is needed).
Omitting the final step – taking the square root – when finding the length of a side.	Students often simply forget this step. Encourage them to check whether their answer seems reasonable. Consider the example below. 2 cm x cm 8 cm If students find the value of x to be $8^2 - 2^2 = 60$, they can compare this answer with the hypotenuse to see that it is longer, and therefore they must have made a mistake.

Developing conceptual understanding

9Gs7 know and use Pythagoras' theorem to solve two-dimensional problems involving right-angled triangles.

- FIX: Before teaching Pythagoras' theorem, check that students can find x from $x^2 =$ constant (some students may think they need to square both sides); or from $\sqrt{x} =$ constant (some students may think they need to square root both sides). If students are unsure how to solve these equations, remind them that squaring and square rooting are inverse functions of each other, and discuss what this means. An outline of how to continue the discussion is given below.

- Think about how to solve the equation $x + 2 = 5$. Below are two different ways to approach this.

  - You can perform the same operation to both sides of an equation, to create a new equation which is also correct. If you subtract 2 from both sides of this equation, you get $x = 3$.

  - To find x you need to 'undo' what has been done to x (adding 2), by performing the inverse function on 5. The inverse function of 'add 2' is 'subtract 2', so you subtract 2 from 5 and find that $x = 3$. (A related way to think about this is to imagine covering the x with your finger and reading the equation as 'something plus 2 equals 5'. From this you can deduce that the 'something' is 3.)

- You can think in similar ways to solve the equation $\sqrt{x} = 5$.

  - If you square $\sqrt{x}$, the definition of $\sqrt{x}$ tells you that you get $\sqrt{x} \times \sqrt{x} = x$. If you square both sides, you get $x = 5^2 = 25$.

- o You need to 'undo' what has been done to x (square rooting), by performing the inverse function on 5. So square 5 to find that $x = 25$. (Or you can read the equation as 'The square root of something is 5. What is the something?')

- You can do the same to help you solve the equation $x^2 = 25$.

  - o If you square root x^2, you get x. If you square root both sides, you get $x = \sqrt{25} = 5$.

  - o You need to 'undo' what has been done to x (squaring), by performing the inverse function on 25. So, take the square root of 25 to find that $x = 5$. (Or read the equation as 'The square of something is 25. What is the something?')

- FIX: The exercises in the Student's Book involve working with right-angled triangles in different orientations, but if students are finding this difficult, suggest that they first rotate the image to an orientation that they find easier to work with.

- FIX: Check that students know how to calculate squares and square roots using a calculator. If a calculation of the form $\sqrt{3^2 + 4^2}$ is typed incorrectly, it can result in the calculation $\sqrt{3^2} + 4^2 = 19$. This can be avoided by using brackets: $\sqrt{(3^2 + 4^2)}$, or on some calculators, by typing the whole expression $3^2 + 4^2$ inside the box inside the square root.

STRETCH: Ask students to rearrange the formula $c^2 = a^2 + b^2$ to make a or b the subject. (Note that when using the formula to find side length a or b, students may find it easier to substitute lengths into the formula before rearranging it.)

End of chapter mental maths exercise

1. A right-angled triangle has shorter sides of length 6 cm and 8 cm. Find the length of the hypotenuse.	3. A right-angled triangle has a hypotenuse of length 5 cm and another side of length 3 cm. Find the length of the third side.
2. A right-angled triangle has shorter sides of length 60 cm and 80 cm. Find the length of the hypotenuse.	4. A right-angled triangle has a hypotenuse of length 50 cm and another side of length 30 cm. Find the length of the third side.

Technology recommendations

- Use the internet for interactive demonstrations.

  The website http://www.interactive-maths.com/pythagoras-theorem.html contains links to a series of interactive demonstrations of Pythagoras' theorem and examples of its use. These can be displayed on the board and used for class discussion, or investigated by students.

- Use the internet for research.

  Students can use the internet to research the many different proofs of Pythagoras' theorem. Some require knowledge and skills that most students will not have at this stage, but others can be understood more easily. The website https://www.cut-the-knot.org/pythagoras/ shows over 100 proofs.

Investigation/research tasks

- ### Non-right-angled triangles investigation   *Problem solving*

    1. Draw at least four different triangles that are not right-angled and which have all three angles less than 90°. Label the longest side of each triangle c, and the other two sides a and b (in any order). (Note that for these triangles c is *not* the hypotenuse, since only right-angled triangles have a hypotenuse.)

    2. For each triangle, measure a, b and c and calculate c^2 and also $a^2 + b^2$. Write your results in a table.

    3. Write down what you notice about the relationship between c^2 and $a^2 + b^2$.

    4. Repeat all of the steps above, but this time for at least four different triangles which are not right-angled and which have one angle greater than 90°.

    5. Write down what you notice about the relationship between c^2 and $a^2 + b^2$ for these triangles.

    6. Summarise what you have discovered about non-right-angled triangles.

Extension: Without drawing, check whether equilateral triangles obey the rules you have found.

Solution:

For triangles with all angles less than 90°, $c^2 < a^2 + b^2$.

For triangles with one angle greater than 90°, $c^2 > a^2 + b^2$.

This means that if we know whether a triangle has an angle greater than 90°, and we know the lengths of two of the sides, we can write an inequality relating the length of the third side to the lengths of the other two sides.

Extension: In an equilateral triangle, all three angles equal 60° and all three sides have the same length. So, if the side length is 1, for example, then $a = b = c = 1$. Then $a^2 + b^2 = 2$ and $c^2 = 1$. So, for this equilateral triangle, $c^2 < a^2 + b^2$, which fits the rule for triangles with all angles less than 90°. In general, for an equilateral triangle with side length x,

$a^2 + b^2 = 2x^2$ and $c^2 = x^2$. So $c^2 < a^2 + b^2$ (specifically, $c^2 = \frac{1}{2}(a^2 + b^2)$ for all possible values of x.

> TIP: Students will need a protractor or set square to ensure that they draw triangles with or without an angle greater than 90° as required.

- ### Pythagorean triples

    The numbers 3, 4, 5 are a 'Pythagorean triple'. This means that they are all integers, and the sum of the squares of the two smaller numbers equals the square of the largest number: $3^2 + 4^2 = 5^2$. So it is possible to construct a right-angled triangle with side lengths 3 , 4 and 5 units. (The units can be centimetres, metres, or any other unit of length).

    Search for other Pythagorean triples with the largest number $c \le 100$. Try to do this in an organised way, keeping a record of your findings. You could use a spreadsheet program for this investigation.

    Extension: The numbers 3, 4 and 5 are described as a 'primitive Pythagorean triple', because they cannot be divided by a common factor. (The numbers 6, 8 and 10 are a Pythagorean triple that is not primitive, since all three numbers can be divided by 2 to give 3, 4 and 5.) Sort the Pythagorean triples you have found into primitive and non-primitive triples, showing your working.

    Adaptation: If students need more support, give some or all of the following guidance on how use a spreadsheet program for this investigation. The guidance below is for Excel.

---

1. Use the top row for values of *a* (the length of one of the two smaller sides). Type the number 1 into cell B1 and type the number 2 into cell C1. Select both of these cells at once, and use the drag handle (a small square at the bottom right of the selection box) to drag to the right until you reach the highest value of *a* you would like to test. This will create a series of consecutive integers.

2. Use the leftmost column for values of *b* (the length of one of the two smaller sides). Type the number 1 into cell A2 and the number 2 into cell A3. Select both of these cells at once, and use the drag handle to drag downwards until you reach the highest value of *b* you would like to test. This will create another series of consecutive integers.

3. In cell B2, type the formula: =SQRT($A2^2+B$1^2) exactly as written here. This will calculate $\sqrt{1^2 + 1^2}$.

4. Select cell B2. Use the drag handle to drag to the right, going as far to the right as the highest value of *a* in the top row.

5. Select the row you have just filled, starting from B2 on the left. Drag the drag handle down, going as far down as the highest value of *b* in the leftmost column.

6. The table now shows values of c^2 calculated from the values of *a* and *b* in the top row and the leftmost column.

BEWARE: When entering the formula =SQRT($A2^2+B$1^2) it is important to type it exactly. The '$' signs tell the program not to change the column reference ('A') in the formula when the formula is copied to the right, and not to change the row reference ('1') when the formula is copied down.

BEWARE: The formatting of the cells affects how easy it is to find the integer values of *c*. Make sure the values in the cells are not rounded to the nearest whole number, or else all possible values of *c* will appear to be integers. In Excel the cell formatting type 'General' displays any integers with no digits after the decimal place and any non-integers with several digits after the decimal place – making integers easy to spot.

Uses of Pythagoras' theorem   *Research*

Use the internet to research uses of Pythagoras' theorem. Find out at least three uses, and for each one, explain how Pythagoras' theorem is used.

TIP: If students are finding it difficult to find suitable websites, suggest that they search for 'uses of Pythagoras theorem'.

TIP: Students could present their work as a poster. Encourage them to aim their writing at other students of their age, and not to write about anything that they cannot understand and explain in their own words.

- **Construct a 3-4-5 triangle inside a square**

   1. Draw a square with side length at least 10 cm.

   2. Find the mid-points of the top and right-hand sides.

   3. Draw lines joining the mid-point of the top to the two bottom corners.

   4. Join the mid-point of the right-hand side to the bottom left corner.

   5. You have now created several triangles. Use a protractor to check which triangles are right-angled.

   6. One of the right-angled triangles is similar to a triangle with side lengths 3, 4 and 5 (which means that its side lengths are in the ratio 3 : 4 : 5). Use measurement and calculation to find out which triangle it is, showing your working.

BEWARE: For this method to work, students need to start with an accurately drawn square. They can either inscribe a square in a circle by construction, or draw the square on squared or graph paper.

TIP: Another method for constructing a right-angled triangle with sides in the ratio 3 : 4 : 5 without using a protractor is to draw a 'daisy wheel', within which a 3-4-5 triangle can be drawn. Instructions for this can be found on the internet.

Solution:

The diagram shows the construction. (The shaded triangle will have lengths 3 cm, 4 cm and 5 cm only if the side of the square has length $2\sqrt{5}$ cm. Otherwise this triangle will be similar to a 3-4-5 triangle.)

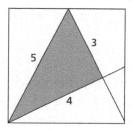

Bearings, maps and loci

Learning objectives

Learning objectives covered in this chapter: 9Gp7, 9Gp8, 9Gp9

- Use bearings (angles measured clockwise from the north) to solve problems involving distance and direction.
- Make and use scale drawings and interpret maps.
- Find by reasoning the locus of a point that moves at a given distance from a fixed point, or at a given distance from a fixed straight line.

Key terms

- bearing
- scale drawing
- locus

Prior knowledge assumptions

- Students can draw and measure angles with a protractor.
- Students can draw parallel lines using a set square and ruler.
- Students can multiply and divide decimal numbers.
- Students can round numbers to a given degree of accuracy.

Guidance on the hook

Purpose: To revise compass points and begin to develop the idea of describing movement in particular directions.

Use of the hook: Ask the students what they know or remember about compass points. Draw a simple compass on the board (four points), and check they know the eight points of the compass by asking 'what is the direction half way between north and east?', etc. Also ask the students about when they look at a map which way is north? How do they know? Discuss the convention of north always being 'up' the page.

Give each of the students a 10 by 10 grid, and explain that one 'move' is from one line intersection to the next (vertically, horizontally, diagonally). Ask the students to mark the point 'A' on the grid, then work through the questions in the Student's Book, with the students working individually, but then checking their solutions in pairs.

What happens if they move the position of point A? How does that change their answers?

Can they make up their own questions about movements and directions? Encourage students to use compass points to describe their moves.

Adaptation: If students find it difficult to visualise moves, you could make this a more practical exercise by using a larger grid with rods or rulers to represent moves.

Extension: If A was in the centre of the grid, are there any intersections/points they would not be able to reach in five moves or fewer?

TIP: Ask students to use different colours to record their answers to different questions, so they can record all their answers on one grid rather than using several grids. Make sure they include a key.

Starter ideas

Mental maths starter

How many metres are there in 2.5 km?	How many centimetres are there in 12.4 m?	How many centimetres are there in 2 km?	How many centimetres are there in 4.2 km?
Round 12.37 to one decimal place.	Round 15.59 to the nearest whole number.	Round 1424 to the nearest ten.	Round 1582 to the nearest hundred.
Calculate 1.4 × 1000.	Calculate 13.65 × 1000.	Calculate 5.86 × 10 000.	Calculate 2.9 × 100 000.
A rectangular garden measures 30 m by 12 m. What is its area?	A rectangular room measures 8 m by 7.5 m. What is its area?	A rectangular field measures 250 m by 120 m. What is its area?	A rectangular garden measures 32 m by 12.5 m. What is its area?
Three lines meet at a point. The angles between them are 60°, 180° and x degrees. What is x?	Three lines meet at a point. The angles between them are 110°, 135° and x degrees. What is x?	Four lines meet at a point. Three of the angles between them are 45°, 65° and 120°. What is the fourth angle?	Four lines meet at a point. Two of the angles between them are 55° and 65°. the other two angles are x and $2x$. What is x?

Compass directions activity

Using parcel tape or chalk, make a large north arrow on the floor of the classroom (or outside). Ask a student to stand at the (non-pointed) end of the arrow and point east/south/west. Ask the other students to check their accuracy.

Ask another student to stand there and point out north east, south east, south west, north west – again ask other students to check/agree directions.

Point out objects in suitable places (for example a window, the door, or if outside, a building or a tree) and ask students to identify the direction of the object. You could 'hot seat' the students in turn at the end of the arrow and do a mixture of direction and object questions to check understanding (fairly quick fire if possible).

Locus activity

This activity can be done in the classroom or outside, depending on the facilities available.

Stand in a space. Tell the students that you are going to ask them to stand in various positions. In each case ask them to check each other's position when they think they are in place:

1. Ask the students to all stand 2 m away from you. Give them a short time to get in position. What shape do they make? Why?

2. Ask the students to stand 2 m away from a straight edge (wall, edge of playground). What shape do they make now?

3. Ask the students to stand the same distance from two straight edges that are at right angles to each other (walls, edges of playground). How can they describe their position?

4. Stand about 2 m from the straight edge. Ask the students to stand the same distance away from you as they are away from the wall. What shape do they make?

5. Hold one end of a metre rule. Ask a student to hold the other end (so that you are two points at the end of a short straight line. Ask the students to stand 2 m away from you. What shape do they make now? How is it similar/different to the first shape they made?

6. Stand two students about 4 m apart. Ask the other students to stand so that they are the same distance from both students. (When they have worked this out, link back to previous work on perpendicular bisectors).

Start point check

Show the students a diagram like the one below:

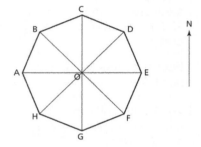

Ask the students:
- Which point lies south of O?
- Which point is west of O?
- Which point is north west of O?
- Which point is south west of O?
- Which point is south east of B?
- Which point(s) is(are) north of G?
- What is size of the angle COE?
- What is the size of the angle COD?

Discussion ideas

Probing questions	Teacher prompts
If the bearing of B from A is 050°, how can we find the bearing of A from B?	Can we draw a diagram? On your diagram, can you find some parallel lines? How can the parallel lines help you? You may need to extend some of the lines to find some corresponding angles.
If a ship sails on a bearing of 162° instead of 161°, how far off course are they after sailing for 50 km? 100 km?	Can we draw a diagram? How could we improve the accuracy of the diagram? Do you think this error would make a significant difference to the ship? How do you think sailors make sure they are accurate with their bearings?

Probing questions	Teacher prompts
What does a scale of 1 : 10 000 represent?	If there was a length of 1 cm on the map, how many cm would that be in real life? How could we write that more neatly? What about if the length on the map was 4 cm? 7 cm? How many cm would represent a length of 1 km? 10 km?
If you wanted to draw a scale diagram of a house measuring 20 m by 32 m, what would be a sensible scale to use?	You need your scale drawing to be big enough to see all the details clearly, but not so big that it doesn't fit neatly on your piece of paper. Measure your paper. What do you think would be a good scale?
How many points are there that are exactly one metre away from a tree trunk? What shape do they make?	Imagine you are above the tree looking down on it. What shape would you see the points make? Can you draw a diagram to show your answer? STRETCH: Imagine you were 3 metres away from the tree looking at it sideways on, what shape would you see?

Common errors/misconceptions

Misconception	Strategies to address
With statements such as 'Find the bearing of A from B' students start from A rather than B.	Ask the students 'how do I get to <a local landmark> from here?' Get them to give directions – where do they begin their directions from? The **from** place – it is the same with bearings, you have to give the direction **from** where you start **to** where you are looking at or wanting to go.
Not realising that the units in a scale are the same so that 1 : 10 can mean 1 cm to 10 cm or 1 m to 10 m or 1 km to 10 km.	Write the ratio with the units in, for example, 1 cm : 10 cm, then multiply both sides by 100 (rules of ratios) to give 100 cm : 1000 cm = 1 m : 10 m. Repeat the process to give 1 km : 10 km. Remind students that if no units are given, the units are always assumed to be the same.
The locus of a set of points around the end of a line are often drawn as a rectangle rather than a semi-circle.	Draw a line segment on a plain A3 piece of paper. Attach a pencil to a piece of string and measure off 5 cm. Ask the students about the points that are 5 cm from the line and draw the straight bits, keeping the other end of the string on the line segment. Ask the students what happens at the end of the line. Keeping the string straight, move the pencil around the end of the line to draw a semi-circle. Repeat down the other side of the line and other end.

Developing conceptual understanding

9Gp7 Use bearings (angles measured clockwise from the north) to solve problems involving distance and direction.

- Check the students' understanding of compass points using the starter activity. How can they describe directions in between the compass points? Explain that more accuracy is needed. This can be demonstrated by showing how quickly angles diverge from two adjacent compass points. Introduce the idea of a bearing as an angle measured clockwise from north, and the convention of writing bearings as three figures.

- FIX: Using the compass points and bearings sheet from the photocopiable resources, ask the students to complete the bearings for the eight compass points (this can then be referred back to as necessary when they are answering questions).

- Consolidate understanding by giving or showing the students a map (such as that in the photocopiable resources) and asking them to find various bearings using questions such as 'What is the bearing of the cave from the lighthouse?' Alternatively, ask the students to work in pairs asking each other questions on bearings from the map and checking each other's answers. Remind the students that all north lines are always parallel to each other.

STRETCH: Give the students the bearing of one place from another and ask them to work out the bearing in the other direction. For example: If the bearing of Alltown from Beston is 150°, what is the bearing of Beston from Alltown?

9Gp8 Make and use scale drawings and interpret maps.

- Use a simple map (such as the one in the photocopiable resources). How far is it from the house to the beach? How do they know? (Answer: they don't!) Introduce the idea of a scale and that a map is a scale drawing. Ask where else scales are used (for example, when drawing plans for a house, diagrams of very small things such as cells or electronic components, scale models). Give the example of drawing a scale plan of the classroom. You wouldn't want to draw it full size, so what scale would be appropriate?

- FIX: Measure the classroom and complete a simple scale drawing of the classroom, showing clearly how the scale is used on the actual measurements of the classroom.

- Give an example of a map scale, such as 1 : 10 000. Ask the students what this ratio means and check they have a clear understanding with a couple of example lengths. For example, how far would 3 cm represent? If a road was 2 km what would it be on the map? How do you work it out?

- FIX: Use the example scale with the map for bearings (in the photocopiable resources) to work out the distances between the places on the island.

- Consolidate calculating with scales using exercises from the Student's Book.

STRETCH: Use some actual maps and ask students to calculate distances between various locations on the map. This can also be done using online maps.

9Gp9 Find by reasoning the locus of a point that moves at a given distance from a fixed point, or at a given distance from a fixed straight line.

- Use the locus starter activity above to introduce the idea of a locus – a collection of points that fit a given rule. Emphasise the need for clear diagrams to scale.

- FIX: Draw a point on the whiteboard and ask students in turn to mark points that are 20 cm away from it, using a ruler as necessary. How can they record ALL the points that are 20 cm from the point? Complete the circle.

- Repeat the process with a line representing a wall, and then with a line segment. Make sure the students appreciate the difference between the two – one you can go all the way around, the other you cannot.

- Consolidate with exercises from the Student's Book, making sure students pay attention to accuracy and correct use of scale. Link back to previous work on constructions as necessary.

STRETCH: Working on plain paper, construct the locus of points that are equidistant between two points, between two lines that intersect at a point, and (if they can) between a point and a line.

End of chapter mental maths exercise

1. If a plane is flying on a bearing of 130° and turns clockwise 45 degrees, what is its new bearing?

2. If I am facing east and turn 20 degrees clockwise, what is the bearing of the direction I am now facing?

3. If a boat is sailing on a bearing of 115° and turns 40 degrees anticlockwise, what is its new bearing?

4. A map has a scale of 1 : 100 000. What is the real distance between two villages if the distance on the map is 6 cm?

5. A map has a scale of 1 : 100 000. What is the length on the map of a lake that is 2 km long?

6. Describe the shape of the locus of points that are 6 cm away from a point.

Technology recommendations

- Use an interactive whiteboard tool to demonstrate measuring with a protractor and setting up diagrams that can then be used to demonstrate bearings and loci.

- Use online maps to demonstrate scales and how using different scales changes the appearance of the map. This can be done down to street level on some map applications.

Investigation/research tasks

- Why do we have 360 degrees in a whole turn? Where does it come from?

- How are degrees sub-divided? Find some examples of how this is done and where and why this is needed.

- Are there any other units used for measuring angles? What are they? Why do you think they are not used as often as degrees?

Probability

Learning objectives

Learning objectives covered in this chapter: 9Db1, 9Db2, 9Db3

- Know that the sum of probabilities of all mutually exclusive outcomes is 1 and use this when solving probability problems.
- Find and record all outcomes for two successive events in a sample space diagram.
- Understand relative frequency as an estimate of probability and use this to compare outcomes of experiments in a range of contexts

Key terms

- mutually exclusive outcomes
- sample space
- relative frequency

Prior knowledge assumptions

- Students can work out the probability of an event not happening, given the probability of it happening.
- Students can make a tally chart.
- Students can solve linear equations.
- Students can add and subtract fractions.
- Students can find equivalent fractions.
- Students can convert between decimals, fractions and percentages.

Guidance on the hook

Purpose: This activity introduces the idea that the different outcomes of an event may not be equally probable.

Use of the hook: Working in pairs, students throw two six-sided dice 100 times, and make a tally chart of the sum of the two numbers thrown (from 2 to 12). Afterwards, ask pairs for their most and least common sums. The most common sum is likely to be 7 (since this is the most probable sum) and the least common sums are likely to be 2 and 12 (since these are the least probable sums).

Have a class discussion, or small group discussions, about the following points:

- why some sums occur more frequently than others
- why not all pairs found the same most common sum (if applicable; or if not, discuss whether it would be possible that you find the most common sum to be a number other than 7)
- what the results might be like if students rolled the two dice only 10 times (and students could be asked to try this).

Adaptation: The activity could be run as a game played as a class or in large groups, in which students start by each choosing a number from 2 to 12. Two dice are rolled repeatedly, and each time a student's chosen sum is rolled, they gain 1 point. You win the game by being first to get 10 points. The results can be displayed on the board using a tally chart.

Extension: Students could think about what results they might get if they found the product of the two numbers on the dice (or alternatively, the positive difference between them) instead of the sum. Ask what outcomes are possible, and which of those outcomes are likely to be relatively common or relatively rare.

Starter ideas

Mental maths starter

Simplify $\frac{12}{18}$.	Simplify $\frac{40}{64}$.	Simplify $\frac{14}{35}$.	Simplify $\frac{24}{144}$.
Calculate $\frac{1}{2} + \frac{1}{8}$.	Calculate $\frac{1}{6} + \frac{1}{3}$.	Calculate $1 - \frac{5}{12} + \frac{1}{2}$.	Calculate $1 - \frac{2}{9} - \frac{1}{3}$.
Write 45% as a fraction in its simplest form.	Write $35\% + \frac{2}{5}$ as a percentage.	Write $20\% + \frac{1}{10}$ as a fraction in its simplest form.	Write $5\% + 0.2 + \frac{1}{4}$ as a percentage.
Solve the equation $2x + 0.8 = 1$.	Solve the equation $\frac{2}{5} + x = 1$.	Solve the equation $x + \frac{1}{4} + \frac{1}{3} = 1$.	Solve the equation $2x + \frac{3}{4} = 1$.
When you roll a fair six-sided dice, what is the probability that it lands on 5?	When you roll a fair six-sided dice, what is the probability that it lands on an even number?	When you roll a fair six-sided dice, what is the probability that it lands on 5 or 6?	When you roll a fair six-sided dice, what is the probability that it lands on a prime number?

Start point check

Probability scale

Draw a probability scale using squared or graph paper. Then add the labels A–H to the scale in the appropriate places, to match the probabilities described below.

A. The probability of rolling an even number on a normal six-sided dice.
B. The probability of picking a yellow ball when picking a ball at random out of a bag containing two red balls and six yellow balls.
C. The probability of rolling 8 on a normal six-sided dice.
D. The probability of spinning 'blue' on a spinner that has a 120° slice coloured blue.
E. The probability of a train being late if its probability of being on time or early is $\frac{3}{5}$.
F. The probability of spinning 'red' on a spinner that is all coloured red.
G. The probability of picking a letter 'A' when picking a letter at random from the word 'ALPHABET'.
H. The probability of rolling 3 or higher on a normal six-sided dice.

Alternatively, instead of giving the descriptions for A–H, ask students to think of their own examples of probabilities to mark on their probability scale.

Activity: Exploring experimental probability

Give each student a six-sided dice and ask them to record the results of the following three experiments, using a separate tally chart for each one:

1. rolling the dice six times
2. rolling the dice 36 times
3. rolling the dice 120 times.

Ask students to draw a bar chart for each of their three experiments.

Share and combine all students' results for 120 rolls.

Discuss what sort of results students were expecting, and which of the sets of results best meets their expectations.

TIP: To save time, groups of two or three students could be given a dice each and combine their results to total the required numbers of rolls. Alternatively, large numbers of coin tosses can be generated quickly using the simulation at http://www.shodor.org/interactivate/activities/Coin/; however, students may be more convinced by real-life results.

Discussion ideas

Probing questions	Teacher prompts
State two events that are mutually exclusive. State two events that are not mutually exclusive.	Students may need to be reminded of the meaning of the term 'mutually exclusive'. You could start by giving the following examples: • mutually exclusive – today being Wednesday and today being Thursday; rolling one dice (once) and getting 2 and 3 • not mutually exclusive – today being Wednesday and today being sunny; rolling two dice and getting 2 and 3.
Three students, Xavier, Yaling and Zaafir are playing a game in which the winner is the first to get 5 points. They toss two coins repeatedly, and after each toss they score points using the rules below. • If both coins land on heads, Xavier gets 1 point. • If both coins land on tails, Yaling gets 1 point. • If one coin lands on heads and one lands on tails, Zaafir gets 1 point. Is this game fair? Try it and see.	Students may assume that the three ways of scoring are equally likely. If so, have them try playing the game a few times to see how it turns out. Discuss why Zaafir is most likely to win. Students may find it hard to see that heads on coin 1 and tails on coin 2 is not the same outcome as tails on coin 1 and heads on coin 2. Demonstrating with two different types of coin may help with this.
If you create a sample space diagram for two events, one of which has two possible outcomes and the other six, how many entries should the diagram have?	If students cannot see the answer, make the question more concrete by specifying one event as a coin toss and the other as a dice roll. When they have tried sketching the sample space diagram and worked out its number of entries, ask how it would change if the dice had eight sides, or ten sides. Then ask if they can generalise – how many entries should the diagram have if the two events have n and m possible outcomes?
Three dice are thrown, and the three numbers are added. Why can you not draw a normal sample space diagram to represent the outcomes? Can you suggest how the outcomes might be summarised?	Students may suggest a 3D sample space diagram, which would work in principle, but is difficult to create in practice. Another way is to draw a separate 2D sample space diagram for each possible outcome of one of the events. This would involve drawing six 6 by 6 diagrams. If students think it is possible to summarise the results in a single, normal sample space diagram, ask them to try it. Students could try drawing sample space diagrams for rolling two six-sided dice and tossing a coin (which can be shown using two 6 by 6 sample space diagrams, one for each possible outcome of the coin toss). Ask students to work out probabilities for different outcomes.

Probing questions	Teacher prompts
Two biased (unfair) six-sided dice are thrown. The probabilities that the dice will land on particular numbers are known. Is it possible to draw a sample space diagram for the outcomes of this event? Is it possible to find the probabilities of different outcomes by counting entries in the sample space diagram? Explain your answers.	Students may assume that, because it is possible to draw a sample space diagram showing all of the outcomes, it is also possible to calculate probabilities by counting outcomes. Discuss the idea that this is only possible when all outcomes have equal probability. Point out that a sample space diagram is of limited use in a situation like this. (Students may later learn to use tree diagrams to calculate probabilities of multiple events having different probabilities for different outcomes.)

Common errors/misconceptions

Misconception	Strategies to address
Thinking that all possible outcomes of an event are always equally likely (for example, it will either rain tomorrow or it will not rain, so $P(\text{rain}) = P(\text{no rain}) = \frac{1}{2}$).	This is true for the outcomes of a fair dice roll or a fair coin toss, and students may assume it is true for all events. In the hook for this chapter, students can discover experimentally that for some events, different outcomes have different probabilities. Ask students to suggest other examples of events whose outcomes are not equally likely. Relatively easy examples to understand are: picking a ball from a bag containing, say, nine red balls and one yellow ball; and spinning a spinner which has unequal sectors. An online spinner simulation with adjustable sectors can be found here: http://www.shodor.org/interactivate/activities/AdjustableSpinner/.
Thinking, for random events such as coin tosses or dice throws, that the outcomes of earlier events affect the probabilities of outcomes of later events. For example, students may think that if a fair coin is tossed six times and lands on heads every time, it is more likely to land on tails the next time. They may think that if the results of a series of tosses do not consist of half heads and half tails, then subsequent tosses will shift the results closer to 50–50.	Ask students to think about whether there is any way that a coin or a dice can have 'memory' of past outcomes. Students may know instinctively that a run of, say, seven heads out of seven coin tosses is relatively unlikely (and they may not realise that in fact, any specific run is just as unlikely). So, after a run of six heads they may think that a seventh head is very unlikely. However, while a run of seven heads may have been unlikely at the start (since it is one of many possible outcomes from seven tosses), *now that we have already had seven heads* it has a 50% chance of happening. In other words, the probability of six heads then one tail is equal to the probability of six heads then one head.
Thinking that the results of repeated trials with two possible outcomes would be unlikely to include 'runs' of one outcome repeated several times.	Ask each member of the class to toss a coin 30 times and record their results in the order they occurred. Then ask who had runs of three, four, five or longer. Students could try the activity, https://nrich.maths.org/6012, which is about real and faked results from repeated coin tosses.
Attempting to find a probability from a sample space diagram by dividing the number of favourable outcomes by the number of unfavourable outcomes, instead of dividing by the total number of outcomes.	Remind students that (when outcomes are equally likely) probability $= \dfrac{\text{number of favourable outcomes}}{\text{total number of outcomes}}$. Try asking students to create a sample space diagram for tossing two coins once. The incorrect

Misconception	Strategies to address
	calculation gives the probability of getting one head and one tail as $\frac{2}{2} = 1$, which is clearly incorrect. Remind students that out of four possible outcomes, two are favourable, so the probability is $\frac{2}{4} = \frac{1}{2}$.
Thinking that relative frequency is the same as probability (rather than being an estimate of probability).	The starter activity 'Exploring experimental probability' involves rolling a dice repeatedly, a small number of times and then larger numbers of times, and comparing the results with what students might expect. Refer back to this when discussing experimental probability.

Developing conceptual understanding

9Db1 Know that the sum of probabilities of all mutually exclusive outcomes is 1 and use this when solving probability problems.

- Start by ensuring that students understand the concept 'mutually exclusive'. Share examples of outcomes that are, or are not, mutually exclusive. Remind students that a probability of 1 (or 100%) means certainty.

- Discuss the implications if the sum of probabilities of all mutually exclusive outcomes were less than 1: if the probabilities of getting the numbers 1–6 on a dice throw added up to, say, 90%, that would imply a 10% chance of getting some other number, or no number at all. Discuss the implications if the sum of probabilities were more than 1, and remind students that nothing can be more probable than certainty.

9Db2 Find and record all outcomes for two successive events in a sample space diagram.

- Introduce sample space diagrams as an organised way to record all possible outcomes of two events. You could start by asking students to write down all of the possible outcomes when throwing two six-sided dice (1 and 1, 1 and 2, etc.) Then ask students to explore different ways of organising these outcomes, to ensure that none are accidentally omitted or repeated. It is quite likely that at least one student in the class will 'invent' a sample space diagram, and can share and explain their diagram for the class.

- To help with creating sample space diagrams, students needing extra support could be given blank sample space diagrams to fill in. The photocopiable resources include sample space diagrams for two events, one with two and one with six outcomes (such as rolling one six-sided dice and tossing a coin), and for two events with six outcomes each (such as rolling two six-sided dice).

- Later on in their studies of probability, students are likely to encounter scenarios involving two successive events, each of whose outcomes do not have equal probabilities. Prepare them for this by discussing the limitations of sample space diagrams, and possible scenarios in which they cannot be used to calculate probabilities.

STRETCH: Introduce the idea of a dice game in which two players each roll a dice, and the player with the higher number scores 1 point. This game is clearly fair if both players use conventional six-sided dice, but what if the two dice show 1, 1, 7, 7, 7, 7 and 4, 4, 5, 5, 6, 6 respectively? Students could invent their own unconventional six-sided dice for this game, and show whether or not the game is fair and work out the probability of winning for each player.

9Db3 Understand relative frequency as an estimate of probability and use this to compare outcomes of experiments in a range of contexts.

- Simulated online dice and spinners can be useful, especially when there is not enough equipment available or when large numbers of trials are to be carried out within a limited time. However, students may be more convinced by real-life probability experiments (which could involve dice, spinners, coins, bags of objects, or sets of cards), where they know the results cannot have been 'fixed'. It is possible to buy dice with 4, 8, 10, 12, 20, 50 and even 100 sides.

End of chapter mental maths exercise

1. A spinner shows four numbers, 1–4. The probabilities of spinning 1, 2 and 3 are each x, and the probability of spinning 4 is $2x$. Find x.

2. The probability that a sports team wins its next match is 0.2, and the probability that the match is a draw is $\frac{3}{5}$. Find the probability, as a percentage, that the team loses the next match.

3. A spinner has two equal-sized sectors, labelled 2 and 3. The spinner is spun twice and the two results are added. Find the probability that the resulting sum is 5.

4. Two coins are tossed. Find the probability that both land the same way up (both heads or both tails).

5. A biased six-sided dice is thrown 200 times. It lands on 6 a total of 72 times. Estimate the probability, as a percentage, of this dice landing on 6 on the next throw.

6. A coloured spinner is spun 60 times. It lands on 'red' eight times. Estimate the probability, as a fraction in its simplest form, that it will *not* land on red when it is spun once.

Technology recommendations

- Use online resources for virtual dice, spinners or coins, for example: http://www.shodor.org/interactivate/activities/Coin/ (toss a coin multiple times and display the results); https://nrich.maths.org/6717 (up to six six-sided dice, and spinners with 2 to 15 numbers); https://nrich.maths.org/8426 (spinner which lands on red or black with equal probability); http://www.transum.org/software/SW/Dice/ (selection of dice, spinners and coins). These can be used to display outcomes on the board.

- If students have studied a computer programming language, they can try writing a program to simulate and display the results of a dice roll experiment. This can also be done using a spreadsheet program which has a function for generating random numbers.

- Use interactive activities on the Nrich website to explore relative frequency and the effect of sample size on probability estimates: https://nrich.maths.org/4304, https://nrich.maths.org/4308.

Investigation/research tasks

- **Probability experiment**

  Give each pair of students ten identical drawing pins (thumb tacks), of the type with a flat metal head, in a cup. Also give each pair a tray or box lid into which they can tip the pins, after gently shaking the cup. Ask each pair to plan and carry out a simple experiment to estimate the probability that a pin will land head down (rather than on its side), recording their data and calculations in a clear and organised way. They will need to tip the pins into the tray or lid, and count and record the total number of pins and the number of pins that landed head down. The more times they repeat this, the more accurate their estimated probability is likely to be.

Allow each student pair to choose their number of throws, and after the activity have a class discussion about the significance of this sample size. Create a table on the board showing sample size and estimated probability. You could also collate the results from all pairs to get the best probability estimate.

An alternative experiment is to estimate the probability of rolling the same two numbers when rolling two dice. The experimental result can be compared with the theoretical probability found from a sample space diagram.

Students could also estimate the probability of getting three consecutive numbers when rolling three dice. Working out the theoretical probability is beyond the scope of this chapter.

- **Relative frequency investigation**

  Collect data and use it to estimate probabilities, as percentages, of the possible outcomes of a particular event, for example:

  - probabilities of colours of the next car to drive past (on a particular street)
  - probabilities that a student picked at random from their class/year/school studies a particular subject, or has a particular favourite subject
  - probabilities of picking particular letters when picking a letter at random from a paragraph
  - probabilities of picking words of particular lengths when picking a word at random from a page.

  The data should be presented in an organised way, and you should show your calculations of probabilities.

- **Probability spinners**   *Problem solving*

  Design a spinner, split into equal-sized sectors, with a number on each sector. (You can use a number more than once.)

  Create a sample space diagram for the scores you can get when you spin two of these spinners and add the scores.

  Predict the probability of each possible score.

  Create two of your spinners (or create one and spin it twice) and collect data to estimate the probabilities of different scores from their relative frequencies.

- **Adaption:**

  There are websites where you can customise an interactive spinner instead of making one, for example https://www.nctm.org/ClassroomResources/Illuminations/Interactives/Adjustable-Spinner/ (which has colours instead of numbers, but you could decide and make a note of which colour corresponds to what number), or http://wheeldecide.com/ (which lets you choose the number of equal-sized sectors, and their labels).

TIP: You can find instructions on websites for how to make a spinner. Some of the simplest designs use thick card for the circle and for the spinning arrow, and a reshaped paperclip to hold them together.
